COLLECTOR'S VALUE GUIDE TO

Early Twentieth Century

AMERICAN PRINTS

Michael Ivankovich

COLLECTOR BOOKS

A Division of Schroeder Publishing Co., Inc.

On the front cover:
Left top: Wallace Nutting, *The Home Room*...14x17"...$230
Left middle: David Davidson, *Old Ironsides*, 16x20"...$170
Left bottom: Sawyer, *A New England Sugar Birth*, 16x20"...$300

Right top: Bessie Pease Gutmann, *Awakening*...14x18"...$115
Right #2 lower top: Fred Thompson, *Fireside Fancy Work*, 14x17"...$175

Right #3 upper bottom: Maxfield Parrish, *The Lute Players*, 18x30"...$675
Right bottom: R. Atkinson Fox, *Dawn*, 11x17"...$125

On the back cover:
Top: Maxfield Parrish, *Daybreak*, 18x30"...$375
Middle: Bessie Pease Gutmann, *My Honey*, 14x21"...$1,000
Bottom: Photographer Unknown, *Maine Fishing Village*, 16x20"...$85

Cover design:
Beth Summers

Book design:
Michelle Dowling

COLLECTOR BOOKS
P.O. Box 3009
Paducah, Kentucky 42002-3009
www.collectorbooks.com

Copyright © 1998 by Michael Ivankovich

The current values in this book should be used only as a guide. They are
not intended to set prices, which vary from one section of the country to another. Auction prices as well as dealer prices vary greatly and are affected by condition as well as demand. Neither the author nor the publisher assumes
responsibility for any losses that might be incurred as a result of consulting this
guide.

Searching For A Publisher?

We are always looking for people knowledgeable within their fields. If you
feel that there is a real need for a book on your collectible subject and have a
large comprehensive collection, contact Collector Books.

Contents

Acknowledgments

Sue...my wife...my best friend...my business partner...the idea person who keyed in most of my changes and who worked as hard as I did on this project...the source of my endless energy...the person who understands how I tick better than anyone else.

My mother Irene...a familiar face to all who have ever attended one of our auctions...and always our biggest supporter and believer.

My sister Lynn and brother-in-law Kevin...who are our right arms at auctions, and always giving of their love and support.

Collaborators...a special thank you goes to each of our collaborators...Sharon & Jim Eckert, Anchor, IL; Debbie Labb & Steve Steinberg, Forest Grove, PA; and Barry & Beth Mroczka, Camp Hill, PA. This book could not have been completed without you.

The Stone family of Delhi & Albany, NY...for sharing their very special Massachusetts getaway cabin with us during the preparation of this book.

Miscellaneous pricing, photograph & background contributors: Alderfer Auction Co. Hatfield, PA; Donald & Alice Davidson, Cumberland, RI; Carol Begley Gray, Nashua, NH; Jan Liberatore, Horseheads, NY; Rick & Charlotte Martin, Columbus, OH; Ed Moody, Schenectady, NY; Doris Myers, Georgetown, MA; and Cindy West, Aliquippa, PA.

Preface

This book originally began as a book exclusively on David Davidson hand-colored photographs. Having already written or published more than 10 works on Wallace Nutting, the next logical publishing step seemed to be another book on Wallace Nutting-like pictures. I have been focusing upon hand-colored photography for more than 20 years and a book on David Davidson, a photographer who sold more hand-colored pictures than all other early twentieth century photographers except Wallace Nutting, seemed to make sense.

Yet when I gathered all of my notes, research, and pricing, I concluded that although I had some very valuable and useful information in this area, it was only a very small part of a much larger picture.

While conducting this research into David Davidson, I had also been doing some expanded research into several other areas of early twentieth century American prints, areas that I had pretty much ignored over the past 20 years. For more than two decades I had been combing antique shows, antique shops, flea markets, auctions, and garage sales looking for hand-colored photographs, pretty much to the exclusion of everything else. I had seen thousands of prints that I had liked, but usually passed them by because I didn't know whether they were common or rare, average or special, bargains or overpriced. When I searched for some value information, I found that the general price guides didn't provide enough information to make informed buying decisions, and I simply didn't have the time to read and digest another entire book on a new subject.

I concluded that other collectors and dealers were probably sharing my frustration. There was no single, concise book which offered helpful background and pricing information on these most popular early twentieth century American prints. Hence, the start of this new book.

I felt confident that my extensive background as a collector, dealer, and auctioneer in early twentieth century American hand-colored photography made me sufficiently knowledgeable to publish another book within this area, especially since our auction prices undoubtedly provide the most accurate and up-to-date value information available anywhere in the country.

However, although I felt quite competent and knowledgeable in the areas of Maxfield Parrish, Bessie Pease Gutmann, and R. Atkinson Fox, I recognized that I was not the ultimate authority. Therefore, I sought out several collaborators who did have a more extensive background than I in these three areas.

The first people I turned to were Sharon & Jim Eckert of Anchor, Illinois. Sharon and Jim have been long-time friends whom I have known for nearly 20 years. While Jim is widely regarded as one of the most knowledgeable Wallace Nutting collectors in the country, Sharon's strength and love has always been with Bessie Pease Gutmann. Together they have major Nutting and Gutmann collections. In 1991, Sharon provided pricing and assistance for a value-based article on Bessie Pease Gutmann for *The Antique Trader*, the first such Gutmann-value article that appeared in any major antique trade paper.

In the area of Maxfield Parrish, I turned to Deborah Labb of Forest Grove, Pennsylvania. Debbie is usually seen wearing her *Maxfield Parrish Wanted* fluorescent reflective vest at many major East Coast antique shows. She is a both a collector and a dealer and has been specializing in Maxfield Parrish for more than 20 years. Debbie and Steve Steinberg also co-sponsor a very well-attended annual Maxfield Parrish show and sale in eastern Pennsylvania. This show brings in Parrish collectors and merchandise from around the country and is a rapidly growing event. And, quite conveniently, Debbie and Steve live only several miles away.

I wasn't really certain where to go at first for an R. Atkinson Fox expert. Debbie Labb suggested that I contact Barry Mroczka of Camp Hill, Pennsylvania, whom she described as a major Fox collector. I met Barry at the Carlisle Antique Show, laid out the outline of this project, and we agreed to work together on the Fox chapter. I gathered my camera and photography equipment, drove to Camp Hill and had my eyes opened. Barry and Beth Mroczka not only have one of the finest R. Atkinson Fox collections in the country, they are without a doubt two of the most knowledgeable Fox collectors as well.

So, these chapters on Maxfield Parrish, Bessie Pease Gutmann, and R. Atkinson Fox are joint, collaborative efforts. I did most of the initial chapter format and work-up, and then submitted the chapter to my collaborators for revision. They in turn added much of the all-important pricing information, numerous collecting tips, and other valuable information. I then edited their changes, added new material, and returned the chapters back to my collaborators, who made new changes and additions. We went back and forth like this a few times and I say "thank you" to each of my collaborators for their endless knowledge, hard work, and limitless patience.

We hope you agree that the end result is a helpful and informative book containing the most current pricing available anywhere today. What we are presenting here are actually seven different price guides within one book, with specialized chapters focusing upon the prints of Maxfield Parrish, Bessie Pease Gutmann, and R. Atkinson Fox, and the hand-colored photographs of Wallace Nutting, David Davidson, Fred Thompson, Charles Sawyer, along with the work of many other lesser-known and unknown photographers. The material you read in this book is intended to be complete yet concise, structured yet interesting, while at the same time providing you with valuable pricing information which will enable you to more profitably buy and sell the items we have covered.

We hope you enjoy reading this book as much as we have enjoyed putting it together.

Introduction

Maxfield Parrish, 1870 — 1966
"...In the 1920s the works of Maxfield Parrish
graced the walls of one out of four American homes..."

Bessie Pease Gutmann, 1876 — 1960
"...so captured the imagination of America
that her prints appeared in almost every
home..."

R. Atkinson Fox, 1860 — 1935
"...there are more reproductions of R.
Atkinson Fox's work than those of any other
living artist..."

Wallace Nutting, 1861 — 1941
"...about ten million of my pictures hang in American
homes..."

David Davidson, 1881 — 1967
"...Hardly a New England wedding went by
where the bride didn't receive a David Davidson
picture..."

Charles Sawyer, 1868 — 1954
"...Sawyer pictures are known throughout New Eng-
land..."

Fred Thompson, 1844 — 1909
"...If you vacationed in Maine after the turn of
the century, you probably took home a Fred
Thompson picture..."

Whether these claims represent complete truths or just marketing hype, there can be no denying that the works of Maxfield Parrish, Bessie Pease Gutmann, R. Atkinson Fox, Wallace Nutting, David Davidson, Fred Thompson, and Charles Sawyer were some of the bestselling prints of their era.

And today, because their pictures were sold in such large numbers, it is nearly impossible to walk through a large antique show, group shop, flea market, or auction where you don't see a variety of their work for sale.

This *Collector's Value Guide to Early Twentieth Century American Prints* brings together two very diverse art forms...the prints of Maxfield Parrish, Bessie Pease Gutmann, and R. Atkinson Fox...and the hand-colored photographs of Wallace Nutting, David Davidson, Fred Thompson, and Charles Sawyer. Surprising as it may be to some, these two seemingly dissimilar subject areas...early twentieth century American prints and hand-colored photography...share many similar characteristics:

* They were both sold during the early twentieth century.
* They were both mass produced in relatively large numbers.
* They both appealed to the broad American middle class.
* They both had peak sales occurring between 1910 and 1930.
* They were both nationally distributed.
* They both sold for a low initial cost.
* They were both found in nearly every American middle-class household between 1900 and 1940.
* Both are worth considerably more today than they were 10 – 15 years ago.

...And both are widely sought after by a larger and more diverse assortment of antique collectors and dealers than ever before.

What is the difference between a print and a hand-colored photograph? Quite simply, a print is a machine-produced image that has been produced by either full-color offset printing or some comparable process, while a hand-colored photograph is a black and white photograph which has been entirely hand colored and produced.

For the purposes of this book, an early twentieth century American print is defined as a machine-produced print, reproduced from an original piece of art, primarily during the 1900 – 1940 period. The print may be machine produced in color, or it may be machine produced in black and white, and then hand colored, to reach the desired effect. Either way, a print was machine produced.

Original prints are, in essence, original reproductions, which were reproduced from an original painting or artwork, around the time that the original artwork was created. This is not to be confused with a later reproductions which were either cheap knock-offs intended for a contemporary mass market, or fakes intended to deceive.

For the purposes of this book, a hand-colored photograph is defined as a black and white photograph whose color was applied entirely by hand.

Because the hand tinting of photographs was a labor-intensive process, only those hand-colored photographs which sold in large quantities were produced in large quantities. Which means that those pictures that were the bestselling pictures during the early twentieth century will be the most commonly found today, while those pictures which were the poorest selling pictures are typically the rarest and most desired pictures today. And original hand-colored photographs are not to be confused with later process prints or facsimile prints which were cheap machine-produced reproductions of some of the most popular hand-colored photographs by the photographers themselves.

The hand-colored photography market is probably one of the least understood segments within the antiques and collectibles field. Collectors usually recognize some of the names associated with this field, but more often than not, will fail to recognize a hand-colored photograph from a machine-produced print.

Confused? Don't worry, because this book will help you to sort all of this out.

It is the objective of this book to help readers obtain a better understanding of the background, subject matter, condition, and most importantly, current values of the most highly collectible early twentieth century American prints and hand-colored photographs. This book will show you how to identify the best and rarest prints, it will tell you what value to expect if selling, and what to pay if buying. It will provide you with reproduction alerts, and it will provide you will more than 600 photographs and more than 100 collecting tips, all designed to help you learn about these prints quickly and easily.

This book also includes some other very special pluses:

* The Bessie Pease Gutmann chapter includes a unique rarity rating which lists several hundred Gutmann titles along with their relative rarity to help you better determine what is common and what is rare.
* The Wallace Nutting chapter includes all-new values and prices.
* The David Davidson chapter includes the largest and most complete alphabetical and numerical index of David Davidson picture titles ever published.
* The final chapter includes the most complete listing of early twentieth century Wallace Nutting-like photographers ever published.
* And there's much, much more.

Early twentieth century American prints and hand-colored photographs which once sold for pennies are now selling for hundreds, and sometimes thousands, of dollars. For example:

* In 1997 a Maxfield Parrish auction saw 40 of 183 lots selling for more than $1,000, with the top Parrish in the auction selling for more than $7,400.
* A rare Bessie Pease Gutmann print recently sold privately for more than $1,600.
* Certain collectors are reportedly paying $500 – $1,000 for the rarest R. Atkinson Fox prints.
* A rare Wallace Nutting picture sold at auction in 1997 for more than $4,500.
* The best David Davidson, Sawyer, and Fred Thompson pictures have neared or passed the $500 threshold, with no end in sight.

Once called poor man's art, these prints are no longer for those on a low budget. Early twentieth century American prints and hand-colored photographs are no longer cheap, inexpensive, or easy to come by. Some are fairly common and still cost $100 or less. Others are extremely rare and bring considerable sums of money today.

How do you tell the difference between a common and a rare print? And once you find a rarity, where do you go to sell it for top dollar?

For the answers to these and other important questions, read on.

Chapter 1

Putting Popular Early Twentieth Century Prints into Perspective

There were literally hundreds of artists and illustrators competing for a share of the art print, book, calendar, magazine, and advertising illustration markets at this time and while some were very successful and became quite famous, most failed to catch the attention of America's rapidly growing population and remained in obscurity.

Today Maxfield Parrish, Bessie Pease Gutmann, and R. Atkinson Fox have become three of the most collectible names within the area of early twentieth century American prints. Each developed their own individual style, and each succeeded in attracting a strong following for their work.

R. Atkinson Fox . . . whose diversified subject matter makes him difficult to stereotype was one of the most popular artists of his time and is just beginning to be discovered and understood by many collectors.

The first half of this book will be devoted to the prints featuring the work of these three artists. We have selected them because in our travels we have found their art to be among the most interesting, the most popular, the most readily available, and most in demand by collectors. This is not to say that the art of many of their contemporaries is not popular, was not as good, or is not in demand. Rather, in our opinion we have found the work of these three artists to be among the most interesting to collect.

It is not our intention to write the most definitive work ever completed on these three artists. Other books have already been written on each. Rather, it is our intention to provide readers with a general understanding and a basic working background on each individual artist. We don't expect these chapters to answer each and every one of your questions. Instead, we would hope that these chapters will answer most of your questions...quickly and easily. We have tried to take all of our research on each artist, and filter it into the fewest number of words, while providing you with as many visual references and research tools as possible. We have tried to give you enough detail to help you make informed buying decisions. And we have tried to arrange each chapter in a manner which provides collectors and dealers with the type of information we think that they need. If we succeeded in that, then we have accomplished what we set out to do. If we

Maxfield Parrish . . . and his famous Girls-on-Rocks and New England landscape scenes painted in his famous Parrish blue is probably the best known and most highly collectible of these three artists.

Bessie Pease Gutmann . . . and her heart-rendering depiction of youthful innocence is very well known to some collectors, yet virtually unknown to many others.

haven't been able to help you answer your questions, at the end of each chapter we tell you where you can go to find more detailed information about the question at hand.

The Growth of Early Twentieth Century Prints

A calendar print, missing the calendar pad

Calendars became a rapidly growing business in the late 1800s. Businesses learned that in addition to building good will, giving away free calendars which contained their advertising message meant a full year of very inexpensive advertising, right in a potential customer's household. Which in turn meant increased business.

By the early 1900s literally millions of calendars were being printed each year, a number which grew by some estimates to approximately 25,000,000 annually by the mid-1920s. This meant that significantly more calendars were being printed than there were American households, which in turn meant that most households would only keep one or two of the many free calendars they received each year, throwing away those that they found least interesting.

As a business owner, if you found that people were throwing your calendar away while keeping another, you would most likely either stop providing free calendars to your customers,

or switch to another calendar company. Either way, that didn't bode well for the publishers and calendar companies. They wanted to sell as many calendars as possible and the only way they could do that was to determine what pictures and images the public desired most, and give the public exactly what they wanted.

Which meant that the leading calendar companies began competing to buy the art of America's leading artists and illustrators. What type of art and subject matter appealed to the widest audiences? Often that depended upon the era in question. What was popular in 1910 was different from what the public wanted in 1920, 1930, or 1940. Popular books and movies greatly influenced what became popular calendar art each year. Important historical events also became popular calendar subjects. Some subjects and artists remained popular for many years, while most others came into and went out of favor very quickly.

Geographical location was also an important determinant of what calendar prints would be used. What was popular with New York City apartment dwellers was not necessarily what appealed to Nebraska's farmers. Different subjects appealed to men and women, young and old, north and south, rich and poor, and to different religious beliefs.

Calendar companies soon learned that whoever had the most popular artists and pictures under contract would sell the most calendars. Enter the likes of Parrish, Gutmann, and Fox.

Maxfield Parrish's art was so incredibly popular that Parrish was pretty much under exclusive contract to produce Edison-Mazda and Brown & Bigelow calendars between 1918 and 1962. If my math is correct, that would make nearly 45 consecutive years that Parrish was commissioned to create the exclusive artwork for a calendar...for only two companies. That in itself is probably some kind of record.

R. Atkinson Fox produced the artwork for so many calendars that his publishers had him use pseudonyms so that their customers would think they had a much larger stable of artists working for them than they actually did. Although most of his work was produced under his own name, Fox also produced art under 25 variations of the 13 different pseudonyms that he used.

Although Bessie Pease Gutmann produced less calendar art than Parrish and Fox, she too was sought out by the calendar companies, providing original artwork to both the Osborne and Brown & Bigelow calendar companies.

And what happened at the end of every year? Most calendars were simply thrown out with the trash. A few calendars were saved in their entirety, while the most popular pictures were cropped down, framed, and hung in another part of the house.

Maxfield Parrish...Girl on Rocks

Bessie Pease Gutmann...adorable infants and children

result you will see a wide variety of art print sizes and shapes today.

Framed art has always been the most popular form of art, and publishers were always looking for new artists or specific prints that had potential to increase their sales. As with calendars, publishers sought out the best artists and tried to sign them to a long-term exclusive contract.

While end-of-the-year calendar art provided free pictures for hanging, art prints had to be purchased. Which generally meant that only the best and most popular pictures were produced as art prints.

The subjects varied widely and so did the sizes. Some art prints only came in a single size, while others came in many different sizes. Print sizes varied by publisher and because art prints were really nothing more than inexpensive machine-produced prints, they were often cropped down to fit a specific frame. As a

R. Atkinson Fox...although sometimes called a Parrish imitator, that couldn't be further from the truth.

Most artists sold their work to the publisher for a single payment or commission. That way, the artists received a predetermined sum (which helped to pay the bills) and it was up to the publisher to make a profit out of that artwork. If the print sold more than enough copies to cover all expenses, the publisher made a profit; if the print failed to sell in any significant numbers, a loss may have been incurred. Some publishers were able to spread the cost of the original artwork over several different projects. For example, the same original piece of art might have been used as a calendar print, an art print, and a jigsaw puzzle. Regardless of how the art was used, the publisher owned all rights to the work and was able to use it themselves, rent it to another company on a one-time or multiple-time usage basis, or sell the artwork outright.

A royalty basis was another preferred compensation arrangement for the artists. Here the artist would receive a commission based upon each individual print sold. The more prints that were sold, the more the artist would make.

And a few select artists were able to work on a commission and royalty basis whereby they received both an up-front payment as well as a per-print royalty.

The Printing Process

What follows is a very simple overview of the process used to create many of the early twentieth century's most popular prints. Although the exact process varied by publishing company or artist, this summary is intended to provide you with a very basic understanding of the role of the artist, the role of the publishing company, and the overall print and production process.

The artist would create the original artwork using his or her preferred medium, either oil-on-canvas, oil-on-board, pen and ink, charcoal, pastel, or whatever worked best for the subject at hand. Sometimes a piece of art was created by the artist who then attempted to sell it to a publisher. Most often the artist completed a work at the direction of a publisher.

If commissioned by a publisher, the artist was usually given very specific direction as to what the publisher was expecting. Occasionally, artists with good reputations and proven track records might be allowed to use their own creativity to satisfy the need of a publisher.

Some artists painted while on location, but travel meant time and money. Therefore it was not uncommon for some artists to paint from memory, while other artists never even saw the subjects they painted, using either a photograph or other image as the basis for their own artwork.

Once the original artwork was completed and met the satisfaction of the artist, it was delivered to the publisher. The publisher would either accept it as-is, reject it entirely, or return it to the artist for correction or revision. The final artwork needed formal approval by the publisher. Sometimes the decisionmaker was a single individual, other times it was a committee who had to give final approval on the art. Either way, it was the responsibility of the final decision makers to see that the artwork would be a quality piece, being both popular with the general public and easily salable to their calendar-buying business clients.

A lithographic press

During most of the nineteenth century, the lithographic printing process was the preferred technique for print production. When you think of large scale lithography, most people first think of Currier & Ives. Currier & Ives prints were actually hand-colored lithographs and they probably used the larger-scale lithographic printing process more successfully than anyone else.

In lithography, the image is actually drawn or created on a special stone which serves as the actual printing surface. The paper is then laid on the stone and using a limited amount of applied pressure, the natural antipathy of water and grease transfer ink from the stone image to the print paper.

The biggest problem with this printing technique was that the image on the lithographic stone had a tendency to wear-out relatively quickly. The first images usually had the sharpest detail but, after several hundred impressions had been made, the image quality began to deteriorate.

Fortunately offset color printing was developed to enable publishers to more quickly and efficiently produce the many tens of thousands of impressions that were needed to satisfy the early twentieth century print market.

A printing plate

An early print room

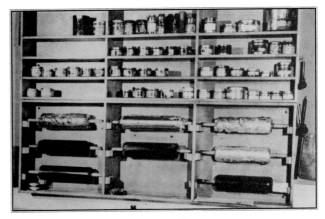

Inks and rollers.

Once approved, the original artwork was taken to the studio to begin the print production process. Preparation for a black and white printing job was relatively easy and only required the use of a single printing plate and a single pass through the printing press.

Color printing became much more difficult and expensive. In color printing, the first step was color separation. This was a fairly complicated process that took the original artwork and broke it down into the primary colors that would eventually be printed. Usually this would vary between four and six different colors. A color separation machine would be used to separate the original artwork into the primary colors, resulting in a separate glass negative for each color.

After some delicate touch-ups, the image on the glass negative would be transferred onto a metal printing plate. Again, a separate printing plate would be needed for each individual color that was to be printed.

The first metal printing plate was then attached to the printing cylinder on the press. The round cylinder was then passed over the blank sheet of paper and the first color of ink would be transferred from the printing plate onto the print paper. Remember that only one single color would be added on this first pass.

After completing the first run, perhaps 5,000 – 25,000 sheets or more, the same process was repeated for the second and subsequent colors. A six-color printing job, for a 25,000 sheet run, meant that a total of 150,000 passes had to be made through the printing press on that particular job. Which meant that everything had to be perfectly in register. Because if only one color was off by $\frac{1}{32}$", the entire printing job would be ruined.

On larger printing presses that utilized larger sheets of paper, multiple images could be printed at the same time, for example, if a job could be printed 4-up, four identical images could be printed on a single sheet of paper and then cut down into identical prints. A 10,000 print job could be completed in 2,500 sheets. And on all but the smallest presses, most jobs were capable of being printed in multiple images per sheet.

Once the printing job was finished and completely dry, the larger sheets were cut down into individual prints. Calendar prints would be glued onto the individual calendars, with the final steps being the attachment of calendar pads, ribbons, any other *bells and whistles*, and then the final packaging.

An ornate frame.

A less ornate frame.

Art prints would either be framed immediately or shipped to the retail store which would handle the eventual framing. Shape and size most definitely helped to sell the print and is especially important to the value of an art print today.

Some artists assigned a title to each of their pictures immediately, and sometimes the title was directed by the publisher. Regardless of whether the title was created by the publisher or artist, the objective of any title was to help to sell the print. Creative titles were sometimes as important in selling the prints as the

Plain and simple oval frame.

actual artwork itself and it wasn't uncommon for a title to change several times before becoming final.

When determining rarity, there are two numbers that should be understood…total number printed and number still in existence. Rarely is either number actually known. Such records which were probably kept by most publishers have long since disappeared. And there is no way to know how many prints are still remaining today. Rather than knowing the exact number still in existence, the estimated number of remaining prints usually becomes a very subjective guess. Experienced collectors can usually make the educated assumption that if they have seen many copies of a particular title in their travels, then there are probably quite a few still in existence. If they have seen very few copies of a given title or image, you can probably assume that the particular image is quite rare, and will be in demand by many collectors. However, rarely will you be able to determine the exact number of prints remaining in circulation.

What happened to all of the original artwork that was purchased by the major publishers? Some is still owned by them. Others were sold off whenever storage rooms began to fill up. Unfortunately, all too often many pieces of original art were simply trashed. Whoever would have expected such items to be in such high demand today?

And quite frankly, no one knows exactly where a large percentage of the original art went. Either a larger percentage was trashed than originally thought, or its still sitting in a warehouse somewhere, just waiting to be found by someone like you.

This chapter was intended to provide you with a very brief and general overview of the early twentieth century print market. Many of these guidelines, in very general terms, can be applied to each of the artists we will cover. The next three chapters will focus upon each of the specific artists and will go into more depth regarding the work of each.

Chapter 2

Maxfield Parrish (1870 – 1966)
by Michael Ivankovich
in collaboration with Deborah Labb & Stephen Steinberg

Maxfield Parrish

"In the 1920s the works of Maxfield Parrish graced the walls of one out of four American homes…(making him) one of the most-reproduced artists ever…"

An Introduction to Maxfield Parrish

Of the three artists covered in this book, the works of Maxfield Parrish are undoubtedly the best known, most expensive, and have the widest following today. During his lifetime Parrish created nearly 900 original works of art and his most popular print *Daybreak* reportedly sold more copies than any other art print of its time. In 1996, the original oil-on-canvas of *Daybreak* sold at auction for $4,300,000! Over his 65-year career, Maxfield Parrish's artwork was imprinted on more than 20,000,000 art prints, calendars, book illustrations, greeting cards, and other printed pieces. Additional magazine covers and advertising illustrations accounted for millions more (one source claims that Parrish's art delivered more than one billion advertising messages), which made Maxfield Parrish a household name during much of his lifetime. Few, if any, artists of his day enjoyed the artistic and financial success of Maxfield Parrish.

> *Parrish Collecting Tip:*
> Maxfield Parrish produced nearly 900 works during his 65-year artistic career.

The Lute Players, 18x30". Est Value: $625 – 675.

Frederick Parrish was born on July 25, 1870, into a family of fairly significant means. The Parrish family at one time owned much of the land now occupied by the city of Baltimore, Maryland, and the Parrishes became successful and financially secure landowners and businessman. His father, Stephen Parrish, was an accomplished artist who was considered one of the top etchers in America.

Early in his career, Fred took his grandmother's maiden name as his middle name and became professionally known as F. Maxfield Parrish or Maxfield Parrish, the name he used for the rest of his life.

An early family trip to Europe greatly influenced young Maxfield and broadened his artistic imagination. The centuries-old European streets, buildings, and architecture stretched his imagination and helped to shape his artistic framework for the coming decades.

Old King Cole triptych (triple picture grouping), 6¼x23". Est. Value: $650 – 700.

Maxfield Parrish, circa 1896.

Parrish Collecting Tip:
Maxfield Parrish's artwork appeared as advertising illustrations, art prints, book illustrations, calendars, magazine covers, greeting cards, and more. All are desirable to Parrish collectors.

While living in Philadelphia, Pennsylvania, Maxfield enrolled in Haverford College but apparently his architecture major failed to stimulate his interest because he dropped out prior to graduation to pursue other interests.

Some of Parrish's earliest works were done in the Philadelphia area. In 1895, he painted his famous *Old King Cole* mural at the University of Pennsylvania and additional commissions at the University of Pennsylvania soon followed. The *Old King Cole* mural led to the opportunity for an 1895 magazine cover for *Harper's Bazaar* which provided Parrish with his first national following.

At this point things began happening quickly for Parrish. In 1895, he married Lydia Austin. In 1897, he was admitted to the Society of American Artists at the early age of 27. And in 1898, Parrish moved to Cornish, New Hampshire, where he built The Oaks, his famous house and art studio where he lived for the rest of his life. Beginning shortly after the turn of the century, Maxfield Parrish basically had all of the work that he wanted and supposedly refused more commissions than he accepted.

The next 20 years became some of Parrish's most productive times where he accepted numerous commissions from magazines and books. His colorful book illustrations for *Poems of Childhood* in 1904 were just what the public wanted and this led to many other book illustration assignments prior to the publication of his final book in 1925, *The Knave of Hearts*.

The ready availability of Parrish's earliest art prints just after the turn of the century also contributed to his popularity and rapidly growing reputation. His unique Parrish blue coloring was like no other artist of his time and certainly became his unique trademark early in his career.

In 1917, Parrish was commissioned by General Electric to paint his first Edison-Mazda calendar. This first calendar, *Dawn*, proved to be so popular that Parrish was signed to several lucrative commission deals to continue painting Edison-Mazda calendars for the next 17 years.

Daybreak, 18x30". Est. Value: $350 — 450.
The better the color, the higher the value.

In 1922, Maxfield Parrish painted his most famous and commercially successful print *Daybreak* which hit a vein with America. Including enchanted gardens, romantic girls, idyllic stone architecture, distant utopian mountains, and the famous luminous Parrish blue coloring, *Daybreak* typified Parrish's Girls on Rocks artistic phase and was widely acclaimed as his best work. *Daybreak* became Parrish's bestselling print ever, and was considered to be the bestselling art print of all time up to that point.

Parrish Collecting Tip:
Daybreak was Parrish's bestselling print and is by far the most commonly found Parrish print today. Millions of copies were originally sold, yet it is still considered to be very popular.

With the onset of the 1929 stock market crash and the depression of the 1930s, demand for Parrish's Girls-on-Rocks type scenes diminished. Just as the public had tired of his Girls-on-Rocks style of pictures, by 1930 Parrish had tired of doing them as well. This stylistic change enabled Parrish to make the transition to an area that he much preferred: *American landscapes*. Immediately upon completing his final Edison-Mazda calendar, Parrish began a new long-term relationship with Brown & Bigelow, the country's leading calendar publisher, where he continued to paint his beautiful landscape calendars for the next 25+ years. Landscapes had become Parrish's favorite subject matter, and, although they failed to achieve the high level of sales and public acclaim of his earlier prints, by any other artist's standards, they were still considered a major success.

Parrish Collecting Tip:
Landscapes represented Maxfield Parrish's favorite subject matter. They typically represented New England summer and winter landscapes, still featured his famous Parrish blue, and usually date a picture after 1930. Many different Brown & Bigelow landscape art prints and calendars appeared in the 1940s, 1950s, and early 1960s. Some of the later landscape production calendar prints were printed on a glossy, shiny stock.

Maxfield Parrish...the later years.

Unlike most artists, Parrish was widely recognized and appreciated as an artist and illustrator, and was financially successful as well. On March 30, 1966, Maxfield Parrish died at the age of 95.

Eventide, a Parrish landscape scene. Est. Value: $250 — 275.

Maxfield Parrish Value Guide

The prices indicated in the Value Guide sections and photograph captions throughout this chapter are based on an overall good print, typically having a grading of 4 as per our Parrish grading scale. If the print is of higher quality than a 4, the price should be adjusted upwards. If the condition is lower than a 4, the price should be adjusted downward. The objective of this Maxfield Parrish Value Guide is not to give you an exact price on each and every print. Rather, it is the objective of this Value Guide to help you to place a ballpark value on any given print.

You should recognize that value will vary based upon many different factors, some of the most important being *condition, condition, condition.* Prices will also vary throughout many different parts of the country. The values quoted here represent estimated prices of what you might expect to fairly pay for any given print at the retail level. If you are looking to sell a print, you should expect that dealers will pay proportionately less.

The Collecting Cycle of Maxfield Parrish Prints

Phase I. Initial Production and Peak Period: Parrish's earliest works were printed in their largest volume between 1900 and 1934. This was his Girls-on-Rocks period and represented the peak of his popularity. By this time he had illustrated all of his books, created the majority of his Edison-Mazda work, and after more than 30 years of artistic success, the public began to tire of his idyllic and utopian scenes.

Phase II. Gradual Market Decline: Unlike other artists who faded away after their peak period of success, by 1935 Parrish had moved on to another totally different phase — *landscapes*, which he painted until 1962. Although not as popular as his earlier Girls-on-Rocks period, his landscapes were considered a major success by most standards.

Phase III. Renewed Collectibility: Just as Parrish's second artistic phase was coming to an end in the early 1960s, collectors were beginning to recognize the collectibility of Maxfield Parrish. By the 1970s, an expanding base of collectors began to push prices upwards and Maxfield Parrish remained a strong collectible area throughout the 1980s and 1990s.

Phase IV. Current Market Status: The current market for Maxfield Parrish can be described as nothing short of very strong. There is considerable interest in all forms of Maxfield Parrish collectibles, and at a recent 1997 Maxfield Parrish mail-order auction, 40 of 183 lots (22%) sold for more than $1000, with the top lot bringing $7400.

What Do Maxfield Parrish Collectors Look For?

Original Maxfield Parrish watercolor. Est. Value: $7,500.

Original Artwork

The most valuable and highly desirable area of Maxfield Parrish would be Parrish's original art, typically oil-on-canvas or oil-on-board artworks. These are extremely valuable and there are a surprising number still in existence today.

Unlike many other artists whose works are not widely appreciated until after their death, the value of Parrish's work was recognized while he was still alive. And being a smart businessman, Parrish recognized that his work carried value in three different areas:

* A commission based upon either a one-time or repeated usage of the original artwork
* A royalty based upon the number of total prints or images sold
* The final selling price of the artwork after its original intended usage had been completed

Parrish's national reputation and popularity gave him leverage with publishers that relatively few other artists of his time had, and he was able to retain ownership rights to many of his original artworks. The average collector today has relatively little chance of discovering a Parrish original, however. Some are already owned by the Maxfield Parrish Family Trust, while others are in private collections or museums. When they do become publicly available, they are usually sold privately through leading art galleries or through major auction houses.

In addition to the recent $4,300,000 selling price of *Daybreak*, some other auction prices of Parrish original paintings would include

* $662,500 for the 1895 Mask & Wig Club mural of *Old King Cole* (Christie's, 1996)
* $398,000 for *Stars*
* $210,000 for *Blue Hose/Yellow Hose* (Christie's, 1996)
* $140,000 for *Egyptian Sculpture*
* Five separate Parrish landscapes sold within the $150,000 – 210,000 range each

Original Artwork Value Guide

Christmas Toast (oil on board)	10x14"	$45,000
Pair of wood gold-leaf columns	1x3"	$800
Trees (watercolor)	4x4"	$7,300

Murals

Parrish also painted several very large murals throughout his career, including

* *Old King Cole* (1906), in the Knickerbocker Hotel, New York City
* *The Pied Piper* (1909), in the Palace Hotel, San Francisco
* *Dream Garden*, which was completed by Louis Comfort Tiffany, based upon a Parrish artwork

Although you will obviously have little opportunity to purchase an original mural, you should understand that art print triptychs of these murals have been produced and are very desirable to collectors.

Art Prints

This is the area that most collectors pursue because individuals prefer to collect things that they can hang on their walls. Art prints represent

Ecstasy, a typical Girl-on-Rocks scene

Silent Night, a typical winter landscape scene

original reproductions of the original artwork, most framed and suitable for hanging.

Because of Parrish's popularity, many different publishers sought his artwork for publication and over the years, various publishers distributed

Maxfield Parrish art prints. Some of these publishers included House of Art, Dodge, P.F. Collier, and Reinthal-Newman, among others.

Art prints came in a variety of sizes, with 6x10", 12x15", and 18x30" often being the most common standard sizes. However, because they were inexpensive, machine-produced prints, they were sometimes cropped down in size to fit a specific frame. As a result, you will see a wide variety of art print sizes.

Art Print Value Guide	Size	Value	Date
Aucassin Seeks Nicolette	11x17"	$700	1903
Air Castles	12x16"	$140	1904
Aladdin (Arabian Knights)	9x11"	$100	1907
Atlas	9x11"	$25	1908
Autumn	10½x12"	$225	1905
Bellerophon	9x11"	$20	1909
Brazen Boatman			
(Arabian Knights)	9x11"	$100	1907
Broadmoor	6¾x8½"	$150	1921
Broadmoor	17¼x22"	$900	1921
Cadmus	9x11"	$100	1909
Call to Joy, A (as single print)	6½x20½"	$350	1915
Canyon	6x10"	$100	1924
Canyon	12x15"	$295	1924
Cassim (Arabian Knights)	9x11"	$100	1906
Centaur			
(or Jason and His Teacher)	9x11"	$70	1910
Circe's Palace	9x11"	$70	1908
City of Brass (Arabian Nights)	9x11"	$100	1905
Cleopatra	6¼x7"	$275	1917
Cleopatra	13½x15½"	$675	1917
Cleopatra	24¼x28"	$1,500	1917
Daybreak	6x10"	$95	1923
Daybreak	10x18"	$240	1923
Daybreak	18x30"	$375	1923
Dies Irae	12x15"	$275	1910
Dinkey Bird	11x16"	$160	1905
Dream Garden	14x24½"	$130	1915
Dreaming	6x10"	$150	1928
Dreaming	10x18"	$440	1928
Dreaming	18x30"	$1,100	1928
Easter	8x10"	$250	1905
Errant Pan	9x11"	$250	1910
Evening	6x10"	$100	1922
Evening	12x15"	$250	1922
Fisherman & Genie			
(Arabian Nights)	9x11"	$100	1906
Florentine Fete, A	6x10"	$125	1916
Florentine Fete			
(Garden of Opportunity)	10¾x20½"	$475	1915
Florentine Fete — Love's Pilgrimage			
(as single print)	6½x20½"	$350	1915
Florentine Fete — A Call to Joy			
(as single print)	6½x20½"	$350	1915
Fountain of Pirene	9¼x11½"	$250	1907
Garden of Allah	4x8"	$95	1918
Garden of Allah	9x18"	$200	1918
Garden of Allah	15x30"	$325	1918
Garden of Opportunity			
(as single print)	10¾x20½"	$475	1915
Garden of Opportunity			
(as triptych)	20½x24½"	$1,600	1915
Gardener	13x19"	$275	1907
Harvest	8x10"	$200	1905
Hilltop	6¼x10"	$100	1927
Hilltop	12x20"	$350	1927
Hilltop	18x30"	$800	1927
Idiot (or The Booklover)	8x11"	$275	1910
Interlude	12x15"	$250	1924
Jack Frost	12½x13"	$300	1936
Jason and the Talking Oak	9x11"	$150	1908
King Black Isles	9x11"	$150	1907
Land of Make Believe	9x11"	$250	1912
Lantern Bearers	9x11"	$350	1910
Love's Pilgrimage			
(as single print)	6½x20½"	$350	1915
Lute Players	6x10"	$150	1924
Lute Players	10x18"	$275	1924
Lute Players	18x30"	$675	1924
Morning	6x10"	$150	1922
Morning	12x15"	$250	1922
Nature Lover	10x13"	$225	1911
Old King Cole	3x11½"	$200	1906
Old King Cole	6¼x23"	$700	1906
Page, The	10x12"	$225	1925
Pandora's Box	9x11"	$275	1909
Pied Piper	6¾x21"	$1,100	1909
Pierrot's Serenade	9x11"	$75	1908
Prince, The	10x12"	$225	1925
Prince Agib (Arabian Nights)	9x11"	$100	1906
Prince Codadad			
(Arabian Nights)	9x11"	$100	1906
Queen Gulnare	9x11"	$225	1907
Quest for Golden Fleece	9x11"	$100	1910
Reveries	6x10"	$125	1928
Reveries	12x15"	$250	1928
Romance	14¾x23½"	$900	1925
Royal Gorge	16x20"	$550	1923
Rubaiyat	2x8½"	$125	1917
Rubaiyat (without verse)	3¾x14¾"	$200	1917
Rubiayat (with verse)	3¾x14¾"	$250	1917

Rubaiyat	7x28½"	$700	1917
Sea Nymphs	9x11"	$180	1910
Search for Singing Tree	9x11"	$200	1906
Sinbad Plots Against the Giant	9x11"	$150	1907
Sing a Song of Sixpence	5¾x14"	$750	1911
Sing a Song of Sixpence	9x21"	$900	1911
Spirit of Transportation	20x16"	$650	1923
Spring	10x12"	$225	1905
Stars	6x10"	$310	1927
Stars	10x18"	$650	1927
Stars	18x30"	$1,800	1927
Sugar Plum Tree	11x16"	$450	1905
Summer	9x12"	$250	1905
Tempest Series —			
An Odd Angle of Isle	7x7"	$175	1909
Tempest Series — As Morning			
Steals Upon the Night	7x7"	$175	1909
Tempest Series — Phoenix Throne	7x7"	$175	1909
Tempest Series —			
Prospero and His Magic	7x7"	$175	1909
Thanksgiving	9x11"	$225	1909
Three Shepherds or Xmas	11x13¼"	$250	1904
Toyland Soldier	8x11"	$450	1910
Valley of Diamonds			
(Arabian Nights)	9x11"	$100	1907
White Birch	9x11"	$100	1931

Wild Geese	15x12"	$150	1924
With Trumpet and Drum	12x17"	$450	1905
Wynken, Blynken & Nod	11x15"	$425	1905

Parrish Collecting Tip:
Many of Parrish's most successful art prints also appeared on calendars, book illustrations, or in some other format.

Cassim. Est. Value: $100.

Cleopatra. Est. Value: $1,500.

Canyon. Est. Value: $275.

Dreaming. Est. Value: $1,100.

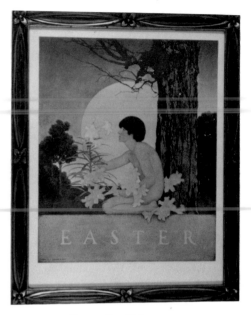

Easter. Est. Value: $250.

Evening. Est. Value: $250.

Harvest. Est. Value: $200.

Errant Pan. Est. Value: $250.

Hilltop. Est. Value: $800.

Land of Make Believe. Est. Value: $250.

Jason and the Talking Oak. Est. Value: $275.

Lantern Bearers. Est. Value: $350.

Pied Piper. Est. Value: $1,100.

Morning. Est. Value: $250.

Pandora's Box. Est. Value: $275.

Rubaiyat. Est. Value: $700.

Sea Nymphs. Est. Value: $180.

Sinbad Plots Against the Giant. Est. Value: $150.

Sing a Song of Sixpence. Est. Value: $900.

Stars. Est. Value: $1,800.

Spirit of Transportation. Est. Value: $650.

Summer. Est. Value: $250.

White Birch. Est. Value: $100.

Wynken, Blynken & Nod. Est. Value: $425.

A Knave of Hearts triptych: The Page (l), Romance (c), The Prince (r). Est. Value: $1,200 – 1,400.

Knave of Hearts Prints

The *Knave of Hearts* was a book by Louise Sanders which Parrish illustrated in 1925. This book contained many different Parrish prints which became very popular and collectible. Most *Knave of Hearts* prints are actually from either hardbound or softbound books. Prints taken from hardbound *Knave of Hearts* bookplates were printed on single-side pages which means that there will be no printing of the back side of these prints, whereas *Knave of Hearts* prints taken from soft-bound books will have printing on the reverse side.

The *Knave of Hearts* print titles include

* The *Knave of Hearts* (front and back cover). Est Value: $80 – 100
* The *Knave of Hearts* (title page). Est Value: $50 – 70
* *Romance* (printed on the cover linings in the front and back of hardbound editions only). Est Value: $80 – 100
* This is the book of (with space for owner's name). Est Value: $80 – 100
* *Lady Violetta About to Make the Tarts...*Est Value: $80 – 100
* *The Characters.* Est Value: $50 – 70
* *The Manager.* Est Value: $90 – 110
* *Two Chefs at the Table.* Est Value: $50 – 70
* *Blue Hose – Yellow Hose.* Est Value: $80 – 100
* *Chef Carrying Cauldron.* Est Value: $50 – 70
* *Entrance of Pompdebile.* Est Value: $80 – 100
* *Chef Between Two Lobsters.* Est Value: $50 – 70
* *Lady Ursula Kneeling Before the King.* Est Value: $80 – 100
* *The Frog and the Prince.* Est Value: $50 – 70
* *Six Little Ingredients.* Est Value: $80 – 100
* *Violetta and the Knave Examining the Tarts.* Est Value: $80 – 100
* *Gardener Wheeling Vegetables.* Est Value: $50 – 70
* *King & Chancellor at Kitchen Door.* Est Value: $80 – 100
* *Two Cooks Peeling Potatoes.* Est Value: $50 – 70
* *The Prince.* Est Value: $115 – 135
* *The Page.* Est Value: $115 – 135
* *Fool in Green.* Est Value: $50 – 70
* *King Tastes the Tarts.* Est Value: $80 – 100
* *The Serenade.* Est Value: $50 – 70
* *The End—The Manager Bows.* Est Value: $80 – 100

Knave of Hearts Value Guide

Large-sized *Knave of Heart* prints (10x12") generally sell in the $90 – 150 range. Small sizes 4x9½" typically sell in the $60 – 110 range.

1921 Edison-Mazda calendar, Primitive Man, small size, 8½x19", with incomplete pad. Est. Value: $1,000 – 1,100.

Edison-Mazda Calendars

Between 1918 and 1934, Parrish painted works for the Edison-Mazda Calendar Series. Commissioned by the Edison-Mazda Division of General Electric, each annual picture focused upon a different aspect of the overall theme of lighting. More than 10,000,000 of these calendars were distributed around America, bringing the work of Maxfield Parrish into most American households and businesses. Although these calendars were commissioned by Edison-Mazda, the name of various Edison-Mazda distributers and related businesses also appeared on these calendars.

Edison Mazda calendars basically fall into four separate categories, with the values varying for each:

a) Large-Complete...which means an original 18x37½" calendar with both the print & calendar intact

b) Large-Cropped...which means a large calendar has been cropped down to the approximately 14½x22½" print

c) Small-Complete...which means an original 8½x19" calendar with both the print & calendar intact

d) Small-Cropped...which means a small calendar has been cropped down to the approximately 6¼x10½" print

complete 12-month pads will be valued higher than calendars with only partial or no pads.

Parrish Collecting Tip:

Edison-Mazda calendars date between 1918 and 1934 and represent one of the most desirable, collectible, and expensive forms of Maxfield Parrish prints. The large, complete calendars are typically valued at $1,400 – 2,900 when in excellent condition.

Edison-Mazda Value Guide	Small Complete 8½x19"	Small Cropped 6¼x10½"	Large Complete 18x37½"	Large Cropped 14½x22½"
1918 Dawn (or Night is Fled)				
	$1,100	$300	$2,900	$950
1919 Spirit of the Night				
	$1,200	$450	$2,900	$1,500
1920 Prometheus				
	$1,200	$500	$3,000	$1,500
1921 Primitive Man				
	$1,100	$400	$2,800	$1,400
1922 Egypt				
	$1,200	$500	$2,900	$1,500
1923 Lampseller of Baghdad				
	$1,100	$450	$2,900	$1,500
1924 Venetian Lamplighter				
	$900	$300	$2,400	$1,300
1925 Dreamlight				
	$900	$350	$2,400	$1,300
1926 Enchantment				
	$950	$400	$2,500	$1,350
1927 Reveries				
	$600	$150	$1,400	$650
1928 Contentment				
	$900	$350	$2,400	$1,300
1929 Golden Hours				
	$700	$200	$1,500	$750
1930 Ecstasy				
	$950	$400	$2,500	$1,350
1931 Waterfall				
	$800	$275	$2,000	$1,000
1932 Solitude				
	$800	$275		
1933 Sunrise				
	$1,100	$450	$3,100	$1,500
1934 Moonlight				
	$1,200	$450		

Quite obviously, large calendars will be worth considerably more than small calendars, and complete calendars are worth considerably more than cropped calendars. Calendars with

Dawn — small cropped, $300; large cropped, $950.

Spirit of the Night — small cropped, $450; large cropped, $1,500.

*Egypt —
small cropped, $500; large cropped, $1,500.*

*Lampseller of Baghdad —
small cropped, $450; large cropped, $1,500.*

*Waterfall —
small cropped, $275; large cropped, $1,000.*

*Venetian Lamplighter —
small cropped, $300; large cropped, $1,300.*

Solitude — small cropped, $275.

Sunrise — small cropped, $450; large cropped, $1,500.

Moonlight — small cropped, $450.

1946 Brown & Bigelow calendar print, jumbo, 24x30".
Est. Value: $500.

Brown & Bigelow Calendars

Between 1935 and 1962, Parrish began producing a series of pictures for Brown & Bigelow calendars and prints which featured his landscape scenes. Landscape scenes were typically New England scenes, featured the famous Parrish blue, and represented Parrish's true love in art. While Brown & Bigelow was the publisher of these calendars, the advertiser's name was usually much more visible and prominent than that of Brown & Bigelow.

Brown & Bigelow calendars and prints came in both summer landscape and winter landscape scenes. Winter landscape prints were sized between 8½x11" and 12½x17", while summer landscape calendars varied in size from 3¼x4" to 24x30". Larger calendars will usually be worth more than small calendars, and complete calendars are worth more than cropped calendars. Calendars with complete 12-month pads will be valued higher than calendars with only partial or no pads at all.

The following prints were issued as Brown & Bigelow Winter Landscape Scenes:

1941	Winter Twilight
1942	Silent Night (or Winter Night)
1943	At Close of Day (or Plainfield, NH, Church at Dusk)
1944	Eventide
1945	Lights of Home
1946	Path to Home (or Across the Valley)
1947	Peace at Twilight (or Lull Brook)
1948	Christmas Eve (or Deep Valley)
1949	Christmas Morning
1950	Afterglow (or A New Day)
1951	Twilight Hour
1952	Lights of Welcome
1953	Peaceful Night (or Church at Norwich)
1954	When Day is Dawning (or Winter Sunrise)
1955	Sunrise
1956	Evening
1957	At Close of Day (Norwich, VT)
1958	Sunlight (or Winter Sunshine)
1959	Peace of Evening (or Dingleton Farm)
1960	Twilight Time (or Freeman Farm)
1961	Daybreak
1962	Evening Shadows

Value Guide for B&B Winter Landscape Calendars:
Sizes: 8½x11" – 12½x17", $250 – 325

The following prints were issued as Brown & Bigelow summer landscape scenes:

1936	Peaceful Valley
1937	Twilight
1938	The Glen
1939	Early Autumn
1940	Evening Shadows
1941	Village Brook
1942	Thy Templed Hills
1943	A Perfect Day
1944	Thy Rocks & Rills
1945	Sun-Up
1946	Valley of Enchantment
1947	Evening & Afterglo (or A New Day)
1948	Millpond
1949	Village Church
1950	Peace of Evening (or Evening Shadows)
1950	Sunlit Valley
1951	Daybreak
1952	Ancient Tree
1953	Evening Shadows

1954	Old Glen Mill
1955	Peaceful Valley
1956	Misty Morn
1957	Morning Light
1958	New Moon
1959	Under Summer Skies
1960	Sheltering Oaks
1961	Twilight
1962	Quiet Solitude
1963	Peaceful Country

Value Guide for B&B Summer Landscape Calendar Samples or Greeting Cards
3¼x4", $30 – 40
4½x6", $40 – 60

Value Guide for B&B Summer Landscape Calendar Prints
Medium, 8x11", $150 – 200
Large, 11x16", $250 – 325
Extra Large, 16x22", 350 – 425
Jumbo, 24x30", $450 – 500
With complete calendar pads: add 25% of the above price.

Twilight Hour. Est. Value: $325.

Parrish Collecting Tip:

Brown & Bigelow calendars date between 1936 and 1963, featured Parrish's landscape scenes, and are generally not considered to be as valuable as the earlier Edison-Mazda calendars. These calendars are typically valued at $100 – 500 when in excellent condition, depending upon size & condition.

Evening.
Medium to Extra Large, Est. Value: $175 – 400.

Path to Home. Est. Value: $325.

At Close of Day. Est. Value: $290.

Daybreak.
Medium – Extra Large, Est. Value: $175 – 425.

Evening Shadows.
Medium – Extra Large, Est. Value: $200 – 425.

The Glen.
Medium – Extra Large, Est. Value: $200 – 425.

Village Brook.
Medium – Extra Large, Est. Value: $175 – 400.

A Perfect Day.
Medium – Extra Large, Est. Value: $175 – 400.

Valley of Enchantment.
Medium – Extra Large, Est. Value: $200 – 425.

Misty Morn.
Medium – Extra Large, Est. Value: $200 – 425.

Under Summer Skies.
Medium – Extra Large, Est. Value: $200 – 425.

Dodge Publishing

Dodge Publishing also released several calendars featuring Maxfield Parrish art.

Business Man's Calendar	6x8"	$75 – 100
Business Man's Calendar (with original box)	6x8"	$100 – 125
Calender of Cheer	6x8"	$75 – 100
Calender of Cheer (with original box)	6x8"	$100 –125
Calendar of Friendship	6x8"	$75 – 100
Calendar of Friendship (with original box)	6x8"	$100 – 125
Calendar of Sunshine	6x8"	$75 – 100
Calendar of Sunshine (with original box)	6x8"	$100 – 125

Italian Villas and their Gardens. Est. Value: $175 – 225.

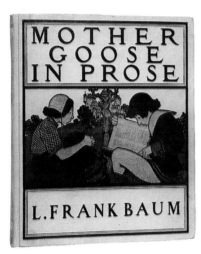

Mother Goose in Prose. Est. Value: $1,800 – 2,200.

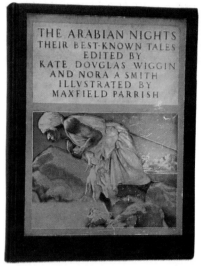

The Arabian Knights. Est. Value: $100 – 150.

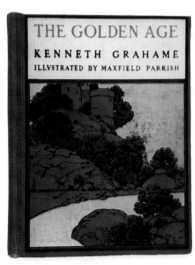

The Golden Age. Est. Value: $90 – 100.

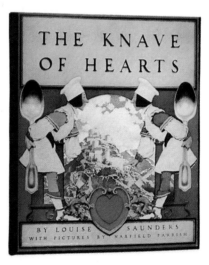

The Knave of Hearts. Est. Value: $600 (softbound), $1,200 (hardbound).

Book Illustrations

In 1897, Maxfield Parrish illustrated his first book, L. Frank Baum's *Mother Goose in Prose*. The success of this book was overwhelming and Parrish's career was on a roll. Between 1897 and 1925, Parrish illustrated more than 20 books.

Book Value Guide

The Arabian Nights, 1945	$65
The Arabian Nights, 1st edition, 1909 with original dust jacket	$200
The Arabian Nights, 1st edition, 1909	$170
Dream Days,1902	$95
A Golden Treasury of Songs & Lyrics, 1st edition	$260
The Golden Age, 1st edition, 1899	$95
In The Beginning, 1976	$40
Italian Villas and their Gardens, 1904	$250
Knickerbocker's History of New York, 1900	$300
King Albert's Book	$85
The Knave of Hearts, 1925	$1,200
The Knave of Hearts, softbound, 1925	$600
The Lure of the Garden, 1st edition 1911	$145
Mother Goose in Prose by L. Frank Baum, 1897	$2,500
Poems of Childhood, by Eugene Field, 1904	$150
Poems of Childhood by Eugene Field, 5th Ed	$85
A Wonder Book and Tanglewood Tales 1st Ed, 1923	$185
A Wonderbook and Tanglewood Tales, later editions	$125
The Early Years, Skeeter's, all editions	$225
The Early Years, Skeeter's, American 1st edition, 1973	$250
The Early Years, Skeeter's, Japanese edition, 1975	$40

Parrish Collecting Tip:

Books illustrated by Maxfield Parrish are highly sought after by collectors. *The Arabian Knights* is the most commonly found book and was reprinted in numerous editions. First editions are the most valuable and most collectible, typically having a value of $100 – 200.

Magazine Covers and Inserts

As his popularity grew, Parrish was commissioned to create covers for numerous magazines between 1895 and 1936, including *Century, Collier's, Harper's Bazaar, Harper's Weekly, Hearst's, Ladies Home Journal, Life, Scribner's*, and nearly 25 other magazines. Today Parrish magazine covers are highly desirable to Parrish collectors.

He also created numerous inserts for these and other magazines and most are collectible and desirable to Parrish collectors.

Harper's Round Table, July 4, 1895. Est. Value: $100 – 125.

Note that in 1895, Parrish's name was still F. Maxfield Parrish.

Harper's Weekly, 1896. Est. Value: $150 – 200.

Charles Scribner's Sons, The Christmas Book Buyer, 1899. Est. Value: $100 – 150.

Magazine Cover Value Guide

Book Buyer's covers	$100 – 150
Century covers	$50 – 75
Collier's covers	$40 – 100
Harper's covers	$40 – 120
Ladies' Home Journal covers	$35 – 95
Life covers	$45 – 120
Scribner's covers	$50 – 100

Magazine Insert Value Guide

Century magazine		$20 – 40	
Community Plate	10x15"	$110	1918
Djer Kiss Elves	9x14"	$125	1918
Djer Kiss Maiden	10x12"	$125	1921
Hires Root Beer	5x7"	$35	1921
Illustrated London News		$100 – 125	
Jell-O-Polly	7x10"	$55	1922
Pandora's Box	9x11"	$85	1908
Sandman, The	5x7"	$45	1905
Swift's Premium Ham	9x12"	$125	1921

Life, March 1, 1923. Est. Value: $125 – 175.

Parrish Collecting Tip:

Magazine covers featuring Maxfield Parrish artwork are highly sought after by Parrish collectors and typically are valued at $50 – 200, depending upon specific issue and condition.

Advertising Illustrations

Once he became a household name, numerous advertisers commissioned Maxfield Parrish to execute art for their respective products. Advertising illustrations were commissioned

Life, March 29, 1923. Est. Value: $125 – 175.

Djer-Kiss advertising piece, 1918. Est. Value: $75 – 125.

by Colgate, Djer-Kiss Perfume & Cosmetics, Ferry Seeds, Fisk Tires, Jell-O, assorted candy boxes, gift boxes, and wide variety of other brand name products.

Jell-O advertising piece. Est. Value: $50 (small) — 100 (large).

Parrish Collecting Tip:

Maxfield Parrish advertising illustrations are highly desireable to Parrish collectors and are typically valued at $25 – 125 when in excellent condition.

Peter Peter pumpkin eater
Had a wife and couldn't keep her
He put her in a pumpkin shell
And there he kept her very well

USE FERRY'S SEEDS

Ferry Seeds poster, 1918. Est. Value: $1,100 — 1,200.

Jack and the Beanstalk poster

Posters

Parrish artwork also appeared on a number of different posters which are quite desirable and collectible. Some examples would include

Poster Value Guide

Century Magazine poster	1902	14x20"	$1,000 – 1,200
Ferry Seed poster	1918		$1,100 – 1,200
Harper's Weekly (National Authority on Amateur Sport)	1897	12¼x16	$1,600 – 1,800
Jack and the Beanstalk			$1,200 – 1,400
New Hampshire Winter Paradise			$400 – 600
Scribner's (Fiction Number)	1897		$1,600 – 1,900

Other Parrish Collectibles

In addition to original artworks, art prints, calendars, book illustrations, magazine covers, posters, and advertising illustrations, there is a wide variety of other Maxfield Parrish items sought after by collectors, including miscellaneous advertising pieces, playing cards, match book covers, correspondence, signatures, photographs, and pretty much anything else containing the art of Maxfield Parrish.

1909 Old King Cole triptik calendar, 12½x29".
Est. Value: $1,500 (very rare).

Triptik with Love's Pilgrimage (l); Garden of Opportunity (c); A Call to Joy (r). 21½x25". Est. Value: $1,600.

1929 Edison-Mazda calendar, Golden Hours, complete calendar, 8½x19". Est. Value: $700.

Tin Edison-Mazda advertising sign (double sided), 21½x26". Est. Value: $2,800 (rare).

Advertising thermometer, 8x10". Est. Value: $275.

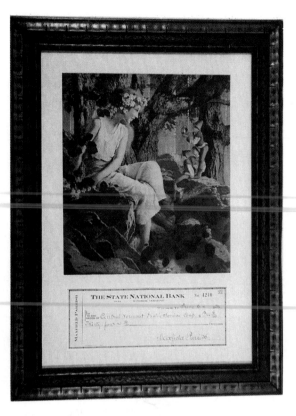

Framed Parrish print and signed check

Framed Broadmoor Hotel collage, including a Broadmoor Hotel
menu, postcard, and match book

Soldier, from a rare 10-Pin Game. Est. Value: $150.

Framed Parrish check and eight playing cards

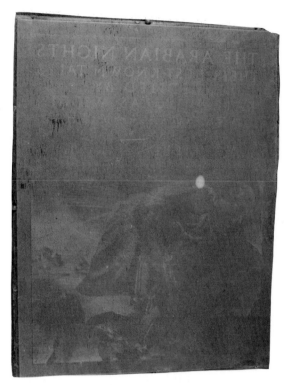

Copper engraving plate from The Arabian Knights.
Est. Value: $400.

Toyland Soldier art print, 9x11". Est. Value: $450.

Framed magazine cover, Life's Christmas Cover. 8x10¾".
Est. Value: $110.

MISCELLANEOUS

Blotter – Twilight		$75	1936
Book matches – The Broadmoor Hotel		$80	1920s
Broadmoor menu	11x15"	$185	1920s
Broadmoor post card	3x5"	$40	1930s
Djer Kiss ad	11x15"	$125	1916
Edison-Mazda pencil		$30	1925
Edison-Mazda Spirit of Night &			
Dawn ad	11x16"	$175	1919
Ferry Seed, Peter, Peter			
Pumpkin Eater ad	16x10"	$125	1919
Fisk Tire ad	11x15"	$85	1919
Hires ad	7x10"	$75	1921
Jell-O recipe booklet —			
Polly Put Kettle and			
The King & Queen		$75	1924
Jell-O, King & Queen Might			
Eat Thereof ad	9x6"	$55	1921
Magazine gift subscription card —			
Castle of Indolence (from			
the Florentine Fete Series)	6x9¾"	$150	1912
Magazine gift subscription card —			
Ladies' Home Journal	7x11"	$125	1913
McClures cover		$70	1904
Playing cards—			
Contentment, full deck with box		$225	1928
Playing cards — Dawn, full deck with box		$250	1918
Playing cards — Egypt, full deck with box		$250	1922
Playing cards — Enchantment,			
full deck with box		$200	1926
Playing cards — In the Mountains,			
full deck with box		$140	1971
Playing cards — Lampseller of			
Baghdad, full deck with box		$225	1923
Playing cards — Reveries,			
full deck with box		$195	1927
Playing cards — Spirit of the Night,			
full deck with box		$250	1919
Playing cards — Waterfall,			
full deck with box		$200	1931
Playing cards — Ecstasy,			
full deck with box		$200	1930
Playing cards — Venetian Lamplighter,			
full deck with box		$200	1924
Stamp — Brill Brothers		$50	
Pamphlet — Scribner's Classics for			
Younger Readers (Wynken, Blynken,			
& Nod)	3½x6"	$65	
Puzzle — Lady Violetta & The Knave		$125	1925
Puzzle — The Page		$125	1925
Puzzle — The Prince		$125	1925

Royal Baking Powder ad		$80	1895
Signed checks		$195	1930s
Single cards		$8, $14	
Soldier game		$1,100	1913
Swifts Ham ad	12x14"	$185	1921
Swift's Ham ad (Jack Sprat)		$125	1921
Tape measure — 2 Knaves		$150	
Theater program for Globe			
Theater	5x7"	$65	1909
Tie rack — Old King Cole		$375	1909

Parrish Collecting Tip:

Basically any item which includes original reproduction Maxfield Parrish art is desirable to Maxfield Parrish collectors.

Reproduction Alert

You should recognize that because of the popularity and value of Maxfield Parrish prints, there is a wide variety of reproductions available, some legitimate, others meant to deceive.

Contemporary limited edition reproduction prints of many of Parrish's most popular prints are available on the Internet or through other more traditional channels in the $150 – 300 price range. These are being honestly marketed and sold as limited edition reproductions.

Color laser copies are the cheapest and most common form of fraudulent reproduction. I was recently at an auction and saw a 12x15" laser copy of *Stars*, framed in an old frame, being sold by the auctioneer as original. It only sold for $35 which told me that most in attendance easily spotted the laser reproduction. After the print was delivered to the purchaser, I saw him continually inspecting the print. He knew that something was wrong with it. He started looking at it from different angles, he held it up to the light. Basically he did everything but take it apart. Eventually he took it home with him where, I suspect, it was ultimately resold to someone else as original.

In addition to limited edition reproductions and laser copies, you should recognize that several beautiful books illustrating the works of Maxfield Parrish in full color have been published. They were large, with many beautiful color pictures. It is fairly common to see pictures cut out of these books and reframed as original. Your best defense against this is to review the original books to determine what these color reproduction book illustrations look like.

How do you tell recent reproductions from original prints? Common sense should help you out. Exceptionally bright and shiny prints will probably indicate newer prints. Grainy prints with somewhat blurry or fuzzy detail are also signs of newer prints. Original Maxfield Parrish prints should have crisp color without looking too florescent, shiny, glossy, or bold.

Don't be deceived into thinking that the print is original just because the backing paper on the frame is old. A common faker's technique is to frame a newer print in an old frame, replace the old nails, and then glue a larger piece of old backing paper to the frame, cropping it to fit exactly. It's very easy to do, and it's done more often than you may think.

Parrish Collecting Tips:

Beware of buying Parrish prints at auctions which offer no guarantee of authenticity. *As is-where is-no returns* auctions tend to serve as a prime dumping ground for many reproduction, doctored, and fake Maxfield Parrish prints. Know what you are bidding on before you raise your hand.

Beware of dealers who have only one Parrish in their booth. Chances are that they are not very knowledgeable in the area of Maxfield Parrish. You might be getting an incredible bargain. Or you might be buying their mistake.

Beware that many other artists were also painting the Enchanted Garden and Girl-on-Rocks styles of pictures. (See Chapter 4 on R. Atkinson Fox as an example.) Many prints in the style of Maxfield Parrish were published during this period, and sometimes dealers who are not familiar with the works of Maxfield Parrish will sell these look-alikes as authentic Parrish prints.

Identifying and Dating Maxfield Parrish Prints

The Signature: Maxfield Parrish prints carry a variety of signatures, each varying by publisher or year of publication. The following represent some of the more common types of Parrish signatures.

Block Maxfield Parrish signature on print

Block M.P. signature on print

Block © Maxfield Parrish, 1909 on print

Block Maxfield Parrish, © BB USA on print
(BB stands for Brown & Bigelow)

Block Maxfield Parrish, © BB on print
(BB stands for Brown & Bigelow)

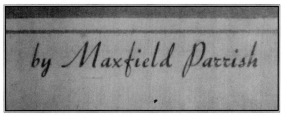

Italicized Maxfield Parrish lower right below print

The Title: The title is sometimes, but not always, found on the print. The following are some examples of how the title may appear.

Old King Cole, title centered under print

The Pied Piper, title centered in box under print

The Twilight Hour, title centered below print on matting

Evening Shadows, title italicized and lower left beneath print

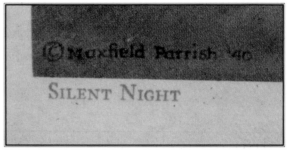

Silent Night, title lower left beneath signature & copyright

The White Birch, by Maxfield Parrish

The Publisher's Marking: Some, but not all, prints also include the publisher's name.

The House of Art

P.F. Collier

Triptych label, Curtis Publishing Co.

Curtis Publishing Co.

Understanding the Main Determinants of Value

The value of a Maxfield Parrish print will depend upon several key factors.

Subject Matter: What is the topic or theme of the print? Is it a calendar or art print? Girls-on-Rocks or landscape print? Edison Mazda or Brown & Bigelow? Is it common or rare? Is it an early or later piece? How many prints were originally produced, and how many are still remaining? How many other collectors are interested in owning that same print? Where else can you go to get a comparable one?

Condition: Is the picture in poor or excellent condition? Is the color sharp or faded? Does the picture have any water stains, foxing, or blemishes? Has it been cropped or cut down? Is the stain, foxing, or blemish major and very noticeable, or minor and barely noticeable? If matted, is the matting blemished or clean? Is the frame an original ornate frame, an original plain frame, or a new frame? What is the condition of the frame? How difficult will it be to find the same print in the same or better condition?

Size: How large is the picture? If matted, how large is both the mat and the picture? Has the picture or matting been cropped down to fit another frame.

Each of these questions must be considered in arriving at a final estimated value.

Parrish Collecting Tip:
The original backing paper is often very important to some Parrish collectors. Unless the picture is extremely dirty and especially in need of a good cleaning, you are probably better off leaving the original backing paper on the frame, although ultimately it is the print itself that is of primary importance and value.

Maxfield Parrish Condition Guide

We typically use a 6-point grading system when evaluating the condition of Maxfield Parrish prints:

Uncirculated: The print looks like it just came off the press and basically was never exposed to the light of day. The original borders will be intact and there can be absolutely no imperfection whatsoever. You will rarely, if ever, find prints in this condition. But if you do, they will command a premium price.

5–Mint: The print must have excellent color and detail, absolutely no foxing, water stains, discoloration, cropping, or tears at all. It must be nearly perfect.

4–Very Good: Although there may be some loss of color due to the natural aging process, there are basically no other imperfections.

3–Good: There is some loss of color due to the natural aging process. There may also be minor blemishes, that are barely noticeable. However, there can be no cropping at this rating.

2–Fair: There is evident loss of color or there are evident blemishes, including, but not limited to, foxing, water stains, discoloration, cropping, or tears. If a print has been cropped or reduced in size, it cannot be graded higher than a 2.

1–Poor: There is major loss of color and/or major blemishes. These prints have minimal value.

Some of the More Commonly Found Maxfield Parrish Prints

* Daybreak
* Garden of Allah
* The Dinkey Bird

* Air Castles
* Prints within the Arabian Knight series
* Wild Geese
* Morning
* Evening
* Canyon
* The Lute Players

Parrish Collecting Tip:

Daybreak was far and away Maxfield Parrish's bestselling print and seemingly there are more *Daybreak* prints in circulation than all other Maxfield Parrish prints combined.

Some of the More Highly Sought After Maxfield Parrish Prints

* Nearly any Edison-Mazda calendar (larger calendars are generally better than smaller ones)
* Lantern Bearers
* Stars
* Cleopatra
* The Pied Piper
* Wassail Bowl
* Dreaming
* Most of the Maxfield Parrish posters
* Most Djer Kiss advertising

Maxfield Parrish Collectors' Club

At the time this book went to press, there was no formal or official Maxfield Parrish collectors' club.

Other Maxfield Parrish Books and Reference Materials

* Cutler, Laurence and Judy Goffman Cutler. *Maxfield Parrish Retrospective*. 1995.
* Cutler, Laurence S. Judy Goffman, and The American Illustrators Gallery. *Maxfield Parrish*.
* Lane, Stephanie. *Maxfield Parrish: A Price Guide*. 1993.
* Ludwig, Coy. *Maxfield Parrish*. 1973.
* Perry, Richard. *The Maxfield Parrish Identification & Price Guide*. 1993.
* Skeeters. *Maxfield Parrish: The Early Years*. 1993.

Maxfield Parrish on the Internet

We found a wide variety of web sites featuring the works of Maxfield Parrish. You can locate any current web sites featuring Maxfield Parrish by simply keying the words Maxfield Parrish into any of the major Internet search engines. We found many visual images of Parrish's work, pictures for sale, assorted books and reference materials, current Parrish news and events, dealers who were both buying and selling on the Internet, educational & informational articles on Parrish prints and Parrish collecting, and much more.

As the Internet is changing so rapidly today, rather than limit you to any of the specific web sites that we found, we would recommend that you surf the net yourself and see what is available on Maxfield Parrish today.

Where to Go If Looking to Buy or Sell Maxfield Parrish Prints

There are many dealers around the country who specialize partially or entirely in Maxfield Parrish. One obvious reference source we would recommend would be our collaborators on this chapter, Deborah Labb and Stephen Steinberg. Their annual Maxfield Parrish Show and Sale in Pennsylvania serves as a major gathering of Parrish collectors and is an excellent source for locating quality Maxfield Parrish prints. Debbie and Steve also appear at a variety of antique shows throughout the eastern portion of the country. They are always actively buying and selling Maxfield Parrish prints and can be reached at Box 461, Forest Grove, PA 18922 (215)794-5507.

Other dealers specializing in Maxfield Parrish can be found in many of the national and regional antiques & collectibles trade papers.

If you would be interested in consigning any Maxfield Parrish prints to our next twentieth century American print catalog auction, you can contact Michael Ivankovich at P.O. Box 1536, Doylestown, PA 18901 (215)345-6094, fax (215)345-6692, or e-mail: wnutting@comcat.com.

Or you can visit the twentieth century American print section of our www.wnutting.com Internet web site.

About Deborah Labb and Stephen Steinberg

Deborah Labb has been collecting Maxfield Parrish since 1976 when a friend introduced her to Parrish prints in her grandmother's house. She acquired quite a few prints herself over the next

Deborah Labb & Stephen Steinberg, at 1997 show

Summary of Key Maxfield Parrish Collecting Tips

* Maxfield Parrish produced nearly 900 works during his 65-year career prior to his death in 1966.
* His artwork appeared on more than 20,000,000 art prints, book illustrations, and calendars, and appeared on many more millions of advertising pieces and magazine covers.
* Parrish was best known for his Girls-on-Rocks (1900 – 1934) and landscape (1936 – 1962) scenes.
* His art appeared on Edison-Mazda calendars between 1918 and 1934.
* His art appeared on Brown & Bigelow calendars between 1936 and 1962.
* His art appeared as illustrations in more than 20 books.
* His art appeared on numerous magazine covers, magazine inserts, posters, and advertising pieces.
* His most popular and bestselling art print was *Daybreak*.
* Original Maxfield Parrish artwork can be very difficult and extremely expensive to locate.
* All Maxfield Parrish prints were machine produced.
* There are many Maxfield Parrish reproductions in circulation and you need to learn to differentiate between original prints and more recent reproductions.

10 years before meeting Stephen in 1985, when she introduced him to the collection. Together they have been dealing in Parrish since the mid-1980s and have accumulated an impressive collection of their own. They continue to pursue their never-ending hunt for the rarest of Parrish finds.

Their Pennsylvania Maxfield Parrish Show and Sale has become an annual event every April since 1990. The show brings together a large selection of original Maxfield Parrish art prints, calendars, books, and advertising, as well as a small assortment of oil paintings, drawings, and estate items offered for show or sale.

The 1997 Maxfield Parrish show opening

* Know who you are dealing with when contemplating a purchase. Do they have considerable experience and a favorable reputation? Do they offer a complete, money-back guarantee if the print is not as described? Are they willing to share information with you to enable you to become a more knowledgeable collector?

Chapter 3

Bessie Pease Gutmann (1876 – 1960)

by Michael Ivankovich
in collaboration with Sharon & Jim Eckert

Bessie Pease Gutmann as a young woman

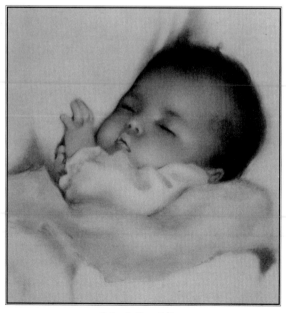

A Little Bit of Heaven

"Bessie Pease Gutmann...so captured the imagination of America that her prints appeared in almost every home..."

An Introduction to Bessie Pease Gutmann

Bessie Pease Gutmann was probably America's most famous artist of infant boys and girls. Born Bessie Collins Pease on April 8, 1876, in Philadelphia, Pennsylvania, she went on to a 50-year artistic career, producing more than 600 works in pencil, pastels, charcoal, oils, ink washes, water colors, and assorted other media. She became one of the early twentieth century's most famous artists and hit a vein in early twentieth century America's tastes that was unparalled by any other female artist of her time.

Gutmann Collecting Tip:
Bessie Pease Gutmann produced more than 600 works during her 50-year artistic career.

Shortly after her birth, her family moved to Mount Holly, New Jersey, where she lived for the next 20 years. Excelling in art at an early age, she began giving art lessons at the age of 12 and, by age 16, had entered numerous art competitions, winning many prizes and awards for her artistic skills.

After graduating from high school, she studied art at the Philadelphia School of Design for Women (now the Moore College of Art). At the age of 17 she attended the Chase School of Art, and later the Art Students' League of New York, where she attracted considerable attention for her artistic talent.

While studying at the Art Students' League in New York she met Bernhard Gutmann. Impressed by her work, Bernhard invited Miss Pease to collaborate with him and his brother, Hellmuth, in their expanding art and advertising business. Their timing was perfect. The formation of Gutmann & Gutmann in 1902 came at the right time as the early twentieth century art print market was beginning to accelerate. With a rapidly expanding middle class, there was increasing demand for low cost, machine-produced prints of popular subjects.

Bessie Collins Pease began working for Gutmann & Gutmann in 1903, and shortly thereafter began accepting commissions and contract jobs from a variety of other companies. Advertising, magazine covers, calendar and book illustrations, postcards, and art prints were all a part of her work.

Gutmann Collecting Tip:

Bessie Pease Gutmann's artwork appeared as art prints, book illustrations, calendars, magazine covers, postcards, and in various other forms of advertising. All are desirable to Gutmann collectors.

In 1906, Bessie Collins Pease became Bessie Pease Gutmann when she married Hellmuth Gutmann. They remained married for 42 years until his death in 1948. They had three children.

The husband and wife team of Bessie Pease and Hellmuth Gutmann proved very effective in the flourishing art print field. At this time there were numerous individuals vying for a share of the rapidly expanding art market. Maxfield Parrish, R. Atkinson Fox, Louis Prang, Wallace Nutting, David Davidson, Fred Thompson, Charles Sawyer, Zula Kenyon, Maud Humphrey, Alphonse Mucha, Harrison Fisher, Howard Chandler Christy, and literally hundreds of other artists, illustrators, and photographers were struggling to find their niche in diverse artistic areas.

Bessie Pease Gutmann found her niche in the gentle and innocent world of children where she ultimately became known as America's most famous baby artist. As early as 1904, she released the first of several hundred art prints focusing upon infants, children, pets, childhood, mothers and the joy of mothering, fathers, love, marriage, and even an ill-timed entry into Wallace Nutting's world of colonial interior scenes. Bessie Pease Gutmann continued releasing new art prints until 1952 at the rate of approximately seven new titles per year, with her highest pro-

duction occurring between 1905 and 1920. After 1920 her output declined to only a few new titles per year, most likely as a result of the public's waning interest in art prints.

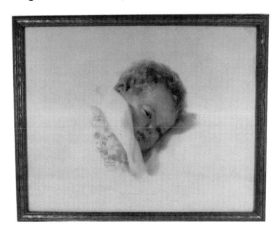

On Dreamland's Border, 14x21". Est. Value: $100 – 150.

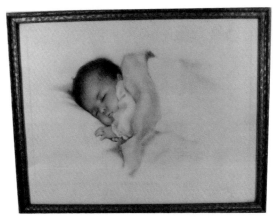

A Little Bit of Heaven, 14x18". Est. Value: $75 – 150.

Awakening, 14x18". Est. Value: $75 – 150.

In 1916, Bessie Pease Gutmann completed her most famous and commercially successful work, *A Little Bit of Heaven*. Several million copies were sold throughout the United States and internationally. In 1918 she completed *Awaking* which sold a comparable number of prints. These were often sold as a pair and, according to some sources, sold more prints than any other art print in history.

In Disgrace, 14x18". Est. Value: $100 – 150.

Gutmann Collecting Tip:

Awaking and *A Little Bit of Heaven* are the two most commonly found Gutmann prints. You will without a doubt see more of these prints, in a variey of frame sizes and shapes, than any other Gutmann prints. Sometimes nicknamed Baby Awake and Baby Asleep, they are often found in pairs. They are also the pictures which are the least expensive because there are so many available.

For nearly 50 years Bessie Pease Gutmann produced creative baby prints using charcoals, crayon, and occasionally watercolor or oil. It was not uncommon for her to complete a work in a single day, although most took considerably longer.

Up to the 1930s, most prints were printed in a single color, usually black or sepia, and then hand colored by a staff artist or colorist. Many early prints had an indented mat. Later prints were produced by color lithography or four-color process printing.

The Reward, 14x18". Est. Value: $100 – 150.

In 1935–36, another very successful pair of Bessie Pease Gutmann prints were produced and became record sellers. *The Reward* and *In Disgrace* featured the same little girl and her puppy, and appealed to a broad spectrum of the public.

Gutmann Collecting Tip:

Some, but not all, of Bessie Pease Gutmann prints were hand colored. Hand-colored prints are typically earlier and are generally more desirable to collectors.

Gutmann Collecting Tip:

The Reward and *In Disgrace* are also two commonly found Gutmann prints. These are from a later period and have a somewhat different color and look from the earlier *Awaking* and *A Little Bit of Heaven* prints.

By the 1920s–30s, a large percentage of American households had one or more Bessie Pease Gutmann pictures hanging on their walls, often times in the nursery or in the children's bedrooms. Reportedly international sales of Gutmann prints nearly equaled American sales.

One sometimes heard criticism of Bessie Pease Gutmann's work was that she rarely spent much time completing detail work on the baby's hands. If you look closely, most baby's hands have very little detail. Perhaps she felt the hands were less important because she spent so much time creating such beautiful detail in the infant's smiles and faces.

Unfortunately, the stock market crash of 1929 and the subsequent Great Depression of the 1930s took their toll on Gutmann & Gutmann and Bessie Pease Gutmann's art. Money was tight for most families and relatively few households were able to devote money to such luxuries as art prints. Gutmann & Gutmann eventually closed its doors in the 1940s.

After the death of Hellmuth in 1948, and as a result of failing eyesight, Bessie Pease Gutmann ceased her commercial art production, working only on personal projects and for her own enjoyment. She died in 1960.

Eda Doench and Meta Grimball

Prints by Eda Doench and Meta Grimball are also of interest to many Gutmann collectors. Both worked for Gutmann & Gutmann for many years (Doench for 10+ years; Grimball for nearly 20 years), and both had styles very similar to Bessie Pease Gutmann. Eda Doench was credited with completing more than 75 works for Gutmann & Gutmann, while Grimball created more than 150 different artworks.

Candle Making, a typical colonial print, 7x9". Est. Value: $50 – 75.

It was Meta Grimball who created most of the charcoal/pencil drawn colonial prints which attempted to compete with Wallace Nutting's colonial interior platinotype pictures. These failed to generate significant sales and are generally regarded as the least desirable form of Bessie Pease Gutmann print. Grimball, along with Bessie Pease Gutmann, produced a series of 60+ postcards for Gutmann & Gutmann.

Eda Doench's subjects were often older children and adults, although her overall artistic abilities were quite varied.

Generally speaking, prints by Eda Doench and Meta Grimball are valued by many collectors at 50–60% of comparable Bessie Pease Gutmann works.

Gutmann Collecting Tip:

Prints by Eda Doench and Meta Grimball which are in the style of Bessie Pease Gutmann are becoming increasingly collectible. However, they are often valued at only 50–60% of a comparable Bessie Pease Gutmann print.

The Collecting Cycle of Bessie Pease Gutmann

Phase I. Initial Production and Peak Period: When first printed between 1905 and 1952, Bessie Pease Gutmann prints were mass produced, inexpensive, and readily available to everyone. Although production significantly declined after 1930, new titles were still being introduced.

Phase II. Gradual Market Decline: As with most other art forms, the general public's tastes gradually shifted to other areas of interest. Between 1940 and 1970, Bessie Pease Gutmann prints became unfashionable. They were either discarded or relegated to attics or basements. The prints were not highly collected at this time, few people wanted them, and prices were generally quite low.

Phase III. Renewed Collectibility: As with so many other items from the twentieth century, collectors eventually began to seek out Bessie Pease Gutmann prints by the 1970s. Auctions, garage sales, antique shows, and flea markets all became fertile ground for collectors. Attics and basements were emptied and the Bessie Pease Gutmann community began to realize what was available to collect — what was common, what was rare and unusual—and what commanded the top prices from serious collectors. Prices began to rise and the number of collectors increased. A collectors' club was formed for several years in the early 1980s prior to disbanding.

Phase IV. Current Market: As we near the end of the 1990s, we are beginning to see a much more sophisticated market than during the 1980s. The release of the book, *Bessie Pease Gutmann: Her Life and Works,* helped to educate collectors about the world of Bessie Pease Gutmann and further stimulated interest in Bessie Pease Gutmann collecting. The current market might be described as firm, but not deep. The lack of a collectors' club, price guide, or a national organization has slowed major growth in national interest. Our prediction is that interest in Bessie Pease Gutmann will continue to grow in the coming years and prices will probably increase for the rarest pictures in the best condition. Condition will become increasingly important.

What Do Bessie P. Gutmann Collectors Look For?

Original Artwork

The most highly desirable Bessie Pease Gutmann collectible is the original artwork which was used in the production of the art prints, book and magazine illustrations, commercial advertisements, magazine covers, etc. Bessie Pease Gutmann executed her original art through a variety of different media. These original pieces of art were given to the individual who commissioned the artwork, ususally the publisher. Although some of the original artwork has survived, most apparently did not. Consider yourself very lucky if you should locate original Bessie Pease Gutmann artwork.

Art Prints

This is what collectors most typically pursue. In a sense, art prints are reproductions because indeed, they are a reproduction of the original artwork. They are machine-produced prints which were printed between 1905 and 1952. It is these art prints, or original reproductions, that are highly sought after by collectors.

Other Items to Look For: Collectors also collect the books, magazine covers, postcards, and magazine advertisements and pretty much anything else of the period which contains the art of Bessie Pease Gutmann.

Illustrated Books

Bessie Pease Gutmann was commissioned to illustrate several books. These are highly prized by collectors and can range in value from $200 to $400. Some of the book titles include

* *Chronicals of the Little Tot*
* *Told to the Little Tot*
* *The Biography of our Baby*
* *A Child's Garden of Verses*
* *Alice's Adventures in Wonderland*

Woman's Home Companion, Aug. '07, magazine cover.
Est. Value: $150 – 200.

Magazine Covers

Bessie Pease Gutmann was also commissioned to illustrate covers for a variety of magazines. Just some of the magazines include

* *The Metropolitan*
* *Pictoral Review*
* *Pearson's Magazine*
* *Woman's Home Campanion*
* *McCall's*

Magazine covers can range in price from $75 to 200.

Postcards

Individual postcards can be worth $30 – 100. Put them in a nice frame with a special matting, and the value can increase significantly.

Four framed postcards, Milestones in a Girl's Life.
Est. Value: $275 – 325.

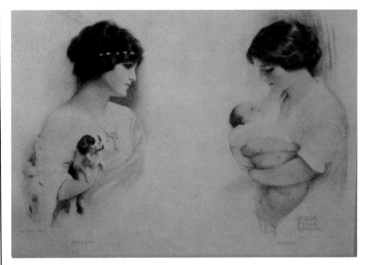

Poverty and Riches. Double images within a single print are quite rare and very desirable.

Round frames are unusual but not rare. Although not universally appealing, they can sometimes add a premium to the value of the print.

Gutmann Collecting Tip:
Special frames which enhance the beauty of the print can increase the value by 10 – 15% or more.

Special frames can also increase the value significantly. Special frames like these with Dancing Infants can make a picture even more special and can increase the value of a print by 10 – 15%.

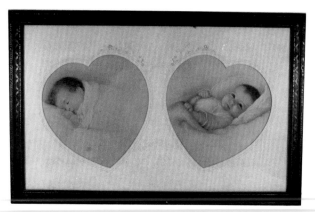

Although these babies appear to be by Bessie Pease Gutmann, they are not.

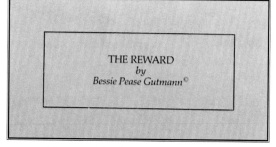

Close-up of The Rewards reproduction title.

Beware of Look-Alikes

Although Bessie Pease Gutmann was the most popular and commercially successful artist of adorable infants and children, she was by no means the only individual catering to this market. A few other artists who specialized in this type of print include

* Charlotte Becker   * Jessie Wilcox Smith
* Maude Fangel   * Ida Waugh
* Frances Tipton Hunter

Reproduction Alert

The Reward, 18x24" reproduction.

13½x16¾" reproduction with a young girl and her pets.

We have seen several different types of Gutmann reproduction art prints in the market place.

One style was 18x24", and had a thin black line around an image approximately 11x15" in size. These were marked "BPG062 Litho in USA" and were published by Portal Publications Ltd...Corte Madera, California. The title was centered below the picture within a small rectangular border. This type of reproduction was printed on a thinner paper and is often cut down in size around the image, framed in either a new or an older, period-type frame, and sold as original.

Another style of reproduction we have seen was 13½x16¾", and was printed on a thicker paper. There was no title, a faint Gutmann signature, and no company marking on this reproduction. This was definitely the better of the two reproduction styles we have seen, easily reframeable into a new or old frame.

Other Gutmann reproductions we have seen included laser copies and photographic copies of prints. These were much easier to detect because of the shiny, glossy surface of the picture.

Art print reproductions are of little interest to most serious collectors.

In addition to art print reproductions, during the mid-1980s to early 1990s a series of addition-al items featuring the art of Bessie Pease Gut-mann were reproduced, including calendars, coffee mugs, crewel embroidery kits, greeting cards, books, bookmarks, wallpaper borders, and even electrical switch plates. These are of minimal interest to serious collectors. However, you should be aware of them because some of these paper items are sometimes cut down, placed in an old frame, and sold as original.

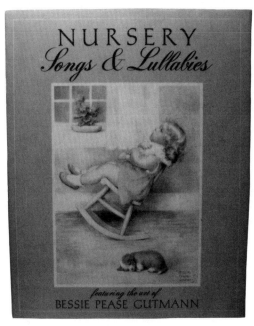

Nursery Songs & Lullabies book

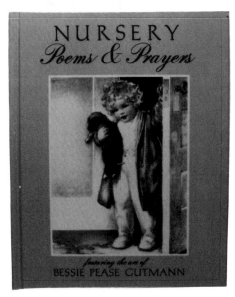

A switch plate

Nursery Poems & Prayers book

Sweet Dreams book

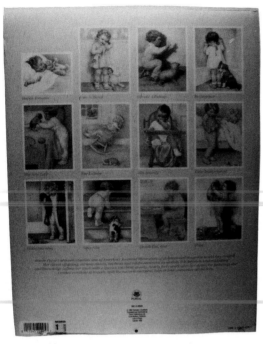

Back of a calendar. Note that calendars were reproduced during the late 1980s — early 1990s, each feature 12 different prints, and are sometimes cut up, framed in old frames, and sold as originals.

Party bag and bookmarks

Greeting cards. Like calendars, these are sometimes cut up, framed in old frames, and sold as originals.

Bookmarkers

Coffee mugs

Identifying and Dating Bessie P. Gutmann Prints

Typically there are three identifying marks that appear on Bessie Pease Gutmann prints:

Bessie Pease Gutmann print signature

The title was usually centered at the bottom of the picture.

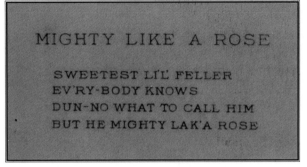

MIGHTY LIKE A ROSE

SWEETEST LI'L FELLER
EV'RY-BODY KNOWS
DUN-NO WHAT TO CALL HIM
BUT HE MIGHTY LAK'A ROSE

Occasionally a verse accompanied the title.

The Title: Bessie Pease Gutmann produced more than 600 pictures, most of which were titled. The title on most art prints will be found centered and just below the picture.

Large Bessie Pease Gutmann print signature

The Signature: Although a few of the early prints will include the artist's maiden name of Bessie Collins Pease, most will include her married name of Bessie Pease Gutmann. Should you find a picture identified as Bessie Collins Pease, you probably have a very early picture because she was married in 1906. The signature will often appear within the lower left or lower right corners of the picture.

The publisher's stock number and name

The Copyright Marking and Publisher's Stock Number: Except for very early works, most Bessie Pease Gutmann prints were given a stock number by Gutmann & Gutmann to help in the identification, marketing, and sale of the prints. Although there was some duplication of numbers, most prints had a stock number unique to each individual print. This will typically be found within the lower portion of the image, or on the matting just below the image.

Gutmann Collecting Tip:

Prints identified as Bessie Collins Pease are very early prints, done prior to her marriage to Hellmuth Gutmann, and are especially desirable to collectors.

Understanding the Main Determinants of Value

The value of a Bessie Pease Gutmann print will also depend upon several key factors.

Subject Matter: What is the topic or theme of the print? Is it common or rare? Does it include a man? Adults? Pets or animals? Young children or infants? How many copies were originally produced, and how many are left? How many other collectors are interested in owning that same print?

Condition: Is the print in poor or excellent condition? Is the color sharp or faded? Is the mat stained or blemished? Is the stain or blemish very small and minor, or does it extend into the picture itself? Is the frame original and attractive, or new or unattractive? How difficult will it be to find the same print in the same or better condition?

Size: How big is the picture itself? How big is the matting? Has the matting been cut down in size to fit another frame?

Each of these items must be considered in arriving at a final estimated value.

Subject Matter

Although there are exceptions to every rule, the following represent some very general guidelines regarding the rarity and desirability of Bessie Pease Gutmann prints. Remember that these guidelines are directed towards those rarest pictures having the highest value to collectors.

In terms of popularity with collectors, infants are still the most popular and bestselling prints, just as they were more than 60 years ago.

*To Have and to Hold.
Est. Value: $300 — 500.*

Typically prints with adults are fairly unusual and quite desirable. Prints with men are rarer than prints with women. One exception: *Home Builders*, which was an especially popular print with newlyweds and is relatively common today.

*Cupid's Reflection (note the reflection in the water).
Est Value: $250 — 350.*

Prints featuring a mother and child can be desirable to collectors.

The New Pet. Est Value: $700 — 900.

Prints featuring children with pets can be unusual and desirable.

The Butterfly. Est Value: $150 – 200.

Prints with children are somewhat more common.

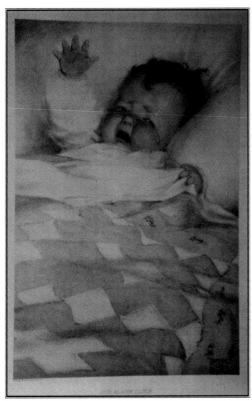

Our Alarm Clock. Est Value: $300 – 400.

Prints with infants as a general rule are fairly common. Some are very rare, others are very common. Only experience will guide you.

Candle Making. Est Value: $50 – 75.

Colonial prints were done primarily in the 1930s by Meta Grimball and were published by Gutmann & Gutmann in an attempt to compete with Wallace Nutting. They failed to sell in any appreciable quantity and are not highly prized by collectors today.

Items that were reproduced in the late 1980s – early 1990s are of minimal interest to today's serious collectors.

Size

The standard original size for a large portion of Bessie Pease Gutmann art prints was 14x21". However, many were cropped down to fit into specific frames, either originally or much later. 14x18" was a common, standard-sized frame, and many Gutmann prints will also be found in this size, but this was by no means the only size of frame used for original art prints.

Bessie Pease Gutmann Condition Guide

While exhibiting at various antique shows we have heard from some dealers that Bessie Pease Gutmann collectors don't really care about condition. If that is true, Bessie Pease Gutmann collectors are indeed unique group. Condition is one of the absolute determinants of value in all other areas of antiques and collectibles, and certainly should be extremely important when considering the purchase of a Bessie Pease Gutmann print.

We consider three primary areas of the overall print when we attempt to determine the value of a Gutmann print: the picture itself, the matting which surrounds the picture, and the frame that the picture is in. Damage to any of these three areas should have a direct impact on value.

What follows is a discussion of how we view the condition of Bessie Pease Gutmann prints we purchase. This guide helps us determine what we will pay and what we will charge for various prints. You are welcome to use it in its entirety, revise it to suit your own collecting style, or ignore it entirely, in your pursuit of Bessie Pease Gutmann prints. The one thing that we will caution you, however, is that, in our opinion, condition will become increasingly important in future years. Failure to pay close attention to condition today could end up costing you dearly when you decide to sell your pictures at some date in the future.

Gutmann Collecting Tip:
We predict that condition will become an increasingly important determinant of value of Bessie Pease Gutmann prints in the coming years.

5. Excellent Condition: Recognizing that most original Bessie Pease Gutmann prints are anywhere from 50 to 100 years old, a print meriting a grading of a 5 must be in mint condition. The picture must have absolutely great color and detail, the matting must be in excellent condition and still retaining its original size, and the frame should be in near perfect condition and appropriate for the period. It doesn't matter whether the paper backing is original or has been replaced. The overall print should look pretty much like it just came out of a box. Very few prints will ever achieve this grading.

4½. Near-excellent Condition: These are prints with practically no visible flaws. To reach this grading, the picture must have great color detail and the mat must be in excellent condition with proper aging. The frame must be attractive, appropriate for the period, but may not be quite perfect. Perhaps there may be a little dirt that needs to be cleaned from the mat or inside glass.

At this grading it might be possible to upgrade to a 5 with a better frame or cleaned glass, but it can never be upgraded to a 5 if the picture and mat are not in perfect condition.

Gutmann Collecting Tip:
Very few pictures will ever be rated a 4½ or a 5.

4. Above-average Condition: These are prints that, although they may not have visible flaws, just don't rate a 4½ or a 5. The picture has very good color and detail, but not absolutely great color and detail, the mat is nice and clean, but perhaps shows a certain amount of aging; and the frame is totally acceptable.

Sometimes a 4 can be upgraded to a 4½ with a better frame or a good cleaning on the inside of the glass.

3½. Slightly Above-average Condition: These are prints that have some noticeable, but minor mat damage, just not as severe or noticeable as a 3 (discussed below). Minor mat blemishes might include a small or barely visible water stain near the edge of the mat, minor foxing on the mat itself, some very noticeable dirt that needs to be removed, or a very minor mat reduction (no more than ½" – ¾"), noticeable frame damage, or any other very minor mat blemish.

A 3½ print whose only blemish is a damaged frame or cleanable dirt can be upgraded to a 4 with a new frame or a good cleaning. However, once the mat has a water stain, has been reduced, or has any other irremovable blemish, it can never be upgraded to a 4.

3. Average Condition: Although the picture must be in good condition, a print being graded a 3 will have major and very visible mat damage. This damage could include major and very noticeable water stains, major and very noticeable foxing, mat creases, mat tears, or other mat blemishes or damage.

A 3 print that is very dirty or has an unsightly frame can easily be upgraded to a 3½ or a 4 with a good cleaning or a new frame.

Gutmann Collecting Tip:
Most pictures will fall within the 3 – 4 category.

Any mat blemish that can be completely covered with an overmat would be considered a 3.

Any print with damage to the actual picture will always be graded below a 3.

2½. Less than Average Condition: These are prints that have modest damage to the actual picture. For example, a noticeable water stain than extends partially into the picture, noticeable foxing that appears on the picture, or any other damage or blemish to the picture itself that cannot be hidden with an overmat.

2. Poor Condition: Prints falling into this category generally have some very significant picture damage. Typically this would include a very major water stain extending through the picture, significant and very visible foxing throughout the picture, a mat crease through the picture, or other major picture damage that cannot be hidden with an overmat.

1 – 1½. Very Poor Condition: Quite frankly you rarely see prints with this grading because by the time they reach this condition, most have been discarded or thrown away. Occasionally they do turn up. Specifically, pictures that are rated a 1 or 1½ will have irreplaceable damage to the picture itself, including, but not limited to, pictures with tears, pictures with unsightly spotting or foxing, or other damage which makes the picture irreparable.

We will once again remind you that this numerical grading system is nothing more than our own personal system for evaluating Bessie Pease Gutmann prints. It is not perfect. It is very subjective. And some individuals may disagree with it or have their own grading system. However, we feel very comfortable using it and, in the absence of any other grading system, we invite you to use it as well.

Some of the More Commonly Found Bessie Pease Gutmann Prints

Home Builders. Est. Value: $150 – 200.

The following titles, in no particular order, represent just some of the Bessie Pease Gutmann titles which are quite common and frequently found by collectors. Other common titles could probably be added to this list as well. This does not mean that they are not desirable to collectors, but rather that they were originally sold in large numbers and are more commonly found today.

* *A Little Bit of Heaven*, sometimes called Baby Asleep

* *Awaking*, sometimes called Baby Awake
* *The Reward*, the happy deed
* *In Disgrace*, the consequences of the happy deed
* *On Dreamland's Border*, common baby in bed
* *Sun-Kissed*, another common infant in bed
* *The Butterfly*, young cupid
* *Chuckles*, baby in bed
* *Home Builders*, happy parents watching bluebird building nest
* *The Message of the Roses*, flapper with box of long-stemmed roses

* *On the Threshold*
* *Speeding*
* *Sunbeam in a Dark Corner*
* *The Kiss*
* *When Daddy Comes Marching Home*

Some of the More Highly Sought After Bessie Pease Gutmann Prints

Lorelei; Est. Value: $800 – 1,200.

When Daddy Comes Marching Home reportedly sold for $1,600 to a private collector in 1996.

Bessie Pease Gutmann Pictures Rarity Rating

The following rarity rating represents actual titles and publisher's stock numbers obtained from a variety of sources, including

* Bessie Pease Gutmann 1929 sales catalog
* Various Bessie Pease Gutmann dealers' for sale mailing lists
* Inspection of numerous pictures found in private collections and dealer inventories
* Pictures we currently have or previously had in our own collections or inventories

The following titles represent some very rare and highly sought-after Bessie Pease Gutmann titles, in no particular order. Although there are certainly more than 10 Bessie Pease Gutmann prints that are highly sought after, the following 10 titles represent, again, in no particular order, prints which in excellent condition can be worth $1,000 or more to certain top, serious collectors.

* *Always*
* *Light of Life*
* *My Honey*
* *Lorelei*
* *Madonna*

Although this is not a complete listing of the 600+ titles attributed to Bessie Pease Gutmann, it does represent a list of many of the most frequently found titles and should help you to confirm the authenticity of many of your pictures.

The letters shown to the right of the studio numbers are what we call the rarity rating and are prioritized as follows:

A – Very Rare
B – Rare

C – Uncommon, but Not Rare

D – Common

E – Very Common

You should understand these rarity ratings are based on our experience and personal opinions, and are very subjective. For example, if in our many years of collecting we have not seen a particular print offered for sale and do not know of any collectors who have the picture, we have to assume it is rare or very rare. However, in the absence of a better and more objective approach to determining rarity, the following represents our best efforts to help you to determine rarity of a picture. You are welcome to use these rarity ratings to give you a very general idea about the rarity of any listed title.

Bessie Pease Gutmann: Alphabetical Index

695 (B)	Aeroplane, The
307 (E)	Afternoon Tea (colonial)
717 (A)	All Mine
774 (B)	Always
711 (B)	An Anxious Moment
725 (B)	Announcement, The (Doench)
694 (E)	Awakening
158 (C)	Baby's First Christmas
605 (C)	Baby's First Christmas
311 (E)	Bedtime (colonial)
712 (C)	Bedtime Story, The
648 (A)	Betrayed by the Sandman
787 (D)	Betty
790 (D)	Billy
654 (B)	Blossom Time
635 (C)	Blossoms
666 (B)	Blue Bird, The
789 (E)	Bobby
714 (B)	Bubbles
619 (B)	Bud of Love
779 (B)	Buddies
782 (C)	Busy Day, A
632 (D)	Butterfly, The
n/k (E)	Butterflies & Daisies
304 (E)	Candlemaking (Colonial)
728 (C)	Chip of the Old Block, A
216 (E)	Chuckles
665 (C)	Chums
n/k (C)	Chums
781 (E)	Contentment
156 (A)	Cupid's Reflection
249 (E)	Cupid, That's Me
644 (C)	Daddy's Coming
634 (A)	Day Dreams
722 (A)	Divine Fire, The
759 (B)	Dove, The (Doench)
643 (C)	Double Blessing, A
735 (B)	Dreaming of You (Doench)
636 (B)	Dreams Come True
763 (B)	Drifting & Dreaming (Doench)
125 (B)	Easter Boy
217 (B)	Easter Girl
755 (B)	Edge of the Pool, The (Grimball)
681 (B)	End of a Perfect Day, The (Grimball)
727 (B)	Eternal Flame (Doench), The
n/k (E)	Excuse My Back
684 (B)	Eyes of Youth (Doench)
659 (C)	Fairest of the Flowers, The
770 (C)	Fairygold
201 (C)	Feeling (Touching)
811 (E)	Feelings
683 (B)	Fire Fly (Doench), The
713 (B)	First Dancing Lesson, The
715 (B)	Forgotten Errand, The (Grimball)
718 (B)	Friend in Need, A
215 (E)	Friendly Enemies
736 (B)	Girl of His Heart (Doench)
682 (B)	Girl of My Dreams (Doench)
747 (B)	Golden Dreams
771 (D)	Goldilocks
201 (C)	Goldilocks
783 (B)	Good-Bye
671 (C)	Good Morning
801 (E)	Good Morning
613 (B)	Good Night
807 (E)	Good Night
678 (B)	Great Love, The
651 (B)	Guest's Candle, The
800 (E)	Happy Dreams
119 (C)	Hearing
209 (D)	Hearing
710 (B)	Heart of a Rose (Doench)
699 (B)	Heart's Ease
754 (B)	Hello Kid! (Grimball)
750 (B)	Help Wanted (Grimball)
109 (E)	Her Wedding Day (colonial)
764 (B)	His Gift (Doench)
721 (B)	His Hour (Doench)
793 (E)	His Majesty
724 (B)	His Message (Doench)
655 (D)	Home Builders
217 (C)	How Miss Tabatha Teaches School
264 (E)	Hush-A-Bye (colonial)
701 (B)	In Arcady

792 (E)	In Disgrace	640 (B)	Poverty and Riches
214 (E)	In Port of Dreams	686 (B)	Prize Winners
259 (E)	In the Library (colonial)	719 (B)	Puss in Arms
646 (B)	Introducing Baby	716 (B)	Reflected Happiness
720 (B)	Intruder, The (Grimball)	768 (B)	Rose (Doench)
707 (B)	Jealousy (Doench)	780 (C)	Rosebud
772 (B)	Kitty (Doench)	753 (B)	Roses (Doench)
805 (E)	Kitty's Breakfast	794 (E)	Reward, The
657 (C)	Knit Two, Purl Two	749 (B)	Saturday Night (Grimball)
101 (A)	Lips that Are for Others	766 (B)	Secret, The (Doench)
650 (E)	Little Bit of Heaven, A	726 (B)	Spirit of the Flowers, The (Doench)
206 (C)	Little Boy Blue	117 (C)	Seeing
205 (C)	Little Jack Horner	211 (C)	Seeing
204 (C)	Little Miss Muffet	697 (B)	Silver Threads Among the Gold (Doench)
803 (C)	Little Mother	208 (B)	Sister
645 (A)	Lorelei	120 (C)	Smelling
223 (E)	Love's Blossom	662 (B)	Smile! Smile! Smile!
652 (B)	Love's Message	751 (B)	Smile for a Smile, A (Doench)
773 (B)	Lucky Dog, A (Doench)	n/k (B)	Snow Bird
819 (E)	Lullaby	777 (B)	Snowbird
739 (C)	Magic Mirror, The	691 (C)	Somebody's Sweetheart (Doench)
641 (C)	Message of the Roses, The	784 (E)	Sonny Boy
n/k (A)	Mermaid Pearls	734 (E)	Sonny Boy
642 (D)	Mighty Like a Rose	743 (B)	Special Delivery (Doench)
798 (E)	Mine	775 (B)	Springtime
729 (C)	Mischief	817 (E)	Star from the Sky, A
217 (E)	Miss Flirt	730 (C)	Sunbeam
769 (B)	Muriel (Doench)	818 (E)	Sunkissed
752 (B)	Music Hath Charms (Doench)	778 (B)	Sunny Sonny
746 (B)	My Darling	202 (D)	Sunshine
610 (B)	My Darling	808 (E)	Sweet Innocence
756 (A)	My Honey	208 (C)	Sweet Innocence
673 (E)	New Lov, Thee	154 (A)	Sweet Sixteen
107 (C)	New Love, The	748 (B)	Sweet Violets
709 (B)	New Pet, The	804 (E)	Sympathy
685	Newcomer, The	702 (C)	Symphony
740 (B)	Night, The Moon, and You, The (Doench)	761 (B)	Tabby
826 (E)	NiteyNite	821 (E)	Television
620 (B)	Now I Lay Me	723 (B)	Temptation (Doench)
690 (B)	Old Friends	822 (E)	Thank You God
692 (E)	On Dreamland's Border	689 (B)	Tiger Rose
704 (B)	On Guard (Grimball)	625 (C)	To Have and to Hold
731 (A)	On the Threshhold	615 (C)	To Love and to Cherish
796 (E)	On the Up and Up	788 (D)	Tommy
150 (B)	Our Alarm Clock	219 (C)	Tom, Tom, the Piper's Son
626 (C)	Our Alarm Clock	706 (B)	True Blue (Doench)
207 (B)	Pals	745 (B)	Twins
776 (B)	Peach Blossom	100 (A)	Twixt Smile and a Tear
825 (E)	Popularity Has Its	767 (B)	Violet (Doench)
744 (B)	Priceless Necklace, A	679 (B)	Watchful Waiting
	Disadvantages	653 (C)	Wedding March, The

Bessie Pease Gutmann Collectors' Club

Although there was at one time a Bessie Pease Gutmann collectors' club, at the time this book went to press the club had been inactive and nonfunctioning for many years.

Other Bessie Pease Gutmann Books and Reference Materials

Christie, Dr. Victor J.W. *Bessie Pease Gutmann, Her Life and Works.* ©1990 (out of print).

Bessie Pease Gutmann on the Internet

At the time this book went to press, we found no significant or helpful web sites related to Bessie Pease Gutmann on the Internet.

Where to Go If Looking to Buy or Sell Bessie Pease Gutmann Prints

There are numerous Bessie Pease Gutmann dealers around the country who specialize partially or entirely in Bessie Pease Gutmann prints. One obvious reference source we would recommend would be our collaborators on this chapter, Jim & Sharon Eckert. They can be reached at P.O. Box 62C, Anchor, IL 61720-0062 or e-mail: anchorsb@ridgeview.org.

Other dealers specializing in Bessie Pease Gutmann can be found in many of the national and regional antique & collectible trade papers.

If you would be interested in consigning Bessie Pease Gutmann prints to our annual twentieth century American print catalog auction, you can contact Michael Ivankovich at P.O. Box 1536, Doylestown, PA 18901 (215)345-6094, fax (215)345-6692, or e-mail: wnutting@comcat.com.

Or you can visit the Twentieth Century American Print section of our www.wnutting.com Internet web site.

About Sharon & Jim Eckert

Sharon and Jim Eckert have been collectors of Gutmann prints since 1985. In addition, they collect prints by Wallace Nutting, Maxfield Parrish, Harrison Fisher, and Zula Kenyon; glass baskets, cast-iron doorstops, horse brass and rosettes, and figurines. While primarily collectors, they do sell on the side to dispose of duplicates and to help finance their collecting.

Sharon works part-time at a bank and spends the majority of her time as a homemaker. Her hobbies are antique collecting and gardening. Jim is also employed at a bank. He enjoys antique collecting and golf. They have one son, James Jr., an industrial engineering student at Bradley University in Peoria, Illinois.

Sharon and Jim can be reached at P.O. Box 62-C, Anchor, IL 61720, or by e-mail at anchorsb@daveworld.net.

Summary of Key Bessie Pease Gutmann Collecting Tips

* Bessie Pease Gutmann produced nearly 600 works of art during a 50-year career prior to her death in 1960, and was one of the most successful female artists of her time.
* Her artwork appeared as advertising illustrations, art prints, books, calendars, magazine covers, postcards, and in many other related forms.
* Bessie Pease Gutmann was best known for her drawings of infants, children, pets, mothers and the joy of motherhood, fathers, love, and marriage.
* Her most popular and bestselling prints were *Awakening* and *A Little Bit of Heaven.*
* Although most Bessie Pease Gutmann prints were machine produced, some earlier works were printed in black and white and then hand colored.
* Eda Doench and Meta Grimball both worked for Bessie Pease Gutmann and their works are collectible in their own right.
* The value of a Bessie Pease Gutmann print is determined by the subject matter, condition, and size.
* Condition will become increasingly important in the coming years.
* There are a variety of art print reproductions and newer items featuring the artwork of Bessie Pease Gutmann. Most are not highly prized by serious collectors and you must learn to differentiate between the original art prints and later reproductions.

* Only the rarest pictures in the best condition, will sell at top prices. More common pictures and those not in the best condition are worth proportionately less and should be valued accordingly.
* Read as much as you can on the subject of Bessie Pease Gutmann. Observe and study as many pictures as possible in order to learn the difference between average, good, and great pictures.
* As with all other forms of antiques and collectibles, buy the best quality that you can afford. Great pictures have the potential to appreciate in value at a faster rate than average pictures.

Bessie Pease Gutmann Value Guide

The prices included in this value guide either reflect actual prices paid, dealer asking prices, or estimated value ranges.

Actual Prices Paid: represent final verified prices paid, either through auction, or through private dealer sales. If the auction included a buyer's premium, it has been included in the reported price.

Dealer Asking Prices: represent what we felt were fair asking prices, as priced by knowledgeable and reputable dealers. These represent prices we observed at antique shows, group and individual antique shops, and dealer mail-order price lists we regularly received. Most prices were personally observed by us; some prices were reported to us by dealers who regularly buy and sell Bessie Pease Gutmann prints. Dealer asking prices which we felt were way out of line as being either too low or too high were omitted from this value guide.

Estimated Fair Market Value: In some instances, we were unaware of an actual price paid, and we were not even aware of a title being offered for sale. Rather than omit the title from this chapter, we have provided what we feel represents a fair market value. You should understand that this fair market value represents nothing more than our opinion as to what a title, in very good condition, may be worth.

Although we would have preferred to have provided you with actual prices paid in each instance, that was simply not possible. At the time this book went to our publisher, no other book had yet attempted to cover in detail the pricing of Bessie Pease Gutmann prints. Therefore, please recognize this value guide for what it is...a guide. It is a first attempt at helping you to better understand the value of Bessie Pease Gutmann prints. If you feel you have a better source for valuing and pricing Gutmann prints, we suggest that you use it. In the absence of a better source, we feel that this value guide represents the most accurate and current pricing of Bessie Pease Gutmann prints available today and hope you find it helpful.

Art Print Value Guide	Size	Value
Aeroplane, The	12x16"	$425
Afternoon Tea (colonial)	7x9"	$75
Afternoon Tea (colonial)	9x12"	$60
Afternoon Tea (colonial)	19x19"	$125
Alice's Adventure in Wonderland Book (1937)		$125
Alice's Adventure in Wonderland (book)		$100 – $175
All is Vanity (postcard)		$45
And They Say School Days Are The Happiest Days (postcard)		$85
Awakening	13x17"	$90
Awakening	14x18"	$115
Awakening	14x21"	$75
Awakening	12x13"	$95
Awakening	13x18"	$150
Awakening	10x13"	$45
Awakening	14x18"	$100
Awakening	13x16"	$125
Be Sociable (Grimball)	5x7"	$30
Bedtime (colonial)	9x12"	$75
Bedtime (colonial)	12x15"	$75
Bedtime Story, The	14x18"	$250
Betty	12x16"	$250
Betty	14x18"	$275
Betty (sepia)	13x16"	$125
Bit of Old China, A (colonial)	11x13"	$75
Blossom Time	14x18"	$350
Blossoms	14x18"	$400
Blue Bird, The	14x18"	$325
Bobby	12x18"	$115
Bobby	14x21"	$80
Bobby	13x18"	$125
Breakfast Hour, The (colonial)	12x15"	$75
Bride, The	14x18"	$600
Bride, The	14x18"	$900
Bubbles	14x20"	$535
Bubbles (magazine cover, 1912)		$135
Butterflies and Daisies	9x12"	$295
Butterflies & Daisies	10x13"	$250

Butterfly, The	14x18"	$275		Feeling (Postcard)		$60
Butterfly, The	10x13"	$160		First Breakfast (colonial)	12x15"	$85
Butterfly, The	14x18"	$210		First Dancing Lesson, The	14x21"	$500
Butterfly, The	13x16"	$150		First Dancing Lesson, The	14x18"	$300
Butterfly, The	13x17"	$110		First Step	14x18"	$180
Butterfly, The	13x17"	$135		First Step	14x21"	$185
Butterfly, The	14x18"	$175		Friendly Enemies	11x14"	$300
Candlemaking (colonial)	11x14"	$95		Friendly Enemies	11x14"	$135
Candlemaking (colonial)	9x12"	$60		Friendly Enemies	11x14"	$55
Candlemaking (colonial)	10x12"	$75		Girl of My Dreams (Doench)	10x13"	$75
Captive, The (postcard)		$85		Goldilocks	11x14"	$30
Child's Garden of Verses, A Book				Good Morning	13x17"	$120
(first edition, 1905)		$225		Good Morning	13x16"	$175
Childhood Days (book, 1912)		$135		Good Night	14x21"	$525
Chip of the Old Block, A	13x17"	$170		Good Night	14x18"	$140
Chip of the Old Block, A	14x18"	$325		Good-Bye	14x18"	$375
Chip of the Old Block, A	14x18"	$225		Grand Finale, The (postcard)		$30
Chip of the Old Block, A	14x18"	$200		Grand Finale, The (postcard)		$55
Chuckles	13x17"	$125		Great Love, The	14x18"	$675
Chuckles	14x18"	$135		Guest's Candle, The	14x18"	$575
Chuckles	13x18"	$150		Happy Dreams	11x17"	$275
Chuckles	11x14"	$85		Happy Dreams	14x20"	$275
Chuckles	10x13"	$50		Happy Dreams	16x20"	$295
Chums	14x18"	$325		Harmony	14x18"	$100
Chums	12x16"	$225		Hearing	9x12"	$250
Contentment	14x18"	$200		Hearing	9x12"	$200
Contentment	12x16"	$155		Hearing	9x12"	$85
Daddy's Coming	14x17"	$400		Hearing	11x14"	$160
Daddy's Coming	14x18"	$250		Hearing (postcard)		$50
Dancing Lesson (colonial)	12x15"	$75		Her Wedding Day (colonial)	6x8"	$45
Dancing Lesson, The (colonial)	12x15"	$75		Her Wedding Day (colonial)	11x14"	$85
Dancing Lesson, The (colonial)	11x14"	$110		His Majesty	14x21"	$210
Day Dreams	14x18"	$750		His Majesty	14x18"	$200
Delighted (postcard)		$45		His Majesty (postcard)		$45
Delighted (postcard)		$85		His Majesty (postcard)		$60
Dessert (postcard)		$30		Home Builders	14x18"	$225
Divine Fire, The	14x18"	$500		Home Builders	14x19"	$160
Double Blessing	12x17"	$290		Home Builders	11x14"	$85
Double Blessing	15x21"	$265		Home Builders	14x18"	$295
Double Blessing	14x19"	$300		Home Builders	13x17"	$125
Double Blessing	13x17"	$295		Home Builders	14x18"	$185
Dreams Come True	14x18"	$400		Home Builders (sepia)	14x18"	$110
Drifting and Dreaming (Doench)	12x16"	$450		How Miss Tabatha Teaches School	13x17"	$325
Events in a Women's Life				Hush A Bye (colonial)	9x12"	$60
(5 framed postcards)		$325		Hush A Bye (colonial)	12x15"	$75
Fairest of the Flowers	13x19"	$275		I Love to Be Loved by a Baby	13x16"	$375
Fairest of the Flowers	16x20"	$265		In Arcady	14x18"	$400
Fairest of the Flowers	13x18"	$295		In Arcady	13x18"	$375
Fairest of the Flowers, The	14x18"	$350		In Disgrace	14x18"	$90
Falling Out (postcard)		$70		In Disgrace	14x18"	$115
Family Album, The (colonial)	11x14"	$75		In Disgrace	14x18"	$110

In Disgrace	13x17"	$175	Mighty Like a Rose	14x21"	$175
In Disgrace	12x16"	$75	Milestones of a Girl's Life, The		
In Port of Dreams	11x14"	$50	(postcard series, framed)		$300
In the Library (colonial)	7x9"	$75	Mine	14x21"	$195
In the Library (colonial)	11x14"	$75	Mischief	14x18"	$295
Introducing Baby	14x18"	$255	Mischief	14x18"	$275
Jealousy (Doench)	13x17"	$225	Miss Flirt	11x14"	$70
Joy Ride, A (Grimball)	5x7"	$30	My Darling	14x18"	$120
Just a Little Bit Independent	14x21"	$135	My Honey	14x18"	$850
Just a Little Bit Independent	11x18"	$220	My Honey	14x21"	$1000
Kitty's Breakfast	14x21"	$160	New Bonnet, The (colonial)	9x12"	$60
Knit Two, Purl Two	14x18"	$325	New Bonnet, The (colonial)	12x15"	$75
Lips that Are for Others	14x18"	$750	New Love, The	5x8"	$100
Little Bit of Heaven, A	14x18"	$110	New Love, The	14x18"	$225
Little Bit of Heaven, A	10x13"	$45	On Dreamland's Border	14x18"	$165
Little Bit of Heaven, A	11x14"	$65	On Dreamland's Border	13x17"	$145
Little Bit of Heaven, A	13x17"	$125	On Dreamland's Border	14x18"	$195
Little Bit of Heaven, A	12x12"	$50	On Dreamland's Border	10x14"	$85
Little Bit of Heaven, A	10x13"	$55	On Dreamland's Border	14x18"	$105
Little Bit of Heaven, A	14x21"	$75	On Dreamland's Border		
Little Bit of Heaven, A	14x18"	$95	with 1935 calendar	14x21"	$100
Little Boy Blue	11x14"	$100	On the Up and Up	14x21"	$140
Little Jack Horner	11x14"	$90	On the Up and Up	14x18"	$225
Little Jack Horner	11x14"	$50	On the Up and Up	14x21"	$145
Little Miss Muffet	11x14"	$175	Our Alarm Clock	14x18"	$70
Little Miss Muffet	11x14"	$225	Our Alarm Clock	14x18"	$350
Little Miss Muffet	11x14"	$185	Pictorial Review magazine cover		$60
Lorelei	14x18"	$1000	Pictorial Review magazine cover		$25
Lorelei	13x17"	$750	Popularity Has Its Disadvantages	14x18"	$120
Lorelei	10x14"	$525	Poverty and Riches	11x16"	$335
Love Bird, The (Doench)	12x18"	$495	Reward, The	14x21"	$135
Love is Blind (postcard)		$55	Reward, The	13x16"	$100
Love's Blossom	11x14"	$80	Reward, The	14x21"	$125
Love's Blossom	11x14"	$110	Reward, The	14x18"	$185
Love's Blossom	11x14"	$40	Reward, The	13x18"	$195
Love's Blossom	10x14"	$75	Reward, The	14x18"	$75
Love's Harmony	14x18"	$275	Reward, The	11x14"	$75
Love's Message	14x18"	$475	Seeing	9x12"	$165
Loving Cup, A (postcard)		$35	Seeing	11x14"	$150
Lullaby	14x21"	$160	Seeing	11x14"	$35
Mending Day (colonial)	12x15"	$50	Seeing	11x14"	$200
Message of the Roses	14x18"	$250	Seeing (postcard)		$45
Message of the Roses (advertising piece)		$350	Smelling	10x13"	$135
Message of the Roses, The	14x18"	$145	Snow Bird	14x18"	$350
Message of the Roses, The	14x18"	$250	Somebody's Sweetheart	13x18"	$150
Message of the Roses, The (sepia)	14x18"	$400	Sonny Boy	14x21"	$135
Mighty Like a Rose	14x21"	$175	Sonny Boy	14x21"	$295
Mighty Like a Rose	10x15"	$75	Sonny Boy	13x19"	$60
Mighty Like a Rose	14x21"	$150	Stitch in Time, A (colonial)	11x14"	$125
Mighty Like a Rose	14x18"	$205	Strenuous (postcard)		$30
Mighty Like A Rose	14x18"	$275	Sunbeam	10x13"	$195

Sunbeam	12x12"	$155	To Love and to Cherish	13x18"	$250
Sunbeam	13x13"	$260	To Love and to Cherish	14x19"	$275
Sunkissed	13x18"	$150	To Love and to Cherish	14x20"	$280
Sunkissed	14x18"	$70	To Love and to Cherish	14x18"	$325
Sunkissed	14x18"	$125	Tom, Tom the Piper's Son	11x14"	$225
Sweet Sixteen	14x18"	$300	Tom, Tom, the Piper's Son	13x18"	$350
Sweetest Joy (postcard), The		$95	Tommy	14x18"	$265
Sweethearts (postcard)		$30	Tommy	14x21"	$195
Sympathy	14x20"	$160	True Blue	14x18"	$325
Sympathy	12x18"	$110	Twixt Smile and a Tear		
Symphony	14x20"	$210	(Bessie Collins Pease)	14x18"	$750
Taste	9x12"	$295	Wedding March, The	14x18"	$500
Tasting	11x14"	$90	When Daddy Comes Marching Home	14x18"	$1,600
Tasting	12x16"	$200	When Signs Fail (Grimball)	11x14"	$60
Tea for Two (colonial)	11x14"	$75	When Signs Fail (Grimball)	11x14"	$55
Television	14x21"	$175	When Signs Fail (Grimball)	11x14"	$175
Television	14x21"	$70	Willing Captive, A (Doench)	12x17"	$175
Television	13x21"	$90	Winged Aureole, The	13x18"	$275
Television	14x18"	$110	Winged Aureole, The	13x18"	$110
Thank You God	14x21"	$170	Winged Aureole, The	14x18"	$315
Through the Looking Glass (book)		$150 – $200	Woman's Home Companion		
Tiger Rose	14x20"	$150	magazine cover (1907)		$25
To Have and to Hold	14x18"	$375	Woman's Home Companion		
To Have and to Hold	14x19"	$275	magazine cover (1907)		$75
To Have and to Hold	14x18"	$400	Wood Magic	14x18"	$350
To Have and to Hold	14x18"	$375	Wood Magic	14x18"	$225

The Bedtime Story. Est. Value: $410.

The Blue Bird. Est. Value: $325.

Blossom Time. Est. Value: $350.

Blossoms. Est. Value: $400.

The Bride. Est. Value: $900.

A Chip of the Old Block. Est. Value: $325.

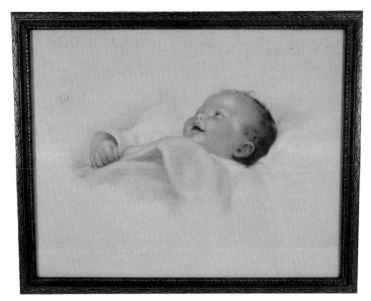

Chuckles. Est. Value: $110.

Chums. Est. Value: $275.

Day Dreams. Est. Value: $750.

The Divine Fire. Est. Value: $500.

Dreams Come True. Est. Value: $400.

The Fairest of the Flowers. Est. Value: $295.

Good Night. Est. Value: $575.

Good-bye. Est. Value: $375.

The Guest's Candle. Est. Value: $525.

Harmony. Est. Value: $300.

Hearing. Est. Value: $200.

How Miss Tabatha Taught School. Est. Value: $325.

In Arcady. Est. Value: $400.

Knit Two, Purl Two. Est. Value: $325.

Little Miss Muffet. Est. Value: $225.

Love's Message. Est. Value: $475.

The Message of the Roses. Est. Value: $350.

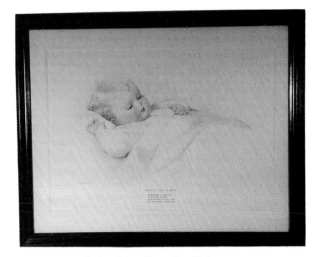

Mighty Like a Rose. Est. Value: $175.

Mischief. Est. Value: $295.

My Darling. Est. Value: $375.

Miss Flirt. Est. Value: $75.

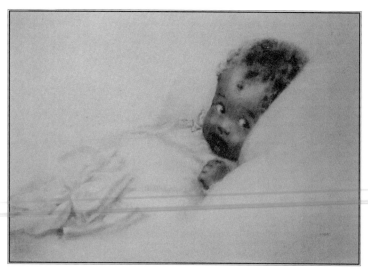

My Honey (rare African American child). Est. Value: $1,000.

Snow Bird. Est. Value: $350.

Sunbeam. Est. Value: $225.

Sunkissed. Est. Value: $125.

Sweet Sixteen. Est. Value: $225.

To Love and to Cherish. Est. Value: $325.

Wood Magic. Est. Value: $350.

The Wedding March. Est. Value: $500.

Chapter 4

R. Atkinson Fox (1860 – 1935)

by Michael Ivankovich

in collaboration with Barry & Beth Mroczka

R. Atkinson Fox

Dawn, 18x30". Est. Value: $150.

"...there are more reproductions of R. Atkinson Fox's work than of any other living artist..."

An Introduction to R. Atkinson Fox

Of the three major artists covered in this book, R. Atkinson Fox is probably the least known outside of Fox collecting circles. He is the individual I knew least about prior to the start of this project, yet he is the artist I found the most fascinating to research and the most challenging to collect.

Brown & Bigelow once stated that more reproductions have been made of R. Atkinson Fox works than of any other living artist at the time. It would seem safe to conclude that the more reproductions in circulation, the more popular the artist, and the work of R. Atkinson Fox was indeed popular. Yet most people purchased works by Fox not because they recognized his name or knew anything about the man, but because they simply liked his work. Fox was a very diversified artist and his broad range of 1,000+ works offered something for everyone. Some works depicted a stark realism, others bordered on an impressionistic flair. Whether he was painting people or animals, portraits or historical events, Fox had a style that appealed to the masses.

The ironic thing is that more often than people knew, prints that carried the name of another artist were by R. Atkinson Fox...using a different name.

Very little was known about R. Atkinson Fox until Rita Mortenson, with the help of *The Antique Trader* magazine and assorted collectors from around the country, began a serious quest for information on Fox in the early 1980s. This fox hunt eventually led to the publication of several books on Fox, the establishment of the R.A. Fox Society, and created a body of knowledge which served to better educate future generations of Fox collectors.

Fox Collecting Tip:

R. Atkinson Fox produced more than 1,000 works during his 50+ year artistic career.

R. Atkinson Fox was born in Toronto, Canada, on December 11, 1860, the son of a Presbyterian minister. He left home in his teenage years to pursue a career in art. Along the way he spent four years working with J.W. Bridgman of the Ontario Society of Artists. From the ages of 17 to 24, he worked as a self-employed portrait artist, painting American Presidents, British Royalty, and other famous subjects. His work was good enough to be exhibited at the Ontario Society of Artists and the Royal Canadian Exhibition. While in his 20s he traveled widely and studied in Europe prior to moving to New York City. In his 30s, he sold some of his work at auction in New York and Boston, presumably to finance future projects.

Although he married early in life, little is known of his first marriage which ended with his wife's death in 1901.

In 1903 he married Anna Marie Gaffney. She was 25 and he was 43. They had eight children together, four boys and four girls, and lived in New Jersey, near the Philadelphia and New York art markets, prior to moving to Chicago.

Fox worked primarily on an assignment basis and would paint whatever subjects his publisher requested. Rarely did he personally visit the sites of his subject matter (e.g., the American west). Rather, he painted mainly from pictures, photographs, or memory, often completing certain paintings in a single day. Working on commission, Fox rarely intended for his works to be considered masterpieces. He produced his work with sufficient speed to please his publishers and made changes wherever so directed.

Beginning collectors and others less familiar with Fox's work sometimes confuse his work with

Maxfield Parrish's Daybreak, Est. Value: $150 – 325.

that of Maxfield Parrish. At times Fox has been accused of being a Parrish imitator. And to a very small extent, that may be true. Maxfield Parrish certainly hit upon an American niche with his Girls-on-Rocks theme and who can blame Fox and others, for attempting to capitalize upon the public's desire for such a theme. *Dawn* and *Love's Paradise*, as well as many other Fox prints, certainly have the look and feel of a Parrish enchanted garden, although perhaps lacking much of Parrish's detail, clarity, and depth.

But while Maxfield Parrish specialized in girls on rocks and New England landscape scenes carrying his famous Parrish blue and where Bessie Pease Gutmann specialized in her darling infants and children, R. Atkinson Fox's subject matter covered a much broader spectrum of subjects. In addition to his own enchanted girls and gardens, Fox became very well known for painting animals (horses, ducks, dogs, elk, and especially cows, "he was considered to be the best painter of cows..."), women and girls, gardens, cottages, ships, Indians, the American west,

R. Atkinson Fox's Love's Paradise, Est. Value: $75 – 150.

flowers, historical figures, American and foreign landscapes, and much more.

An Approaching Storm. Fox was considered to be an excellent painter of cows. 6x10".
Est. Value: $50 – 75.

Chs. Wainright was actually a pseudonym for R. Atkinson Fox.

One of the most difficult and confusing aspects of Fox collecting was Fox's use of pseudonyms. Although more often than not he signed his work with his own name either R. Atkinson Fox or R.A. Fox, quite often he would sign his work with either a slight variation on his own name or another name entirely. Apparently this was done for several reasons. Sometimes he used a different name to sign works that either did not please him or work that he felt was not up to his high standards, and did not want his own good name associated with it.

Other times Fox would use a pseudonym at the direction of a publisher. For example, often times calendar salesmen would approach potential customers with a salesman's sample which offered potential advertisers the choice of several subjects by several different artists. Apparently although the subject matter may have varied greatly, the different works were all done by R. Atkinson Fox, using some of his alias names, with the client none the wiser.

Regardless of why Fox used pseudonyms, the following pseudonyms have been confirmed by the Fox children, publishing records, or various research. Many other signatures are probably also Fox's, but we may never know for certain. If you find a print carrying any of the following confirmed Fox pseudonyms, the picture will actually be an R. Atkinson Fox:

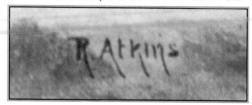

R. Atkins

R. Atkins	H. Musson
L.H. Banks	Geo. W. Turner
L. Capelli	Chas. Wainright
G. Blanchard Carr	Chs. Wainright
B. Carr	C. Wainright
John Colvin	C.N. Wainright
J. Colvin	Thomas Wainright
DeForest	F. Wainwright
Arthur DeForest	(note the extra "w")
Dupre	Geo. White
Elmer Lewis	Geo. W. White
E. Lewis	G. White
Musson	George Wood
Edw. Musson	

L.H. Banks

John Colvin

DeForest

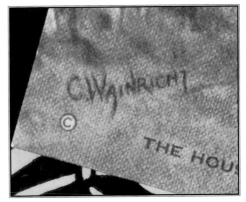

C. Wainright

Arthur DeForest

C.N. Wainright

Dupre

The Sunny South, 7x9". Est. Value: $75.

Fox Collecting Tip:

Fox used many pseudonyms when signing his prints, and in most cases, a Fox pseudonym is just as collectible as a print signed R. Atkinson Fox.

The Sunny South

From an ORIGINAL OIL PAINTING
By R. ATKINSON FOX

◈◈◈

LAZY days…sweet summer days…river drifting slowly, quietly…tropical calm over all…fleecy clouds…swishing palms, and a safe haven for the pirates' vessel, guarded by the protecting fort of a renegade governor's castle. Centuries ago the bold brave buccaneers ventured forth on the southern seas. Once they captured their booty, they would make for their favorite lair—a safe harbor, near a town where the authorities shut their eyes to the misdeed of their guests—where there was wine and women aplenty for the visiting pirate men.

Here the raider of the seas is resting, secure in the beauty and peacefulness of this island in the Sunny South. Banners flap idly in the summer breeze. Sails hardly move as the light zephyrs try in vain to billow them. While the reflection of the galleon appears on the clear blue surface of the waters of the bay.

R. A. Fox painted this scene. He has painted portraits of royalty and Presidents of the United States, but his chief delight is landscapes—landscapes rich and warm, with colors which simultaneously soothe and stimulate the eye.

The Sunny South, biographical backing label.

SECURITY

Reproduced from an original oil painting by Elmer Lewis, for A. M. Collins Mfg. Co., Philadelphia.

THIS striking painting demonstrates to a marked degree the skill of Elmer Lewis, both as a colorist and as a student of wild animal life.

High in the cliffs above the plain, concealed by overhanging vegetation and secure from the attacks of enemies, the lions have found a den. The playful cubs, tired from their frolics, are resting in the genial heat of the afternoon sun. The tawny lioness, with the pride of motherhood showing forth from her beautiful eyes, lies beside them, alert for any danger, while the "father of the family," a monarch indeed, strong, fierce and majestic, stands like a statue, on an out-jetting rock, and scans the distant hills and plains in search of prey.

Elmer Lewis is a native of Brooklyn, N. Y. His art education was acquired in the Art Students' League, New York, and in various schools in Europe. He has been very successful and his pictures have been exhibited at the Architectural League, The National Academy of Design and the Water-Color Society.

Elmer Lewis, Security, biographical backing label.

Sometimes the publishers of Fox's work would produce a biographical backing label which would be used to better describe the work and to give a little more background on the artist to help sell the print. *The Sunny South* label talks about "Lazy days…sweet summer days…fleecy clouds…swishing palms…," etc, followed by a discussion of the merits of Fox as a painter.

The *Security* backing label goes on to discuss the merits of Elmer Lewis as a painter to help sell the print… "a native of Brooklyn…various schools in Europe…his pictures have been exhibited at the Architectural League…." This confuses things even further, because this publisher even provided a biography on a pseudonym! Remember, there was no Elmer Lewis! Elmer Lewis was a pseudonym for Fox and this label demonstrates the lengths that some publishers went to deceive the public.

And if diverse subject matter and different signatures don't confuse things enough for Fox collectors, some pictures were titled while others did not carry a title. Sometimes one publisher would use a picture and include the title, while another publisher would use the exact same picture without listing the title, or use an entirely different title. Fox's prints generally ranged in size from 1½x2½" to 20x40", and publishers would sometimes crop the same picture differently, giving the same picture several different appearances. And it was not at all unusual for the same picture to appear on several different media (art prints, calendars, jigsaw puzzles, magazine or book covers, etc.), in many different sizes and shapes.

Although Fox most likely had a title in mind for each picture he created, he never kept a master title list. And since most of his works were subsequently owned by his publisher, the publisher usually had final control of the title. Sometimes they used Fox's title, sometimes they created their own title, sometimes they changed the title several times, and sometimes they printed the picture without a title.

Fox Collecting Tip:
A Fox print is called an untitled print until the actual published title can be confirmed by collectors.

Fox collecting can be so confusing that Fox collectors have established an entire category of items called *Fox maybes*. The accepted rule of Fox collectors, established by Fox collectors themselves, basically states that a picture thought to be by R. Atkinson Fox cannot be considered a Fox, until that exact picture is confirmed to be a Fox with a 100% degree of certainty. Confirmation of an unsigned or untitled work can be accomplished pretty much only by ascertaining that another identical Fox picture exists in signed form or with a publisher's attribution. And until an unconfirmed picture is confirmed to be a Fox, it is called a Fox maybe. Sounds complicated, but the process seems to work.

Fox, yet are still considered to be Fox maybes because they have yet to be substantiated.

E. West	W.M. Childs
Chs. Morgan	C.E. Dillsworth
Chs. Wilson	Vandervoort
R. Wilson	J.A. Atkins
C. Weeks	Chs. Stacey
H. Lewis	C. Wild
Henri G. Reynard	Geo. A. King
H. Whitney	Fred Atkins
J. Watson	T.C. Carr

Fox Collecting Tip:
A picture is called a Fox maybe when, although an unsigned or untitled picture is suspected of being a Fox, it has not yet been confirmed to be a Fox with a 100% degree of certainty.

A Sunset Symphony, 1926 calendar. F.A. Robert pseudonym.

A good example of a Fox maybe would be *A Sunset Symphony*. Although never officially confirmed as R. Atkinson Fox, F.A. Robert is obviously a variation of Robert A. Fox. This is a highly desirable print which has all of the characteristics of a typical Fox print, yet is still considered a Fox maybe.

Are These Signatures Also R. Atkinson Fox?

The following signatures appear on prints that have all the characteristics of an R. Atkinson Fox, are thought to possibly be an R. Atkinson

One of the most unusual advertising prints was commissioned by Churchill Downs to promote Derby Day, May 13 at Churchill Downs, Louisville, Kentucky. R. Atkinson Fox painted a portrait of Old Rosebud, the 1914 Kentucky Derby Winner, which became the centerpiece of a poster advertising the 1916 Derby. In addition, Old Rosebud was also produced on tin, approximately 18"x30", and provided to local businesses to further promote the derby. It is believed that only 100 of these tins were produced.

Touring America salesman's sample.

Touring America was a salesman's sample of 12 different calendar scenes, most of them depicting a Model-T automobile in a scenic location in America. This Touring America series was

All 12 Touring America scenes.

intended to be a monthly mailing series, complete with a monthly calendar and appropriate advertising message. In this case, the advertising was aimed at automobile dealerships. Often the monthly calendar also served as an ink blotter, a very useful item in the 1920s and 1930s.

More salesman's samples.

This typical salesman's sample depicts different calendar prints available complete with an advertising message. In this case, four of the five prints are confirmed Fox's, although only one has his signature. This is another excellent example of how publishers wanted to present the illusion of having many different artists working for them.

Washington the Soldier and *Washington the Surveyor* are two of three different Fox works which were part of 12 monthly mailing cards titled Washington Thrift Series. Produced by the Thomas D. Murphey Co. in 1926, this is just another example of how Fox's art was used for a wide variety of purposes.

Although financially successful as an artist, Fox's work, like many other accomplished illustrators of his time, did not receive a great deal of respect from the artistic community. Demand for his work remained strong until he passed away in 1935. His work even continued to sell for several years after his death, still appearing on calendars and in other various forms. With the breakout of World War II in Europe, and America's subsequent involvement in it, the subject matter of calendars shifted towards more religious and political themes and away from the more traditional work of R. Atkinson Fox. As color photography became

Washington the Soldier and Washington the Surveyor.

more prevalent, demand for the work of R. Atkinson Fox all but ceased.

Three Other Foxes: Garnet Bancroft Fox, W. Gordon Fox, and A. Fox

G. Bancroft Fox signature

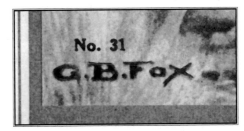

G. B. Fox signature (small)

Garnet Bancroft Fox, The Champion

G. B. Fox signature (large)

There are three other Foxes who you should be aware of, none of which were R. Atkinson Fox, but whose works are sometimes confused with his because of the similarity of the names and style.

Garnet Bancroft Fox and W. Gordon Fox were actually R. Atkinson Fox's nephews. Although each developed his own style, they did adopt certain portions of their well-known uncle's style. The works of Garnet Bancroft Fox and W. Gordon Fox are signed in a variety of ways, some with their real name, some with shortened versions of their real name, and some with pseudonyms, including

G. Bancroft signature

Garnet Bancroft Fox	G. Bancroft Fawkes
G. Bancroft Fox	Guy Fawkes
G.B. Fox	G.B. Fawkes
G. Fox	G. Fawke
G. Bancroft	W. Gordon Fox
Garner Fox	Gordon H. Fox
Garnet W. Fox	

G. B. Fawkes signature

W. Gordon Fox signature

You should be aware that R. Atkinson Fox, Garnet Bancroft Fox, and W. Gordon Fox are actually three totally different artists with very similar styles.

Prudential Fox magazine cover

Prudential Fox signature

At least ten *Prudential* magazine covers produced in the early 1930s, each depicting infants or children, were signed Fox. Barry & Beth Mroczka are of the opinion that they are G.B. Fox, not R. Atkinson Fox. The style is too cute, too unorthodox, and not serious enough to be R. Atkinson Fox. And the plain Fox signature is also representative of the unusual signatures G.B. Fox used. He alone would have embraced the simplicity of simply signing Fox.

A. Fox had no connection with R. Atkinson Fox, Garnet Bancroft Fox, or W. Gordon Fox.

A. Fox actually had no connection whatsoever to R. Atkinson Fox, but because of the same last name, is sometimes confused with Fox. A. Fox was actually a publishing company from Philadelphia. Most of its work is farm scenes.

The Collecting Cycle of R. Atkinson Fox Prints

A 1913 calendar, for a Livestock & Poultry Co., with cows

Phase I. Initial Production and Peak Period: 1900 – 1939 was the peak period for R. Atkinson Fox. Although the art print market slowed during the Depression of the 1930s, demand within the calendar market remained strong (regardless of the economy, people still needed calendars). And despite Fox's death in 1935, demand for Fox's calendar art remained strong for several years after his death.

Phase II. Gradual Market Decline: 1940 – 1970s. The start of World War II in Europe changed the focus of many calendars to more religious and political themes and interest in Fox's calendar art began to wane. Color photography on calendars also became more prevalent after the war.

Phase III. Renewed Collectibility: 1970s – 1980s saw a renewed interest in these prints as more collectors began to discover Fox. Rita Mortenson's 7-part Fox Hunt series in *The Antique Trader*, and several subsequent books on Fox in the 1980s, also contributed to this renewed interest. And perhaps just as importantly, many collectors began turning to Fox because they were either unwilling or unable to pay the higher prices needed at that time to acquire Maxfield Parrish prints.

Phase IV. Current Market: The current Fox market, although not necessarily hot at the time this book went to press, is undoubtedly strong. An R.A. Fox Society collectors' club, periodic club newsletters, an annual convention for Fox collectors, and the continued sighting of new finds keeps attracting new Fox collectors.

What Do R. Atkinson Fox Collectors Look For?

Original Art Works

The original artwork (oil-on-board, oil-on-canvas, etc.) that Fox completed for his publishers is undoubtedly the most highly sought after of all of his work. Unfortunately, there seems to be very little of it remaining. The Fox family is known to possess a number of his original works, and others are known to be in the hands of private collectors. However, pending some type of warehouse find, there are relatively few pieces of Fox's original artwork known to still exist, probably because most were discarded by the publisher after the original intended use. In any event, it is fairly unlikely that the average collector today will ever run across a Fox original.

Original Art Prints

Original art prints were machine produced and come in a wide variety of sizes, shapes, sub-

Fox Collecting Tip:
Original Fox oils are very difficult to appraise. The limited market is extremely speculative...an oil is worth only what the buyer is willing to pay and the seller willing to accept. It is not uncommon for a seller to not find a buyer because of a high asking price.

ject matter, and condition, and art prints are what today's collectors are most likely to find.

A wide variety of sizes were provided by the publishers so that any conceivable use would be satisfied and so that all price ranges would be covered. Of course, the smaller prints usually cost the least. Most of these sizes were intended for various forms of advertising, e.g., calendars, blotters, thermometers, puzzles, fans, etc. Calendar prints ranged in size from 1½x2½" to at least 22x16".

Sometimes prints are framed; often they are unframed. Many businesses purchased prints to frame and sell. Even calendars eventually became framed prints, usually being trimmed to fit a frame. Unfortunately, all too often portions of the print were cut off in the process.

Advertising, Commercial & Novelty

Because the work of R. Atkinson Fox was printed by so many different publishers, in so many different forms, there is much for Fox collectors to seek out. The artwork of R. Atkinson Fox is also found on a wide variety of products and items, including but not limited to the following

* Advertising	* Magazine covers
* Beer trays	* Mirrors
* Blotters	* Newspaper inserts
* Book jackets	* Playing cards
* Calendars	* Postcards
* Candy boxes	* Prints (framed &
* Catalog covers	unframed)
* Children's books	* Scrapbook covers
* Fans	* Serving trays
* *Farmer's Almanac*	* Sewing kits
covers	* Thermometers
* Handkerchief	* Tins
boxes	* Towel racks
* Jewelry boxes	* Wooden plaques
* Jigsaw puzzles	* Writing tablet covers
* Lamp shades	* More

Advertising piece, Deering Co., 19x12". Est. Value: $125 — 175.

Advertising piece, Chain Frame, 6x8". Est. Value: $125 — 175.

Advertising shadow box, Music of the Waters. Est. Value: $60 — 80.

Beer tray, Fraternally Yours, 4x14". Est. Value: $100 — 150.

Blotter, Three of a Kind, 3x4". Est. Value: $90 — 100.

*Book cover, Little Lassie's Book, 6x8".
Est. Value: $90 — 100.*

Blotter, Niagara Falls, 2x3". Est. Value: $30 — 50.

*Calendar, 1932, Nature's Silvery Retreat, 7x9",
Est. Value: $100 — 150.*

Calendar, 1908, Too Late, 4x12". Est. Value: $125 — 145.

Candy box, alias: Deforest, On Treasure Isle, 11x13".
Est. Value: $150 — 200.

Magazine cover, 1930, Hunter's Paradise, 8x10".
Est. Value: $40 — 60.

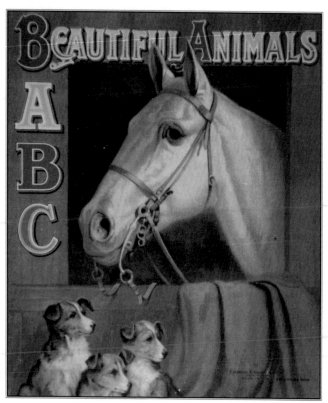

Children's book, Beautiful Animals, 10x12".
Est. Value: $90 — 100.

Farmer's Almanac, 1917, Friends, 5x4".
Est. Value: $125 — 175.

Jewelry box, Art Deco, Sunrise, 5x7". Est. Value: $75 — 150.

Handkerchief box, Pleading at the Bar, 4x8".
Est. Value: $60 — 80.

Jewelry box, enameled. Est. Value: $50 — 100.

Jigsaw puzzle, The Royal Outlaw, 7x11".
Est. Value: $125 — 175.

Mirror, A Canadian Landscape. Est. Value: $60 — 80.

Newspaper insert from Pittsburgh Sun Telegraph, 12/22/24,
Surf Fishing, 8x6". Est. Value: $150 — 200.

Playing cards (framed), Old Faithful Geyser, 2x3".
Est. Value: $30 — 50.

Postcards. Est. Value: $30 — 40 each.

Scrapbook, 9x12", The Barefoot Boy.
Est. Value: $75 — 100.

Serving tray, Oaks by the Roadside, 10x16". Est. Value: $50 — 75.

Sewing kit, Nature's Grandeur, 2x3".
Est. Value: $40 — 75.

Thermometer, advertising, Abe Lincoln, 8x10".
Est. Value: $100 — 150.

Thermometer, silhouette-advertising, The Snow-Capped Mountain.
Est. Value: $40 — 60.

Writing tablet cover, Washington at Valley Forge, 7x8".
Est. Value: $65 — 85.

Wooden Plaques, Music of the Water and The Snow-Capped Mountain.
Est. Value: $25 — 50 each.

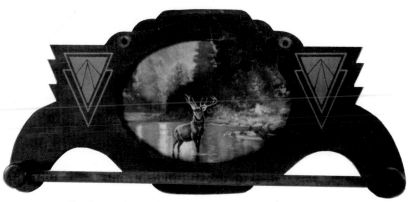

Towel rack, At the Foot of Mt. Rainier. Est. Value: $75 — 100.

Reproduction Alert

Basically there are two different types of Fox reproductions.

Of course there are the standard laser reproductions. These usually have a shiny surface and are not too difficult to detect. They are usually in an old frame to make them appear older, and it is not unusual for them to have old backing paper, which is a result of a larger piece of old paper being added to, and cut to fit, a smaller frame. Caveat Emptor...Let the buyer beware.

Other reproductions have been mass produced and are done very well. They actually appear to be old and some have age defects such as foxing (mildew type stain). They are originally sold as a new reproduction, but as they progress further along the collector-dealer chain, they will eventually be sold as originals. Some unscrupulous dealers even frame them in original period frames in order to make them look older.

There is nothing wrong with acquiring a reproduction as long as it is sold as such, and for an appropriately inexpensive price.

The following titles have been reproduced at the time this book went to press:

* *An Old Fashioned Garden*
* *Daughters of the Incas*
* *Daughter of the Setting Sun*
* *Giant Step Falls*
* *June Morn*
* *Romance Canyon*
* *Sunrise*
* *Sunset Dreams*
* *Where Brooks Send Up a Cheerful Tune*

In addition to the above, a very unique reproduction that Barry & Beth Mroczka are pleased to have in their collection is *The Right of Way* by R. Atkinson Fox. It is a limited edition (650) reproduction of an original oil painting done in 1986 by Daniels Limited Editions. The owners of the oil paid to have it reproduced. It is similar in quality to the museum reproductions of the impressionists, and it has great color and definition.

Identifying and Dating R. Atkinson Fox Prints

Aside from calendars, the dating of R. Atkinson Fox prints is usually difficult to do. Recognizing that Fox's work was typically published from 1900 to his death in 1935, that narrows the range

The Lone Eagle, 1929 calendar with Charles Lindbergh, after his 1927 trans-atlantic flight.

for most (but not all) down to a 35 year period. Certain titles or subjects, such as *The Lone Eagle* (featuring Charles Lindbergh), circa 1927, can help to target the date of a print more precisely.

Although black and white prints were generally produced before 1910, color prints were also produced both before and after 1910.

But realistically, most Fox prints are difficult to precisely date. Even calendars are deceptive — the same print was used in different years, often spanning decades.

Identifying Fox prints is somewhat easier and can be done in several ways.

R. Atkinson Fox signature on print

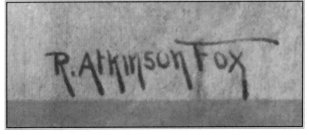

R. Atkinson Fox signature, with different letter characteristics, on print

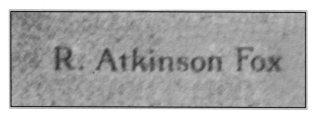

R. Atkinson Fox typeset signature on print

R. Atkinson Fox typeset signature on print border

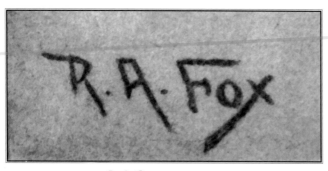

R. A. Fox signature on print

Fox prints can usually be identified by the R. Atkinson Fox or the R.A. Fox signature on the picture (not to be confused with A. Fox).

The Morning Call, title on print

Tom and Jerry, title on print border

Some Fox prints will carry the title which can help to identify a picture, although most will not.

Understanding the Main Determinants of Value

The value of an R. Atkinson Fox print will depend upon several key factors.

Subject Matter: What is the subject or theme of the print? Is it common or rare? How many copies were originally produced, and how many are left? Under what name was it signed? Is the title known or unknown? How many other collectors are interested in owning the same print?

Condition: Is the print in poor or excellent condition? Is the color sharp or faded? Is the print stained or blemished? Is the stain or blemish very small and minor, or does it extend into the image itself? Is the frame original and attractive or new and unattractive? How difficult will it be to find the same print in the same or better condition?

Size: How big is the print? Is it the original size, or has it been cut down in size to fit the frame?

Some of the More Commonly Found R. Atkinson Fox Prints

Although the following list is quite sizable, these titles represent some of the more common R. Atkinson Fox prints, broken down by category:

Women
- *Daydreams*
- *Dawn*
- *Life's Greatest Gift*
- *Love's Paradise*
- *Spirit of Youth*
- *Sunset Dreams*

Dogs
- *A Reliable Guardian*
- *Hunter's Paradise*

Animals
- *The Silent Rockies*
- *Indian Summer*
- *A Sheltering Bower*
- *Good Morning Deer*

Gardens
- *Blue Lake*
- *Venetian Garden*
- *Dreamland*
- *Nature's Beauty*
- *Garden of Love*
- *Promenade*
- *English Garden*
- *Land of Dreams*
- *Moonlight and Roses*
- *Garden of Romance*
- *Midsummer Magic*

Cottages
  An Old Fashioned Garden
  Where Nature Beats in Perfect Tune
  Enchanted Steps
  The Old Home
  Memories of Childhood Days
  Home Sweet Home
  When the Day is Over
  Blossom Time
  Russet Gems
  The Old Mill
Landscapes
  Perfect Day
  Nature's Sublime Grandeur
  Moonlight on the Camp
  Glorious Vista
  Inspiration Inlet
  Where Peace Abides
  Guardian of the Valley
  An Old Oak
  Mountain Valley
  A Song of the Evening
  Autumn Gold
  Sunland
  Path to the Valley
  An Inviting Pathway
  Stately Sentinels
  The Good Luck Line
  Oaks by the Roadside
  The Road of Poplars
  A Rustic Bridge
Ships
  Good Ship Adventure
  River of Romance
  Clipper Ship
Indians
  Indian Paradise
  The Buffalo Hunt
George Washington
  First Raising of the Stars & Stripes at Valley Forge
Flowers
  Poppies
Pseudonyms
  Musson: *A Thoroughbred*
  Turner: *Silvery Divide*
  Wainright: *Nature's White Mantle*
    Two Medicine River Falls, Montana
    Sentinels of the Pass
    Paradise
    The Echoing Call

White: *All Set*
  At the Foot of Mount Rainier
  Silvery Wonderland
  Silvery Grandeur

Some of the More Highly Sought After R. Atkinson Fox Prints

Many Fox collectors would include in this category any Fox print not in their collection. Certain subjects are more highly sought than others. Indians, beautiful women, women with horses, horses, dogs, lions, tigers, and children are considered the most popular. Garden scenes, though most are fairly common, should also be included. A print does not have to be scarce to be highly sought after.

Women
  June Morn
  Elysian Fields
  In the Valley of Enchantment
  Sunrise
  Twilight
  Music of the Waters
Animals
  Old Rosebud (on tin) — horse
  A Royal Outlaw — tiger
  In the Enemy's Country — lions
  Play While You May — foxes
  Monarch of the North — polar bears
  Strength and Security — lion
  Security — lion
  Battle of the Wild — moose and wolves
Indians
  In Meditation Fancy Free
  Daughter of the Setting Sun
  Daughters of the Incas
  White Feather
Other
  The Good Shepherd — religious
  Supremacy — naval battle
  Through the Mountain Pass — stagecoach
  Out of the Sky He Comes — Lindbergh
  Aces All — tractor

R. Atkinson Fox Society

There is a very active R. Atkinson Fox collectors' club called the R.A. Fox Society. This group publishes a newsletter, holds an annual convention, and actively works to promote the works of R. Atkinson Fox. Dues in 1997 were $25/single; $35/family.

The officers rotate among the members. For the sake of continuity, if you would like to receive information about joining the R.A. Fox Society, contact my collaborators, Barry & Beth Mroczka, 8 Blackmore Court, Camp Hill, PA 17011 (717)732-6798. Please include a SASE and they will send the current membership information.

Other R. Atkinson Fox Books and Reference Materials

* Mortenson, Rita C. *R. Atkinson Fox: His Life and Works.* 1991, with prices revised in 1994.
* Rita C. Mortenson. *R. Atkinson Fox: Volume 2.* 1992.
* Patricia L. Gibson. *R. Atkinson Fox: Identification & Price Guide.* 1995.
* Rick and Charlotte Martin. *Vintage Illustrations.* 1997.
* *"The Fox Hunt"*... a 7-part series on *"The Search for R. Atkinson Fox." Antique Trader.* 1980 – 1983.

R. Atkinson Fox on the Internet

At the time this book went to press, we found no active web sites devoted to R. Atkinson Fox on the Internet.

Where to Go If Looking to Buy or Sell Fox Prints

There are numerous R. Atkinson Fox dealers around the country who specialize partially or entirely in R. Atkinson Fox prints. One obvious reference source we would recommend would be our collaborators on this chapter, Barry & Beth Mroczka. They can be reached at 8 Blackmore Court, Camp Hill, PA 17011 (717)732-6798.

Another possibility would be to join the R.A. Fox Society and contact various members through the club.

Several antique dealers actively advertise their interest in buying and selling R. Atkinson Fox through various antique trade papers.

If you would be interested in consigning any R. Atkinson Fox prints to one of our upcoming twentieth century American print auctions, you can contact us at The Michael Ivankovich Antiques & Auction Co., Inc. at P.O. Box 2458, Doylestown , PA 18901 (215)345-6094, fax (215)345-6692, or e-mail: wnutting@comcat.com.

The Mroczka's dining room.

A Fox collector's dream...Barry Mroczka's study.

About Barry & Beth Mroczka

Barry and Beth Mroczka have been collecting Fox prints since 1975, the year they met and married. They began their collection by accident. Barry bought some old frames (with prints) with the intention of removing the old prints and framing Picasso and Van Gogh calendars. Beth liked the old prints that were in the frames (so did Barry). The prints and frames remained intact and became a grouping in their dining area. Several were signed R. Atkinson Fox. More old prints were bought, most of them also signed R. Atkinson Fox. Soon, they were buying Fox exclusively. Twenty-two years later, they have 760 different Fox prints. Counting the same prints more than once (calendar, puzzle, fan, print, etc.), they have more than a thousand. They also have more than 300 Fox unsigned maybes.

They go Fox hunting at least once each weekend. They are both employed by the Commonwealth of Pennsylvania.

Summary of Key Collecting Tips

* R. Atkinson Fox produced more than 1,000 works during his 50-year career prior to his death in 1935.
* Although sometimes labeled a Parrish imitator, Fox was an extremely prolific artist, painting animals, women and girls, gardens, cottages, ships, Indians, the American west, flowers, historical figures, American and foreign landscapes, and many more different subject areas.
* Fox also painted under more than 13 pseudonyms, most of which are as collectible as those carrying the R. Atkinson Fox signature.
* Many prints do not have signatures or attributions. Final identification was often provided by other means including publisher's records, the Library of Congress, publisher's catalogs, comparisons with original oil paintings, and by various other means.
* A Fox print is considered untitled until the actual published title can be confirmed by collectors.
* A picture is considered a Fox maybe until an unsigned or untitled print suspected of being a Fox can be confirmed to be a Fox with a 100% degree of certainty.
* Garnet Bancroft Fox and W. Gordon Fox were R. Atkinson Fox's nephews, yet neither they, nor R. Atkinson Fox, had any connection with a publishing company named A. Fox.
* Fox's prints appeared on an extremely wide variety of items, most of which are highly desirable to Fox collectors.
* Value will be impacted by a variety of factors including
    * rarity of the print
    * popularity and desirability of the print
    * subject matter
    * condition...condition...condition
    * size
    * framed or unframed
    * attractiveness of the frame
    * medium (calendar, puzzle, print, etc.)
* To many collectors, condition is paramount. No damage whatsoever will be tolerated or accepted.
* You should be aware that there are Fox reproductions in circulation.
* There is an active R. Atkinson Fox Society which serves as a primary source of information for Fox collectors.
* Prices will vary geographically. Certain prints are common in some areas and rare in other areas, depending upon how the publishers originally marketed and distributed their work. Prices in western states tend to be higher than in other areas of the country.
* Rare Fox prints are not always popular prints. Only serious collectors will pay top prices for items they do not already have. High prices will often deter the average buyer or collector.
* Some collectors only collect certain subject areas (e.g., horses, cows, gardens, women, landscapes, etc.).
* Many Fox prints fall into crossover collectible categories. For example, a Charles Lindbergh scene by R. Atkinson Fox might be considered collectible by Fox collectors, Lindbergh collectors, and aviation collectors. Indians, animals, and historical subjects can also fall into these crossover collectible categories.

R. Atkinson Fox Value Guide

Pricing Fox prints is extremely subjective and very difficult. If most collectors think these prices are too high and most dealers think these prices are too low, then they are probably just right. Many factors determine the price.

Condition: These prices assume that the print is in very good to excellent condition with no major flaws and bright colors.

Rarity: The scarcer the print, the higher the price.

Desirability: The more desirable prints will always command higher prices.

Size: Larger prints are generally worth more than smaller prints. The ranges provided here reflect the variations.

Complete print vs. partial print: Partial prints are worth less than complete prints.

Medium: Postcards, fans, and blotters are generally worth less than prints. Complete calendars are usually worth more. Jigsaw puzzles are only worth more to jigsaw puzzle enthusiasts. The average Fox collectors do not seem to be enthusiastic about puzzles.

Size limitations of this chapter made it impossible to list and price all the prints, various sizes, and different mediums.

Title	Rarity	Est Value
Abraham Lincoln	Uncommon	$140 – 175
Aces All	Scarce	$150 – 180
Afternoon Call, An	Uncommon	$150 – 175
Ambassador of Good Will, An	Uncommon	$110 – 135
Among the Daisies	Scarce	$150 – 175
Approaching Storm, An	Common	$50 – 75
Approaching Storm, The	Uncommon	$70 – 90
Armful of Joy	Uncommon	$90 – 120
Artist Supreme, The	Uncommon	$75 – 110
At the Foothills of Pike's Peak	Common	$40 – 60
Autumn Gold	Common	$20 – 40
Battle of the Wild	Uncommon	$75 – 110
Be It Ever So Humble, There's No Place Like Home	Uncommon	$90 – 110
Best Pie Maker in Town, The	Scarce	$150 – 175
Between Two Fires	Scarce	$175 – 225
Birch Bordered Waters	Common	$40 – 60
Blooming Time	Uncommon	$70 – 90
Blossom Time	Common	$80 – 100
Blue Lake	Common	$40 – 60
Bonnie J., International Champion	Uncommon	$125 – 160
Bred in the Purple (also found with two horses)	Common	$80 – 110
Brother Elk, A	Scarce	$150 – 175
Buffalo Hunt, The	Common	$70 – 90
By the Campfire Glow	Uncommon	$80 – 100
By the Winding Stream	Uncommon	$60 – 80
Canadian Landscape	Common	$50 – 75
Capital and Labor	Uncommon	$125 – 150
Challenge, The (Leopard)	Scarce	$175 – 225
Chicago, Milwaukee, St. Paul & Pacific (Trains)	Uncommon	$140 – 170
Clipper Ship (also Rough Seas)	Common	$40 – 60
Colbourne, Buttes, Colorado	Uncommon	$60 – 80
Columbia River, Oregon	Uncommon	$75 – 90
Comrades	Scarce	$110 – 130
Cottage By the Sea, The	Uncommon	$75 – 95
Crick and Cran (Spick and Span)	Uncommon	$110 – 125
Dandelion Time	Common	$50 – 75
Daughters of the Incas	Scarce	$175 – 250
Daughter of the Setting Sun	Scarce	$175 – 250
Dawn	Common	$50 – 150
Day Dreams	Common	$40 – 70
Days Work Done, The	Uncommon	$100 – 125
Deering	Scarce	$150 – 180
Departure of Columbus	Uncommon	$125 – 150
Discovery of the Mississippi, 1541	Scarce	$175 – 250
Down by the Bridge	Uncommon	$60 – 80
Down on Granpa's Farm	Scarce	$90 – 125
Down on the Farm	Scarce	$150 – 175
Dreamland	Common	$20 – 30
Dreamy Paradise	Common	$40 – 70
Duke	Uncommon	$125 – 160
Edge of the Woods	Common	$40 – 50
Elysian Fields	Uncommon	$90 – 120
Emperor, The	Scarce	$130 – 160
Enchanted Steps, The	Common	$50 – 70
English Garden	Common	$40 – 60
English Garden, An	Common	$120 – 160
Evening Call, The	Uncommon	$90 – 110
Eternal Hills	Uncommon	$60 – 75
Fair Guide, A	Scarce	$175 – 225
Faithful and True	Scarce	$200 – 225
Faithful Friends	Uncommon	$140 – 160
Fallen Monarch, A	Common	$50 – 75
Falls of the Yellowstone	Uncommon	$60 – 80
Feeding Ground, The	Scarce	$110 – 125
Fish Story, The	Scarce	$140 – 170
Flight to Egypt (untitled)	Uncommon	$75 – 100
Flower of the Forest	Uncommon	$70 – 95
Flowerland	Uncommon	$125 – 160
Fooling Him	Scarce	$150 – 180
Forest Fire	Uncommon	$90 – 120
Forest Ranger, The	Uncommon	$90 – 125
Four Chums	Scarce	$110 – 135
Fraternally Yours	Scarce	$125 – 160
Friends (also Two Families)	Scarce	$140 – 175
Gage's Surrender	Scarce	$150 – 190
Garden Gate	Uncommon	$65 – 90
Garden of Contentment	Uncommon	$70 – 95
Garden of Happiness	Uncommon	$70 – 95
Garden of Hope	Uncommon	$70 – 90
Garden of Love	Common	$50 – 75
Garden of Nature	Uncommon	$60 – 85
Garden of Rest	Uncommon	$75 – 90
Garden of Romance	Common	$30 – 70
Garden Realm	Uncommon	$50 – 100
Garden Retreat	Uncommon	$60 – 85
General Foch, Pershing, and Haig Receiving Their Victorious Troops	Scarce	$150 – 190
General Mad Anthony Wayne at the Battle of Stony Point	Scarce	$140 – 170
Geyser	Uncommon	$125 – 150
Girl of the Golden West	Uncommon	$90 – 135
Glories of Autumn	Uncommon	$95 – 130

Glorious Vista	Common	$50 – 125	Leader, The	Scarce	$150 – 175
Going After the Big Ones	Uncommon	$110 – 140	Legal Holiday, A	Scarce	$150 – 175
Going to Sun Mountain	Uncommon	$60 – 75	Life's Greatest Gift	Common	$75 – 90
Golden Gate at San Francisco, The	Uncommon	$70 – 90	Life Saver, A	Scarce	$200 – 250
Good Guide	Uncommon	$140 – 170	Look Me in the Eye	Scarce	$85 – 110
Good Morning Deer	Common	$50 – 75	Look Pretty	Scarce	$175 – 200
Good Shepherd, The	Common	$50 – 125	Lookout Mountain	Scarce	$85 – 110
Good Ship Adventure	Common	$40 – 75	Lost Sheep, The	Uncommon	$90 – 110
Great Falls of Yellowstone	Uncommon	$60 – 75	Love Birds (also Castle of Dreams)	Uncommon	$75 – 90
Guardian of the Valley	Common	$50 – 75	Lovers Bower	Uncommon	$75 – 100
Harvesting	Scarce	$90 – 120	Love's Paradise	Common	$70 – 150
Head of the Herd	Scarce	$85 – 110	Magic Forest, The	Uncommon	$75 – 95
Heart's Desire	Common	$60 – 100	Magic Pool, The	Uncommon	$60 – 80
Heights of Quebec	Uncommon	$60 – 75	Me and Rex	Scarce	$140 – 175
His Last Cartridge	Uncommon	$75 – 100	Memories of Childhood Days	Common	$50 – 95
Holding an Investigation	Common	$40 – 50	Mid Mountain Verdure	Uncommon	$60 – 90
Home of the West Wind	Uncommon	$75 – 100	Mid Summer Magic	Common	$60 – 80
Horse Pasture, The	Uncommon	$125 – 150	Mill and the Birches	Uncommon	$80 – 110
Hunter's Paradise	Common	$60 – 80	Minnehaha Falls	Uncommon	$75 – 100
In a Lovely Garden Where Dreams			Mirror Lake	Scarce	$85 – 110
Come True	Uncommon	$75 – 100	Mischief Maker, A	Scarce	$125 – 160
In America's Wonderland	Common	$60 – 90	Monarch of the North, The	Uncommon	$95 – 125
In Flander's Field	Common	$60 – 90	Mystic Hour, The	Uncommon	$70 – 95
In Meditation Fancy Free	Uncommon	$150 – 300	Moonbeam Enchantment	Uncommon	$80 – 110
In Moonlight Blue	Uncommon	$125 – 160	Moonlight and Roses	Common	$70 – 95
In My Garden of Dreams	Uncommon	$95 – 125	Moonlight on the Camp	Common	$50 – 75
In New York Bay	Uncommon	$60 – 75	Morning Call, The	Uncommon	$90 – 110
In the Enemy's Country	Uncommon	$150 – 175	Morning Mists	Uncommon	$80 – 110
In the Heart of the			Mount of the Holy Cross, The	Uncommon	$80 – 110
Sierra Nevadas	Uncommon	$45 – 140	Mountain in All Its Glory, The	Uncommon	$70 – 95
In the Land of the Sky	Uncommon	$70 – 100	Mountain Trail, The	Uncommon	$90 – 125
Indian Paradise	Common	$75 – 100	Mountain Valley	Common	$50 – 70
Indian Summer	Common	$50 – 75	Mt. Hood	Uncommon	$70 – 90
Inspiration Inlet	Common	$40 – 60	Mt. Rainier — Growing in Rosy		
Iron Horse, The — Driving the			Splendor	Uncommon	$70 – 90
Golden Spike	Scarce	$175 – 250	Mt. Shasta	Scarce	$85 – 110
It's Only a Cottage, But It's Home	Uncommon	$75 – 110	Music of the Waters	Uncommon	$75 – 125
Jealousy	Scarce	$150 – 200	My Castle of Dreams	Scarce	$110 – 150
Journey's End Oregon	Scarce	$150 – 175	My Favorites	Scarce	$200 – 300
June Morn	Uncommon	$125 – 150	Native Son, A	Scarce	$150 – 200
Just Out	Common	$40 – 50	Natural Bridge of Virginia	Uncommon	$45 – 65
King of the Clouds	Scarce	$85 – 110	Nature's Beauty	Common	$30 – 70
King of the Silvery Domain	Uncommon	$70 – 90	Nature's Charms	Uncommon	$125 – 150
Lake Louise in the Canadian			Nature's Grandeur	Uncommon	$90 – 125
Rockies (also A Crystal Gem			Nature's Hidden Places	Uncommon	$75 – 100
in Nature's Crown)	Uncommon	$70 – 90	Nature's Mirror	Common	$95 – 140
Lake Louise, Alberta	Uncommon	$90 – 125	Nature's Retreat	Uncommon	$50 – 100
Land of Dreams	Common	$40 – 70	Nature's Sentinels	Scarce	$90 – 130
Land of the Herd	Scarce	$125 – 160	Nature's Silvery Retreat	Uncommon	$120 – 140
Land of the Sky Blue Waters	Uncommon	$75 – 95	Nature's Sublime Grandeur	Common	$60 – 90
Land Where the Shamrock Grows	Common	$75 – 95	Nature's Treasures	Uncommon	$125 – 175

Near Close of Day	Scarce	$95 – 125	Pride of the Farm (cows)	Uncommon	$75 – 110
Neath Turquoise Skies	Uncommon	$75 – 95	Prize Winners (cows)	Uncommon	$90 – 125
Neighborly Call, A	Scarce	$150 – 175	Promenade	Common	$60 – 90
New England Coast, A	Scarce	$85 – 110	Purple Majesty	Uncommon	$75 – 100
New England Hills (also Inviting			Quiet Pool, A	Uncommon	$75 – 100
Pathway)	Uncommon	$75 – 90	Ready and Willing	Scarce	$140 – 175
New Overland Express	Uncommon	$110 – 140	Ready for Anything	Uncommon	$80 – 110
Niagara Falls	Scarce	$75 – 100	Ready for the Day's Work	Uncommon	$125 – 150
Night Call, The	Uncommon	$90 – 125	Reliable Guardian, A	Common	$50 – 70
No One at Home	Common	$40 – 65	Rest Haven	Common	$50 – 70
Northward Bound	Scarce	$130 – 160	Returning from Pasture	Uncommon	$90 – 120
Oaks by the Roadside	Common	$45 – 65	River of Romance	Common	$50 – 80
October Days	Uncommon	$60 – 85	Road of Poplars, The	Common	$40 – 60
October Sport	Scarce	$125 – 150	Rocky Mountain Grandeur	Uncommon	$75 – 95
Off Treasure Island	Uncommon	$75 – 95	Rocky Waterway	Uncommon	$125 – 150
Oh Susanna —			Romance Canyon	Common	$65 – 95
The Covered Wagon	Scarce	$160 – 200	Rose Bower	Uncommon	$70 – 95
Old Fashioned Garden, An	Common	$60 – 80	Rosy Glow of the Land of Promise	Uncommon	$75 – 125
Old Ironsides	Uncommon	$90 – 135	Rough Seas (also Clipper Ship)	Common	$45 – 65
Old Mill, The	Common	$50 – 75	Roundup, The	Uncommon	$75 – 100
Old Oak, An	Common	$50 – 60	Rover	Uncommon	$120 – 150
Old Oaken Bucket, The	Scarce	$150 – 190	Royal Outlaw, A	Scarce	$200 – 250
Old Pals	Scarce	$125 – 160	Ruins of Ticonderoga	Scarce	$150 – 175
Old Rosebud	Scarce	$175 – 250	Russet Gems	Common	$50 – 100
Old Rosebud (on tin)	Scarce	$425 – 475	Sapphire Sea	Uncommon	$75 – 110
On Guard (dog)	Uncommon	$75 – 100	Scotch Shorthorns	Scarce	$110 – 140
On the Way to the Mill	Scarce	$100 – 130	See America First	Scarce	$125 – 150
One Strike (black & white)	Scarce	$140 – 165	Seeking Protection	Uncommon	$125 – 150
Original Oil Painting		$3000	Sentinel of the Ages	Uncommon	$75 – 95
Oriental Dreams	Uncommon	$75 – 110	Sentinel, The	Uncommon	$95 – 125
Out of the Sky He Comes	Scarce	$170 – 200	Sheltering Bower	Common	$60 – 75
Over the Top	Uncommon	$125 – 150	Shorthorns	Uncommon	$110 – 140
Palisades of the Hudson	Uncommon	$85 – 110	Shorthorns Nooning	Uncommon	$95 – 125
Pals (also The Barefoot Boy)	Uncommon	$75 – 100	Silent Rockies, The	Common	$50 – 75
Paradise (also Dreamy Paradise)	Common	$150 – 180	Sitting Pretty	Scarce	$85 – 110
Pasture Lane, The	Scarce	$125 – 150	Skyline, The	Scarce	$225 – 250
Path to the Valley	Common	$50 – 75	Snow-Capped Mountain Lifts		
Patriarch, The	Scarce	$85 – 115	It's Crest, The	Common	$50 – 90
Peace and Plenty	Scarce	$125 – 150	Song of Evening	Uncommon	$75 – 95
Peace and Sunshine	Common	$70 – 100	Spic & Span (also Crik and Cran)	Scarce	$125 – 150
Perfect Day	Common	$75 – 100	Spirit of Adventure	Uncommon	$60 – 90
Perspective	Common	$40 – 65	Spirit of the Harvest	Scarce	$175 – 225
Picnic Days (1932)	Scarce	$95 – 125	Spirit of Youth	Uncommon	$125 – 150
Play While You May	Scarce	$90 – 125	Spring Beauties	Uncommon	$60 – 90
Playmate Guardian	Uncommon	$75 – 100	Springtime	Scarce	$150 – 175
Political Argument, A	Uncommon	$90 – 120	Stairway, The	Uncommon	$50 – 80
Political Argument, The	Uncommon	$60 – 100	Stately Sentinels	Uncommon	$75 – 95
Poppies (also Red Poppies)	Common	$90 – 160	Summer's Glory	Uncommon	$95 – 150
Port o' Heart's Desire, The	Common	$65 – 85	Summertime at Grandpa's	Scarce	$175 – 150
Portrait of George Washington	Uncommon	$90 – 150	Sunland	Common	$40 – 70
Precious	Scarce	$125 – 175	Sunrise	Common	$75 – 125

Sunrise, Coast of Maine	Scarce	$125 – 150
Sunset Dreams	Common	$50 – 150
Sunset in the Big North Woods	Scarce	$140 – 175
Supremacy	Uncommon	$100 – 140
Surf Fishing	Scarce	$200 – 250
Surrender of Cornwallis at Yorktown	Uncommon	$125 – 150
Sweet Ole Spot (or Dear Ole Spot)	Uncommon	$75 – 100
There's No Place Like Home	Uncommon	$75 – 125
Three Twins, The	Uncommon	$120 – 150
Thrill Before Breakfast, A	Scarce	$150 – 175
Through the Mountain Pass	Scarce	$140 – 180
Tom and Jerry	Uncommon	$130 – 160
Treasure Fleet, The	Uncommon	$75 – 100
Twilight	Uncommon	$100 – 140
Twilight Glories	Uncommon	$60 – 90
Two Families (also Friends)	Scarce	$150 – 175
Two Old Cronies	Scarce	$150 – 175
Untitled Blimp/Slogan	Uncommon	$65 – 85
Untitled – Ducks	Scarce	$75 – 90
Untitled – Road/Bridge/Stream	Common	$40 – 60
Valley of Enchantment	Uncommon	$90 – 125
Valley of Golden Dreams	Uncommon	$75 – 95
Venetian Garden	Common	$75 – 125
Village Belle, The	Scarce	$200 – 250
Vigilance	Uncommon	$75 – 95
Waiting for their Master	Scarce	$150 – 175
Warm Friends	Uncommon	$70 – 95
Washington at Valley Forge	Common	$50 – 75
Washington the Soldier	Scarce	$150 – 175
Washington the Surveyor	Scarce	$150 – 175
Watering Place, The	Common	$40 – 60
Water Lilies	Scarce	$170 – 200
Wayside House	Uncommon	$125 – 175
Well Done	Scarce	$125 – 150
Wending Their Way Homeward	Uncommon	$95 – 125
When Brooks Send Up a Cheerful Tune	Uncommon	$75 – 110
When Evening Shadows Fall (cows)	Uncommon	$75 – 100
When Shadows Lengthen	Uncommon	$75 – 110
When the Day Is Done	Uncommon	$70 – 95
When the Day Is Over	Uncommon	$75 – 100
Where Dreams Come True	Uncommon	$75 – 100
Where Giants Wrought (also To Stand Forever)	Scarce	$95 – 125
Where Nature Beats in Perfect Tune	Uncommon	$75 – 100
White Feather	Scarce	$250 – 350
Who Are You?	Common	$40 – 65
Who's Jealous	Uncommon	$150 – 175

Prints Signed Wain(w)right
(C., Chs., C.N., F., or C. Wain)

At Sundown in the Golden West	Uncommon	$45 – 65

Being Helpful	Scarce	$150 – 175
Campers, The	Scarce	$75 – 90
Echoing Call, The	Uncommon	$50 – 75
Flavor of Fall, The	Uncommon	$50 – 70
Garden of Flowers, A	Uncommon	$45 – 70
House By the Side of the Road	Uncommon	$50 – 75
Maid in the U.S.A.	Scarce	$90 – 125
Midsummer	Uncommon	$50 – 70
Nature's White Mantle	Common	$40 – 60
Old Fishing Hole, The	Uncommon	$45 – 65
Old Pathway, The	Uncommon	$50 – 70
Overlooking Emerald Bay	Uncommon	$50 – 75
Paradise	Common	$40 – 50
Paradise Valley	Uncommon	$45 – 65
Quiet Solitude	Uncommon	$75 – 100
Sentinels of the Pass	Common	$40 – 50
Two Medicine River Falls	Common	$40 – 60
Under the Greenwood Trees	Uncommon	$50 – 70
View Through the Timber, A	Uncommon	$50 – 70
Washington & Lafayette at Valley Forge	Scarce	$150 – 200

Prints Signed George Turner (also Geo.)

Neath Sunset Skies	Uncommon	$60 – 75
Off New England Shores	Scarce	$80 – 90
Silvery Divide	Common	$40 – 50

Prints Signed DeForest or Arthur DeForest

Adventuress, The	Scarce	$125 – 150
As Twilight Approaches	Common	$50 – 60
Barrel of Fun, A	Uncommon	$95 – 110
Childhood Days	Uncommon	$75 – 100
Curly Locks	Uncommon	$75 – 100
Garden Spot, A	Common	$50 – 60
Meditation	Uncommon	$75 – 95
Mighty Like a Rose	Uncommon	$90 – 110
Mutual Surprise	Scarce	$75 – 90
On Treasure Isle	Uncommon	$100 – 125
Perfect Melody, A	Scarce	$125 – 150
Playmates	Uncommon	$70 – 90
Pride of the Blue Ridge	Uncommon	$100 – 125
Speak Rover	Uncommon	$100 – 125

Prints Signed Dupre

At Peace with the World	Uncommon	$90 – 100
By the Zuyder Zee	Common	$50 – 60
Chieftains Pride	Uncommon	$90 – 110
Dreamy Valley	Uncommon	$90 – 100
Grandeur of Nature	Common	$50 – 60
In the Land of the Sky Blue Waters	Uncommon	$90 – 110
Wanetah	Uncommon	$90 – 110

Prints Signed Elmer Lewis (also E. Lewis)

Battle Royal, A	Uncommon	$130 – 170
Discretion is the Better Part of Valor	Uncommon	$150 – 175
Ever Watchful	Scarce	$140 – 175
Guardian, The	Scarce	$175 – 200
Old Ocean Roars/The Jungle Answers	Uncommon	$150 – 175
On the Lookout	Uncommon	$125 – 160
On the Trail	Uncommon	$75 – 125
Royal Pair, A	Scarce	$175 – 225
Safely Guarded	Uncommon	$150 – 175
Security	Scarce	$175 – 225
Strength and Security	Scarce	$250 – 300
Untamed Monarchs	Scarce	$150 – 175
Untitled – lion & the moon	Scarce	$150 – 175
Washington at Headquarters	Uncommon	$125 – 150
Washington at the Battle of Monmouth	Uncommon	$125 – 150

Prints Signed George White
(also Geo. White, G. White, G.L. White)

All Set (Hunter's Friend)	Common	$40 – 60
At the Foot of Mt. Rainier	Common	$45 – 65
Cozy Cottage	Uncommon	$75 – 90
Garden Home, The	Uncommon	$50 – 75

Girl of the Golden West, The	Uncommon	$75 – 100
Grandeur of Summer, The	Uncommon	$75 – 90
Haven of Splendor, A	Uncommon	$75 – 90
On the Trail	Uncommon	$50 – 75
Scenting the Trail	Common	$40 – 60
Sentinel of the Night, The	Uncommon	$50 – 75
Silvery Grandeur	Common	$45 – 65
Silvery Wonderland	Common	$45 – 65
Watching	Uncommon	$50 – 70

Prints Signed John Colvin
(also J. Colvin, John Calvin)

Chums	Scarce	$175 – 250
Faithful	Uncommon	$75 – 90
Guardian, The	Scarce	$175 – 200
Their First Lesson	Uncommon	$125 – 150
Their Great Day	Uncommon	$100 – 125

Prints by George Wood
(not to be confused with the landscape artist)

By a Falling Crystal Stream	Uncommon	$50 – 75

An Old Fashioned Garden. Est. Value: $60 – 80.

A Barrel of Fun. Est. Value: $95 – 110.

An English Garden. Est. Value: $120 – 160.

An Old Oak. Est. Value: $50 — 60.

Being Helpful. Est. Value: $150 — 175.

Blossom Time. Est. Value: $40 — 60.

Blue Lake. Est. Value: $75 — 100.

Clipper Ship. Est. Value: $75 — 100.

Dreamy Valley. Est. Value: $90 — 100.

Dawn (18x30"). Est. Value: $150 — 275.

Down on the Farm. Est. Value: $150 — 175.

Forest Fire. Est. Value: $90 — 120.

Garden of Romance. Est. Value: $60 — 110.

Glorious Vista. Est. Value: $50 — 125.

Harvesting. Est. Value: $90 — 120.

Good Ship Adventure. Est. Value: $75 — 100.

Heart's Desire.
Est. Value: $60 — 100.

In Meditation
Fancy Free.
Est. Value: $150 — 300.

Memories of
Childhood Days.
Est. Value: $50 — 95.

Hunter's Paradise. Est. Value: $60 — 80.

Autumn Gold. Est. Value: $40 – 60.

Mutual Surprise. Est. Value: $75 – 90.

Nature's Beauty. Est. Value: $75 – 150.

My Favorites. Est. Value: $200 – 300.

Mountain Valley. Est. Value: $50 – 70.

Nature's Sublime Grandeur. Est. Value: $60 — 90.

Northward Bound. Est. Value: $130 — 160.

On the Way to the Mill. Est. Value: $100 — 130.

One Strike (black & white).
Est. Value: $140 — 165.

Poppies. Est. Value: $90 — 160.

Ready and Willing. Est. Value: $140 — 175.

River of Romance. Est. Value: $60 — 90.

Rover. Est. Value: $120 — 150.

Russet Gems. Est. Value: $50 — 90.

See America First. Est. Value: $125 — 150.

Seeking Protection. Est. Value: $125 – 150.

Springtime. Est. Value: $150 – 175.

Sunland. Est. Value: $60 – 80.

Sunset Dreams. Est. Value: $100 – 200.

The Best Pie Maker in Town. Est. Value: $150 – 175.

The Battle Royal (Elmer Lewis). Est. Value: $130 – 175.

The Emperor. Est. Value: $130 — 160.

The Enchanted Steps. Est. Value: $50 — 70.

The Evening Call. Est. Value: $90 — 110.

The Monarch of the North. Est. Value: $95 — 125.

The Morning Call. Est. Value: $90 — 110.

The Road of Poplars. Est. Value: $65—85.

Untitled (Ducks). Est. Value: $75—90.

The Three Twins. Est. Value: $120—150.

Who's Jealous. Est. Value: $150—175.

Untitled (Mountain Lion-Elmer Lewis). Est. Value: $125.

Untitled (Road/Bridge/Stream). Est. Value: $40—60.

Tom and Jerry. Est. Value: $150—275.

A Mischief Maker
Est. Value: $125 – 160.

Water Lilies. Est. Value: $170 – 200.

A Political Argument (1903). Est. Value: $90 – 120.

Comrades (1907). Est. Value: $110 – 130.

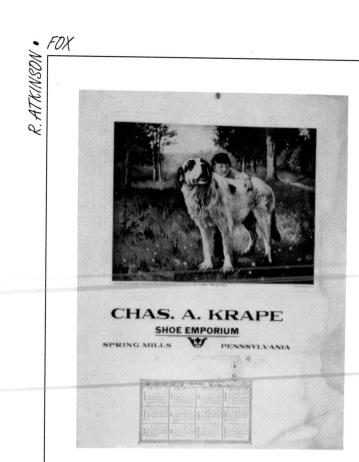

Me and Rex (1909). Est. Value: $140 – 175.

Fooling Him (1911). Est. Value: $150 – 180.

Faithful Friends (1914). Est. Value: $140 – 160.

Through the Mountain Pass (1917). Est. Value: $140 – 180.

Strength (Elmer Lewis-1918). Est. Value: $250 — 300.

Good Guide (1918). Est. Value: $140 — 170.

Maid in USA (C Wainright-1922). Est. Value: $90 — 125.

*Untitled Blimp/Slogan (1924).
Est. Value: $100 — 175.*

Mighty Like a Rose (DeForest-1926). Est. Value: $90 – 110.

Land of the Sky Blue Waters (Dupre-1927).
Est. Value: $75 – 95.

In Moonlight Blue (1927).
Est. Value: $125 – 160.

Aces All (1929). Est. Value: $150 – 180.

An Ambassador of Good Will (1931).
Est. Value: $110 — 135.

Nature's Silvery Retreat (1932).
Est. Value: $120 — 140.

Picnic Days (1932). Est. Value: $95 — 125.

The Good Shepherd (1949). Est. Value: $50 — 125.

NOTE: A Sunset Symphony (FA Robert–1926) is shown on page 85.

Chapter 5

A Collection of Some Beautiful and Unusual Early Twentieth Century American Prints

Maxfield Parrish

Old King Cole, a large triptych

Waterfall, Edison-Mazda calendar

Old King Cole, the only known copy of this calendar

Daybreak, Maxfield Parrish's most popular and bestselling print

Canyon, common, yet very popular

The Lute Players, very similar to Interlude

Hilltop, another common, yet very popular print

Reveries, cropped calendar top

Toy Soldier, art print

Playing cards, Edison-Mazda

Bessie Pease Gutmann

Lorelei, difficult to find

The Guest's Candle, an unusual evening scene

Good Night, another unusual evening scene

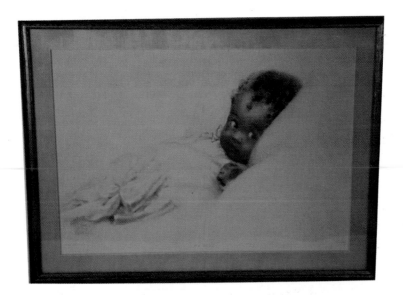

My Honey, an exceptionally rare Gutmann featuring a black baby

Love's Message, quite unusual

The New Pet, pets are always popular

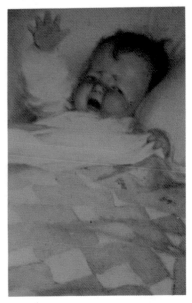

Our Alarm Clock, rare baby scene

A Chip of the Old Block, the title is correct

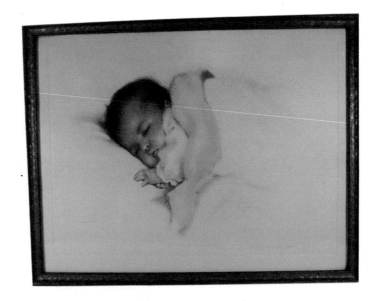

A Little Bit of Heaven, the bestselling Gutmann print of all

How Miss Tabitha Taught School, unusual
and very popular

R. Atkinson Fox

An Approaching Storm, Fox was considered an excellent painter of cows

Precious, certainly has the look and feel of a Bessie Pease Gutmann

Between Two Fires, this could very well have been a Currier & Ives subject (but it wasn't)

Untitled Fisherman, the great outdoors

Supremacy, Military battles

The Lone Eagle, Charles Lindbergh after his conquest

My Favorites, Fox excelled at girls and animals

Daughter of the Setting Sun, beautiful Indian maidens were a
popular publishing topic

Faithful and True, a girl and her friend

Strength and Security, the king of all animals, an Elmer
Lewis pseudonym

Wallace Nutting

Apple Blossoms, Nutting's most popular and common theme

Larkspur, an extremely popular and common foreign thatch-roofed cottage

An interior scene, how Nutting viewed the Colonial Revival Movement

The Guardian Mother, stills holds the Nutting auction record at $4,950

A Dutch Knitting Lesson, a triple rarity, a foreign scene with a man and a child

The Meeting Place, a very popular and expensive animal scene

Florals, were arranged by Mrs. Nutting and are considered rare and very popular

Snow Scenes, are probably the rarest of all Wallace Nutting pictures

The Coming Out of Rosa, is probably Nutting's most popular picture

Silhouettes, Nutting sold more than 40 different silhouette scenes

David Davidson

Berkshire Sunset, exteriors were Davidson's
bestselling pictures

Vanity, some of Davidson's interiors were as
pretty as Nutting's

Easter Bonnet, a Davidson
miscellaneous unusual scene

Porch Beautiful, a fairly common picture

Maytime Fragrance, another girl by a house

The Seine Reel, an unusual and desirable picture

The Governor's Mansion, a fairly unusual scene

The Squire's Note,
fairly common,
but very pretty

Spring Delights, Davidson sheep scene

Whittiers Hearth, very colorful interior

Sawyer

Echo Lake, sometimes called Echo Lake, Franconia Notch, was Sawyer's bestselling picture of all time

The Afterglow, an exterior with excellent coloring

To Join the Brimming River, a typical Sawyer river scene

Cypress Point, an unusual California seascape

Majestic Waters, another colorful exterior

The Original Dennison Plant, Brunswick, Maine,
the same picture was sold by both Nutting and
Davidson

Lake George, close framed

Autumn's Reflection, colorful fall scene

San Juan Capistrano, unusual California mission

Surf at Pinnacle Rock, a Sawyer seascape

Fred Thompson

The Old Toll Bridge, another of Thompson's bestselling pictures
(and fairly common today)

Lombardy Poplar, a very common Thompson exterior
scene

Schooner Lawrence, sailing ships from Maine's coastal ports were another
popular Thompson subject, and very popular with collectors today

Mother's Joy, Thompson didn't produce many pictures with children

Portland Head, most visitors to southern Maine probably returned home with one of these

Brook in Winter, snow scenes are fairly unusual

Toiler of the Sea, one of the rarest of all
Thompson pictures

Fireside Fancy Work, shot in Nuttinghame

The Dancing Lesson, men are quite rare in Thompson pictures

The Old Pilot, perhaps the very best and
rarest Thompson scene

Lesser Known and Unknown Photographers

Porcupine Island, J. Carleton Bicknell

The Old Chaise, Chas R. Higgins

Lover's Road, Gibson

Untitled snow scene, Lamson

From Black Bear Mountain, Inlet, NY, Harris

Going Shopping, Higgins

The Old Well, Villar

Goin to Within, Turner

photographer unknown, Rocky Shoreline point, probably from someone's vacation

photographer unknown, untitled dog, would you want
this dog hanging in your house?

Chapter 6

Putting Early Twentieth Century Hand-Colored Photography Into Perspective

An early twentieth century photographer in the field.

Some people say the current interest in hand-colored photography is because it is affordable; others say it is a result of the renewed interest in the Colonial Revival movement; some say that the high quality of this work is finally becoming recognized; while still others are simply trying to cash in on what they perceive to be the low end of a market.

Collecting Tip:

The term Wallace Nutting-like picture is used to denote any early twentieth century hand-colored photograph dating between 1900 and 1940 that resembles the look and process of a Wallace Nutting picture.

Early twentieth century hand-colored photography, and Wallace Nutting pictures in particular, have become increasingly popular with collectors in recent years. The number of collectors has been growing and good quality pictures at reasonable prices have become more difficult to locate.

What's the cause for all this interest in Wallace Nutting and Wallace Nutting-like pictures? Some people call it nostalgia. Young people love these pictures because they show America as it once was, the way they have never seen it. Older people love them because of memories of simpler days past — no skyscrapers, no telephone poles, no superhighways, no pollution.

Wallace Nutting, circa 1936

Regardless of the causes for all this interest, the hand-colored photography market has indeed been hot, and Wallace Nutting has been in the center of it. What is it that makes these pictures so universally popular with collectors today?

To clearly understand the hand-colored photography market, you must first understand the Wallace Nutting market, and the fact that there are actually three different and distinct segments within the Nutting market. This chapter will attempt to put the overall market of early twentieth century hand-colored photography in perspective, and the remaining chapters will focus more in-depth upon each of the leading photographers and segments within this market.

Nutting was an accomplished author who published nearly 20 books between 1912 and 1936, including his 10-volume States Beautiful series, various other books on furniture, photography, clocks, as well as his own personal biography. He also contributed many photographs which were published in magazines and other books, and as a result of the in-depth research he did for his books, Nutting became widely regarded as the father of American antiques.

A typical Nutting exterior scene

Wallace Nutting was best known for his hand-colored pictures. He sold literally millions of his platinotypes between 1900 and his death in 1941. By 1925, hardly an American middle-class household was without one.

A Nutting reproduction carver arm chair

Wallace Nutting States Beautiful Books

The distinctive Nutting block furniture brand

Nutting also became widely renown for his reproduction furniture. His Massachusetts furniture shop reproduced literally hundreds of different furniture forms of clocks, stools, chairs, settles, settees, tables, stands, desks, mirrors, beds, chests of drawers, cabinet pieces, and treenware, most of which was clearly marked with his distinctive paper label, or the hard-to-miss block or script signature, which was literally branded into his furniture. Today, Wallace Nutting reproduction furniture is almost universally considered to be the finest bench-made reproduction furniture produced in the twentieth century and is highly collectible by all levels of collectors.

Wallace Nutting *pictures*, Wallace Nutting *books*, Wallace Nutting *furniture* are three separate and distinct markets, each with their own group of collectors and enthusiasts. Synergy means that the product is greater than the sum of all of its separate and individual parts. This is what places Wallace Nutting as the most collectible of all early twentieth century hand-colored photographers. The overall synergy of the Wallace Nutting name has made just about anything Wallace Nutting extremely collectible today. The legion of Nutting collectors has grown significantly in recent years, and today there are more people actively seeking Wallace Nutting pictures than ever before.

Collecting Tip:

Wallace Nutting was widely known for the millions of hand-colored pictures he sold, for the nearly 20 different books that he published, and for the thousands of pieces of furniture he reproduced.

A Wallace Nutting catalog auction

In very simple economic terms, when too many people are chasing after too few goods, prices have a tendency to rise. This is exactly what is happening within the Wallace Nutting market today. Too many collectors and dealers are chasing after too few pictures with the net effect being that prices for those pictures remaining in circulation now often cost more than they did several years ago.

It's not that the number of Wallace Nutting pictures is decreasing. Rather, as the number of collectors has grown, an increasing number of pictures are being purchased and held in private collections. These are usually the best pictures, in the finest condition which, in effect, takes them out of circulation. With fewer pictures remaining in circulation, and more people actively pursuing them, the asking prices on those pictures still in circulation are generally higher than they were 12–24 months ago. And because so many collectors are unable to find the rarer pictures in excellent quality, many are paying more for lower quality pictures, while others have slowed down their volume of Wallace Nutting purchases.

And as Wallace Nutting pictures have become increasingly more expensive and difficult to find, more collectors have been gravitating to the comparable, increasingly collectible, yet less expensive, pictures of other early twentieth century photographers.

What many collectors are now beginning to learn is that although Wallace Nutting was widely recognized as the country's leading producer of hand-colored photographs during the early twentieth century, he was by no means the only photographer selling this style of picture. Throughout the country literally hundreds of regional photographers were selling their own brand of hand-colored photographs from their home regions or travels.

Collecting Tip:

There were literally hundreds of professional and amateur photographers who were also selling hand-colored photographs on a full-time and part-time basis between 1900 and 1940.

Wallace Nutting-Like Photographers of the Early 20th Century

Wallace Nutting

"The Big 3"
Davidson...Fred Thompson...Sawyer Art Co.

*Lesser-Known Photographers ****

Unknown Photographers

The inverted pyramid of early 20th century hand-colored photographers

Understanding the Key Players and Segments within the Early 20th c. Hand-Colored Photography Market

The key to understanding the hand-colored photography market rests upon developing an understanding of the important photographers within this market. The following summaries are designed to provide a very brief overview of each major market segment, while the inverted pyramid graphic is intended to help to visually demonstrate the current inter-relationship between the four primary segments within the hand-colored photography market.

A typical Wallace Nutting colonial interior scene

Level 1... Wallace Nutting Pictures

Background

Wallace Nutting was the unquestioned leader within the field of early twentieth century hand-colored photography. Starting on a part-time basis in

1898, Nutting worked in Southbury, Connecticut, from 1905 until 1912, and in Framingham, Massachusetts, from 1912 until his death in 1941.

Level 2...Major Nutting-like Photographers...The Next Three Largest Photographers

Background

David Davidson, Charles Sawyer, and Fred Thompson each operated relatively large photography businesses and, although not nearly as large or well known as Wallace Nutting, they sold a substantial volume of pictures which can still be readily found today — often at undervalued prices. The vast majority of their work was photographed in their home regions of New England and sold primarily to local residents or visiting tourists.

Each of these three photographers had ties to Wallace Nutting.

A typical David Davidson picture

David Davidson: Second to Nutting in overall production, worked out of Providence, Rhode Island, and sold his pictures primarily in the Rhode Island, and Southern Massachusetts area. While a student at Brown University around 1900,

Davidson learned the art of hand-colored photography from Wallace Nutting, who happened to be the minister at Davidson's church. After Nutting moved to Southbury in 1905, Davidson graduated from Brown and started the successful David Davidson Studios in 1907 which he operated until the 1950s.

A typical Fred Thompson picture

A typical Sawyer picture

Sawyer: A father & son team, Charles H. Sawyer and Harold B. Sawyer, operated the very successful Sawyer Pictures Company from 1903 until the 1970s. Beginning in Farmington, Maine, the Sawyer Pictures Company moved to Concord, New Hampshire, in 1920 to be nearer their primary market of New Hampshire's White Mountains. Charles H. Sawyer briefly worked for Nutting in 1902–03 while living in Farmington. Sawyer's total production ranked #3, behind Wallace Nutting and David Davidson.

Fred Thompson: Frederick H. Thompson and Frederick M. Thompson were another father and son team, operating the Thompson Art Company from 1908 until 1923, in the Portland, Maine, area. We know that Thompson and Nutting collaborated because Thompson widely marketed

an interior scene he had taken in Nutting's Southbury home. The production volume of the Thompson Art Company ranked #4, behind Nutting, Davidson, and Sawyer in that order.

Davidson—Sawyer—Thompson Collecting Tips:

*There is an increasing number of collectors who are focusing their collections on David Davidson, Fred Thompson, and Sawyer pictures.

*When taken as a group, there are more Wallace Nutting pictures in circulation than all Davidson-Sawyer-Thompson pictures combined.

*When taken as a group, there are more Davidson-Sawyer-Thompson pictures in circulation than all of the lesser-known and unknown photographers combined.

*With few exceptions, the prices of Davidson-Sawyer-Thompson pictures are lower than comparable Wallace Nuttings, and are higher than all comparable lesser-known and unknown photographers combined.

Level 3...Lesser-known Wallace Nutting-like Photographers
Background

Hundreds of other smaller local and regional photographers attempted to market hand-colored pictures comparable to Nutting-Davidson-Sawyer-Thompson pictures from the 1900s to the 1940s. Although often quite attractive, most were not as appealing or as well mar-

A typical colonial scene by a lesser-known photographer

keted as the better known Nutting-Davidson-Sawyer-Thompson names. As we all know, collectors always buy the name and the most famous of all early twentieth century photographers were Nutting, Davidson, Thompson, and Sawyer. However, as the price of Wallace Nutting pictures has escalated, the work of these lesser-known photographers has become increasingly collectible and are still quite affordable.

Collecting Tip:

The term lesser-known photographer is used to denote any early twentieth century hand-colored photographer, other than Wallace Nutting, David Davidson, Sawyer, and Fred Thompson, whose work is either signed or directly attributable to a specific photographer.

Lesser-Known Photographer Collecting Tips:

*The lesser-known photographers are typically not as widely collectible or desirable as Wallace Nutting, David Davidson, Fred Thompson, or Sawyer.

*Most pictures within this category are collected within the very broad spectrum of early twentieth century photography rather than by the desirability of the individual photographer.

*Price and condition are typically the primary buying motivators within this category. That is, if the price is low enough and the subject matter and condition are good enough, some collectors will want the picture; if the price is too high, or if the subject matter and condition are either uninteresting or of poor quality, few collectors will want it.

*There are a limited number of collectors who are focusing their collections on several specific lesser-known photographers including, but not limited to Chas. R. Higgins, J. Carleton Bicknell, H. Marshall Gardiner, and W.H. Gardiner.

*When taken as a group, there are fewer lesser-known pictures available to collect than either Level #1 (Nutting) or Level #2 (Davidson-Sawyer-Thompson).

*When taken as a group, there are more lesser-known pictures available to collect than in the entire unknown photographer category.

*With few exceptions, the prices of lesser-known photographers are lower than Level #1 (Nutting) and Level #2 (Davidson-Sawyer-Thompson), but are higher than most pictures by Level #4 unknown photographers.

Level 4...Unknown Photographers

Background

These are hand-colored pictures that are not attributable to any specific photographer by a signature, backing label, or by any other means.

A triple grouping by an unknown photographer

Since collectors typically collect the name, pictures by unknown photographers are the least collectible of all hand-colored photographs. Hence, price, subject matter, and condition will be the primary determinants of value.

Collecting Tip:
The term unknown photographer is used to denote any early twentieth century photograph that is not attributable to any specific photographer with a 100% degree of certainty.

Unknown Photographer Collecting Tips:
*Subject matter typically consists of such topics as people, animals, houses, landscapes, specific places, etc.
*When taken as a group, there are fewer pictures by unknown photographers available than all other individual categories.
*When taken as a group, prices for pictures within this group are typically lower than any other categories.

Collecting Tip:
With very few exceptions, usually relating to subject matter, hand-colored photographs by unknown photographers are the least desirable to collectors.

The Hand-Colored Photography Process
What follows is a very broad and general overview of the process used by many early twentieth century hand-colored photographers. Although the exact process may have varied slightly by photographer, this summary will provide you with a basic understanding of the overall hand-colored photograph picture process.

Collecting Tip:
A hand-colored photograph is just what the name implies: each picture was individually hand colored. It was a labor-intensive process, and the fact that each picture was an individually colored piece of art is what makes them all so different and so interesting to collectors.

The photographers typically owned the business and took their own pictures. They would determine the subject, location, angle, lighting,

David Davidson's camera

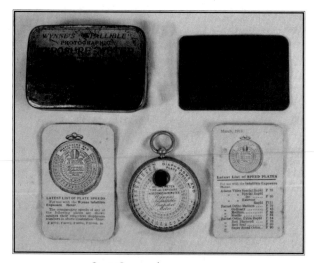

David Davidson's exposure meter

and positioning of the camera, and would shoot many pictures throughout the day.

Upon returning to the studio, each day's pictures were developed in the dark room. Glass negatives, often 5x7", 8x10", or 11x14" in size, were used to print the pictures onto sheets

Original glass negative

of special photographic paper. Earlier photographers (1900 – 1920) typically used a special paper which contained a higher concentration of platinum. These pictures were called platinotypes. After 1920, the platinum paper became more difficult to obtain and most photographers switched to a paper having a higher silver concentration. Relatively few collectors today can detect the difference between the earlier platinum and later silver prints.

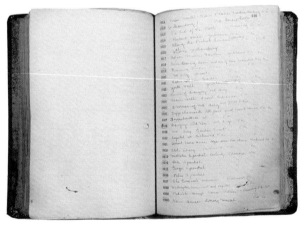

Wallace Nutting's studio log book

The better pictures would be identified, assigned a tentative title, and entered into a studio log book. Pictures were provided with a special unique identifying studio number to help identify loose and unmounted pictures while in the studio and this studio number was typically written on the back of the picture. Unacceptable pictures were usually discarded.

Titles were created by either the photographer or his employees. The primary objective of the picture title was not only to provide a descriptive name to the picture, but to help sell the picture. Catchy titles helped to sell pictures and it was not uncommon for the title on certain pictures to change several times before a title was finalized.

Model picture

Once the picture was developed, titled, and entered into the studio log book, the next step was to determine how the picture should be colored. Although the objective was to color the picture as close to reality as possible, it was not uncommon to have certain enhancements to the picture coloration in order to make the picture appear better than reality. In smaller studios, the photographer was also the colorist; in larger studios, the photographer had colorists to do the actual coloring. Once the final coloring determination was made, a written set of coloring instructions was made and attached to the model picture to help other colorists color subsequent pictures.

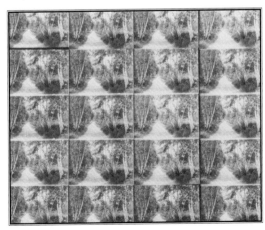

Picture proof sheet

Water colors and porcelain palette

Once the model picture was colored and approved, subsequent pictures were colored following the model picture as closely as possible. Typically, a single colorist would apply all the colors of a picture, rather than each colorist applying only a single color. Larger pictures would have only a single picture on a sheet; smaller pictures could have up to 20 pictures on a single sheet, all 20 of which would be colored by a single colorist. Picture colors were produced by several companies, but the preferred colors were imported directly from the Winsor & Newton Company in England. There were hundreds of different colors and shades available in both tubes and cubes, and each colorist would mix her own colors in her own porcelain color palette.

Colorists

In smaller companies, the actual colorists would approve the final picture; in larger companies, either the head colorist (supervisor of colorists) or the photographer himself would

approve the final colored picture prior to sale. If the picture was approved, it would be mounted on the matboard; if the picture did not meet the studio standard, it was discarded or destroyed.

Most typically, the picture was mounted on a mat board having a slight plate mark indentation around the entire picture, although other matting variations were used by different studios. Once mounted, the title and photographer's name were added, usually below the pic-

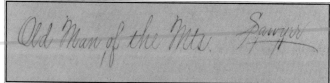

Title and signature

ture. Most studios positioned the title below the lower-left corner of the picture, while the photographer's name was placed below the lower right corner of the picture.

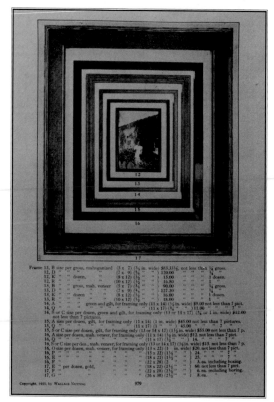

A variety of different frames were available.

146

The final step was the framing. Frames were sometimes supplied by the photographer's studio; other times they were selected by the purchaser at the point of purchase. Volume purchasers of pictures, usually department stores or gift shops, purchased their pictures unframed, which enabled them to sell both the picture and the frame. Some customers even framed their pictures themselves. Frames were usually narrow in proportion to the picture, often mahogany or gold/brown in color, although other types of frames were used to suit individual preferences and tastes. As a result, you will find a wide variety of frames on early twentieth century hand-colored photography.

A Sawyer exterior scene

Subject Matter

New England was the home of most early twentieth century hand-colored photographers and New England is where most hand-colored pictures were sold. The most popular subject matter of New England photographers was outdoor, pastoral, exterior scenes — apple blossoms, birches, rivers, streams, lakes, ponds, country lanes, hills, and mountains were among the most popular subjects. Photographers sold what the public would buy and the vast number of basic outdoor scenes remaining today would seem to confirm that outdoor scenes were far and away the most popular subject matter of most photographers during the early twentieth century.

However, since hand-colored photographs were often sold as gifts or vacation memories, some photographers from outside of New England specialized in selling pictures taken in their home region, with Bermuda, Florida, Colorado, the Rocky Mountains, various National Parks, the Grand Canyon, and the American southwest all being popular picture locations for many photographers.

Collecting Tip:
Outdoor pastoral scenes were the most common type of picture sold by nearly all early twentieth century hand-colored photographers.

Davidson interior scene

Colonial interior scenes were also popular with some photographers. The Colonial Revival Movement was in full swing during the early twentieth century, fostered in part by a wave a patriotism brought about by World War I, and for the first time, twentieth century America began to appreciate its colonial heritage. Photographers would re-create a colonial setting, typically with a woman performing eighteenth century household chores near a roaring fire. Although these interior scenes sold very well for certain photographers, they did not sell nearly as well as the exterior scenes and are considered somewhat rarer today.

Collecting Tip:
Interior scenes were not nearly as popular as the exterior scenes, selling only approximately 10% of the number of exterior scenes.

This Wallace Nutting foreign scene, Venice's Chief Glory, sold at auction for $575 in June 1997.

Some photographers sold foreign scenes as well, with Europe, and Great Britain in particular, usually being the bestselling foreign pictures.

This Wallace Nutting miscellaneous unusual scene, The Old Cabinet Maker, sold at auction for $4,510 in June 1997.

Today, any pictures that fall outside the categories of exterior, interior, and foreign scenes are called miscellaneous unusual scenes. These pictures include such subjects as seascapes, animals, snow, gardens, floral still-lifes, churches and cathedrals, bridges, cottages and castles, and pictures featuring children and men, both of which were very poor selling subjects. (For whatever reason, the buying public preferred women over children and men.) Relatively few foreign and miscellaneous unusual pictures were produced and, because of their rarity, they are very popular with collectors today.

Collecting Tip:
Foreign and miscellaneous unusual scenes are the rarest today and are usually the most sought after by collectors.

Picture Size

Just as you can take a negative to a camera shop today and have it developed into many different sizes, early twentieth century hand-colored photography can come in many different sizes, ranging from 1x2" to 30x50". The general rule of thumb of the larger the picture, the greater the value holds true only to a certain extent. The most popular sized pictures are typically within the 11x14" and 16x20" sizes. These pictures are large enough to show considerable color and detail, yet small enough to fit most wall spaces.

Pictures, 10x12" and smaller, although still very popular, often don't provide the excellent color and detail of the larger pictures and are not as highly valued as the 11x14" and 16x20" pictures.

Pictures larger than 16x20" are sometimes difficult to sell. Although they are rarer, show considerable color and detail, and cost significantly more when originally sold, too few households today offer the ideal wall space for such a large picture. And all too often, such larger pictures were the more popular and common scenes, not the rarities that collectors so highly prize.

Collecting Tip:
The larger the picture, the more desirable it is to collectors, and the more expensive it will be up to the 16x20" size. Pictures larger than 16x20" are often more difficult to sell because of their extremely large size.

Condition

Once you have determined the subject matter and size of the picture, the next step in determining the value is to assess its condition because condition is the most important determinant of value. Over the past five years, condition has become increasingly important as astute collectors have developed a better eye for differentiating between good, better, and best pictures. Conversely, some pictures in average–below average condition aren't bringing the prices they did five years ago because today's collectors have become more discriminating.

Hand-Colored Photography Condition Guide

This numerical grading system is something that we developed when cataloging pictures for our hand-colored photography auctions. Pictures are assigned a grading of 1.0 – 5.0, with 5.0 being mint, 1.0 being the worst. In order to arrive at the appropriate numerical grading, we have developed the following guidelines.

We should remind you that this numerical grading system is nothing more than our personal system for evaluating hand-colored photographs. It is not perfect, and it is very subjective. However, we feel comfortable using it and, in the absence of a better system, you are welcome to use it as well.

5. Excellent Condition: Recognizing that they are nearly 100 years old, these are pictures with absolutely no visible flaws. The picture has great color and detail, the mat is in excellent condition with proper size and aging, and the frame should be in near perfect condition and appropriate for the period. Very few pictures will ever achieve this grading.

Only titled pictures can receive a 5. Smaller untitled pictures will generally not be graded a 5 because they are so typical and common.

4½. Near-excellent Condition: These are pictures with practically no visible flaws whatsoever. To reach this grading, the picture must have great color and detail, and the mat must be in excellent condition with proper aging. The frame must be attractive, appropriate for the period, but may not be quite perfect. Perhaps there may be a little dirt that needs to be cleaned from the mat or inside glass.

At this grading, it might be possible to upgrade it to a 5 with a better frame or cleaning, but it can never be upgraded to a 5 if the picture and mat are not nearly perfect.

4. Above-average Condition: These are pictures that, although they may not have any visible flaws, just don't rate a 4½ or 5. The picture has very good color and detail (but not great color and detail), the mat is nice and clean (but showing a certain amount of aging), and the frame is totally acceptable. Occasionally, a 4 can be upgraded to a 4½ with a better frame or with a good cleaning on the inside of the glass.

The highest grading an untitled picture can receive is a 4.

3½. Slightly Above-average Condition: These are pictures that have minor mat damage, but not as extensive as a picture graded 3. Minor blemishes might include a small and barely visible stain, very minor foxing or dirt, a very minor mat reduction (no more than ½" – ¾"), or any other minor blemish.

Minor picture blemishes could also cause a picture to be graded a 3½. An example of a minor picture blemish would be a few small, white spots on the picture. Or, a slightly damaged frame could cause a picture to be graded a 3½.

A 3½ picture whose only blemish is a slightly damaged frame or cleanable dirt or film on the glass can be upgraded to a 4 with a new frame or a good cleaning.

However, once the mat has a water stain, foxing, or has been reduced, it can never be upgraded to a 4.

3. Average Condition: Although the picture must be in good condition, there will usually be some major visible mat damage. This damage could include water stains that are large and clearly visible, overmats, foxing, major dirt under the glass, mat creases or tears, or other significant blemishes. Remounted or re-signed pictures would also fall into this category.

A 3 picture that is very dirty or that has an unsightly frame can easily be upgraded to a 3½ or 4 with a good cleaning or a new frame.

Any mat blemish that can be completely covered with an overmat would be considered a 3.

Collecting Tips:

*An overmatted picture can never be rated higher than 3.

*A remounted or re-signed picture means that the matting and/or signature are not original. A picture that has either been remounted or re-signed is not a very desirable piece and can never be graded higher than a 3.

*Most pictures will fall within the 3.0 – 4.0 category.

2½. Less than Average Condition: These pictures have some major picture blemishes. For example, a water stain that extends through the title or signature, some fairly major white spots on the picture, or an overmat that is in very poor condition.

2. Poor Condition: Pictures falling within this category generally have some very significant flaws or blemishes. Damage to the picture would include faded picture coloring, noticeable tears or corner chips, or highly visible white spots.

Major mat damage would include things like large tears or creases, a very dark mat, water stains that cover all or a portion of the title or signature, or other major damage that cannot be entirely covered with an overmat.

Other examples of flaws that could cause a picture to be graded a 2 would be broken glass or a frame that is so damaged or unsightly that someone would probably not be interested in hanging a picture with such a frame.

Pictures that have broken glass or a horrible frame can be upgraded with the appropriate corrective action. Even an attractive picture with major mat damage might be upgraded to a 3 by re-mounting the picture.

However, there is little that can be done to upgrade pictures with major picture damage.

1 – 1½. Very Poor Condition: Quite frankly you very rarely see pictures with this grading because by the time they have reached this level, most have been trashed or thrown away. However occasionally they do turn up. Specifically, pictures that are rated 1 or 1½ have irreparable damage to the picture itself. Specific examples would include pictures with major tears, pictures with unsightly spotting, pictures with ink spots, or other major damage making the picture unrepairable.

I can't think of any instance where a picture graded a 1 could be upgraded to a 2. In order to be graded a 1, the picture must be so bad that it is basically beyond repair.

Collecting Tip:

There will be relatively few pictures in the 1.0 – 1½ categories because by the time they reach this condition, they have either been discarded or thrown away.

Summary of Key Points

* The term Wallace Nutting-like picture is used to denote any early twentieth century hand-colored photograph done in the style of Wallace Nutting.

* A hand-colored photograph means that the picture was colored using the hand-tinting process and was in no way machine printed or produced.

* Wallace Nutting sold more hand-colored pictures than any other photographer.

* David Davidson ranked #2 in total output, selling more pictures than all other early twentieth century photographers except Wallace Nutting.

* Sawyer pictures ranked #3 in total output, selling more pictures than all other early twentieth century photographers except Wallace Nutting and David Davidson.

* Fred Thompson ranked #4 in total output, selling more pictures than all other early twentieth century photographers except Wallace Nutting, David Davidson, and Sawyer.

* The term lesser-known photographers denotes a hand-colored photograph that is directly attributable to a specific photographer other than Nutting, Davidson, Sawyer, and Thompson.
* The term unknown photographer denotes a hand-colored picture that is not directly attributable to any specific photographer.
* Outdoor pastoral or exterior scenes are the most common type of hand-colored picture.
* Colonial interior scenes are also quite common, but significantly rarer than exterior scenes.
* Usually the most valuable pictures fall within the foreign and miscellaneous unusual categories.
* The value of any hand-colored photograph will be determined by four points:
  1) name of photographer
  2) subject matter
  3) condition
  4) size
* Overall condition depends upon three key items:

  1) the picture itself
  2) the matting
  3) the frame
* Damage to any of these will tend to reduce values.
* Condition is of primary importance to collectors. A badly damaged Wallace Nutting picture is not considered a highly desirable piece; nearly any mint or excellent condition hand-colored picture, regardless of photographer, is still a very desirable piece.
* As a general rule, pictures with titles are more desirable to collectors than untitled pictures.

This chapter has been intended to provide you with a very brief and general overview of hand-colored pictures and the overall hand-colored photography market. These guidelines will apply to all early twentieth century hand-colored photographs, regardless of the photographer. The remaining chapters will focus upon each of the specific photographers and go into more depth regarding the different segments within this market.

Chapter 7

Wallace Nutting (1861 – 1941)

Wallace Nutting, circa 1936

began touring the New England countryside by carriage or car, taking photographs of rural America. Nutting was one of the first to recognize that the American scene was rapidly changing, that industrialization was altering the way America looked, and our pure and picturesque country would never look the same again. He seemed to feel it his divine calling to record the beauty of America for future generations.

Beginning first in Vermont, then Massachusetts and Connecticut, and eventually throughout the rest of New England, Nutting began photographing country lanes, streams, orchards, lakes, and mountains. Wallace Nutting would take the photograph, assign a title, and instruct his colorists how it should be hand tinted. Each picture that met Nutting's high standards of color, composition, and taste would be affixed to its matting and signed by his employees with the famous Wallace Nutting name. (He hardly ever signed any pictures himself.) Those pictures that did not meet his strict standards were destroyed.

*Decked as a Bride . . . very popular wedding gift in 1920, 14x17".
Est. Value: $100 – 175.*

"...about ten million of my pictures hang in American homes..."

An Introduction to Wallace Nutting Pictures

Wallace Nutting retired from the ministry in 1904 due to ill health. As part of his recovery, he

A Birch Hilltop, 11x14". Est. Value: $100 – 175.

His most popular and bestselling images included *exterior* scenes (apple blossoms, country lanes, orchards, streams, and the rural American countryside), *interior* scenes (usually featuring a colonial woman working near a

152

hearth), and *foreign* scenes (typically thatch-roofed cottages). His poorest selling pictures, which have become today's rarest and most highly collectible Nutting pictures, are classified as *miscellaneous unusual* scenes and include animals, architectural, children, floral still-lifes, men, seascapes, and snow scenes.

SPECIAL NOTE: This chapter is designed to provide you with a general overview of Wallace Nutting pictures and their approximate values. If you are interested in learning more about Wallace Nutting pictures, we would refer you to *The Collector's Guide to Wallace Nutting Pictures: Identification & Values.* This 176 page book includes hundreds of photographs and goes into considerably more detail on the subject of Wallace Nutting pictures and Wallace Nutting books. There are also reference books available on the subject of Wallace Nutting furniture.

Beginning first with exterior scenes in New England, Nutting eventually traveled throughout the United States and Europe, taking photographs in 26 states and 17 foreign countries between 1900 and 1935. Overall, he took more than 50,000 pictures, 10,000 of which he felt met his high standards. The balance were destroyed.

Good Night!...a Wentworth-Gardner House interior, 13x16". Est. Value: $250 – 325.

It was around 1905 that Nutting began taking his first interior pictures. Supposedly one day while it was raining outside, Mrs. Nutting suggested that he take a more "personable" picture indoors. So he set up a colonial scene, had an employee dress up in a colonial fashion, and took several different pictures. These sold rela-

tively easily which encouraged him to expand more into this area.

Nutting's love of antiques, his passion for the pilgrim period, and his unquestionable desire to turn a profit led him to eventually purchase and restore five colonial homes:

* Webb House, Wethersfield, Connecticut
* Wentworth-Gardner House, Portsmouth, New Hampshire
* Cutler-Bartlett House, Newburyport, Massachusetts
* Hazen-Garrison House, Haverill, Massachusetts
* Saugus Iron Works (Broadhearth), Saugus, Massachusetts

Nutting purchased these homes because he felt each represented a different period of early colonial American style and taste. It was here, along with his own homes, Nuttinghame (Southbury, Connecticut) and Nuttingholme (Framingham, Massachusetts), that the majority of his interior pictures were taken.

Nutting's desire to provide the most correct and appropriate settings for his interior scenes led him in his quest to gather one of the best collections of early American furniture ever assembled. He would use the best examples of early American furniture in his interior scenes and, when he couldn't find the best, he would reproduce it.

Working in Southbury from 1905 to 1912, and then in Framingham from 1912 until his death in 1941, Nutting sold literally millions of his hand-colored photographs. He claims to have sold around 10,000,000 pictures although, knowing his habit of exaggerated salesmanship, that number is probably somewhat high.

Whatever the true number, it was large. Wallace Nutting pictures were sometimes called poor man's prints. Sold throughout the first quarter of the twentieth century, well before the invention of color photography, these pictures initially sold literally for pennies. His market was primarily the middle and lower middle class households of New England—those households which could not afford finer forms of art. Because of their low price, Wallace Nutting pictures were purchased in large numbers and by 1925, hardly an American middle-class household was without one. They were purchased as gifts for weddings, showers, holidays, birthdays, and for just about any other reason imaginable.

Nutting sold many pictures directly through his studios where he also provided his own framing. But he also sold his pictures through many other outlets as well: department stores, drug stores, and gift shops, all around the country. He even had full-time salesmen on the road whose sole job was to sell his pictures to these retail establishments (salesmen whom, he claims, sold enough pictures to retire quite handsomely themselves).

A group of Nutting colorists, circa 1920

The height of Wallace Nutting picture popularity was 1915 – 30. During this time Nutting had nearly 100 colorists in his employment, along with another 100 employees who acted as framers, matters, salesmen, management, and assorted administrative office personnel. Let there be no mistake about it...Wallace Nutting pictures were big business.

But by the late 1920s, people began to tire of Nutting pictures. As with any other fashion or style, tastes began to change. Wallace Nutting pictures became passé and sales showed a steady decline. Even the introduction of different matting styles, greeting cards, pentype silhouettes, and lower priced machine-produced process prints could not rejuvenate sales.

The Wall Street crash of 1929 and the following depression all but sealed the fate of the Wallace Nutting picture business. Few new pictures were introduced after 1930 and Nutting basically sold pictures remaining in existing inventory throughout the 1930s.

Wallace Nutting died on July 19, 1941. Although the picture studio remained open for several years after his death, the output was inconsequential after the mid-1930s.

The Collecting Cycle of Wallace Nutting Pictures

Phase I. Initial Production and Peak Period: Wallace Nutting began selling his pictures on a part-time basis as early as 1900. He went into business on a full-time basis in 1905, with his pictures achieving a peak of popularity between 1915 and 1930. He worked out of Southbury, Connecticut, from 1905 to 1912, and Framingham, Massachusetts, between 1912 and 1941.

Phase II. Gradual Market Decline: With the stock market crash of 1929, the sale of Wallace Nutting pictures declined significantly. Sales remained low throughout the 1930s and, with Nutting's death in 1941, never regained the high level of popularity of the 1915 – 30 period.

Phase III. Renewed Collectibility: By the late 1960s, a few people began actively collecting Wallace Nutting pictures. The Wallace Nutting Collectors' Club began in 1973 with nine members. Throughout the 1970 – 90s, interest in Wallace Nutting pictures rose and the Wallace Nutting Collectors' Club now boasts more than 400 members nationwide.

Phase IV. Current Market: Wallace Nutting pictures are extremely popular today with, among other honors, *Country Home Magazine* naming Wallace Nutting as one of its 10 hottest collectibles in 1997. Wallace Nutting pictures have established themselves as the most popular and collectible of all early twentieth century photographs and the number of collectors has been increasing.

Wallace Nutting Pictures: What Are They?

Hand-Colored Pictures: Most Wallace Nutting pictures are black & white photographs with all coloring being hand applied. These typically come in three different mounting styles:

Indented Mats: Indented mats with the picture, title, and signature included within the platemark is the most popular form of matting. Probably 85 – 90% of all Nutting pictures will have an indented-platemark matting.

Black Borders: Black borders around the pic-

Most pictures had the photograph, title, and signature set within an indented platemark border.

Black borders around the picture appeared in the late 1920s – 1930s.

An Eventful Journey, in 7x9" frame

Nutting label on the backing, or have the Wallace Nutting picture copyright serving as official confirmation that the picture is a Nutting. And sometimes loose and never-mounted pictures from the studio, or pictures which have been reclaimed from extremely damaged mats, have been close framed. Close-framed pictures are usually less desirable than indented or black-bordered mats.

Nutting Collecting Tip:
Wallace Nutting pictures having the picture, title, and signature within an indented platemark are usually the most popular with collectors.

ture appeared in the late 1920s and early 1930s. Mats with the picture within a black or colored, non-indented border, and having the title and signature below the border, were introduced in the late 1920s – early 1930s. Although these very colorful pictures have a strong following, most collectors prefer the indented mat.

Slack Waters, in original 20x40" frame

Close-Framed: Close-framed pictures having a frame but no matting, often have a title or signature on the picture itself, have a Wallace

Among October Birches, 16x20" process print. Est. Value: $10 – 25.

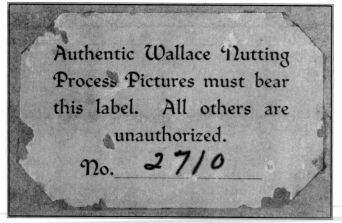

If the backing label says "Authentic Wallace Nutting Process Pictures must bear this label...," it is a process print with minimal value.

4x4" Nutting silhouette. Est. Value: $25 – 50.

Process Prints: Between 1938 and 1942, twelve of Nutting's more popular titles were issued in machine-produced pictures which he called *process prints*. All process print pictures measure 12x15", and if matted, the 12x15" print is placed on a 16x20" mat, with the signature being eliminated, and the title being moved from the lower left corner to the lower right below the picture. Any backing label which contains the word process means that the picture is a process print. The process print titles include

A Barre Brook	Decked as a Bride
A Little River	A Garden of Larkspur
A Sheltered Brook	Nethercote
All Sunshine	October Glories
Among October Birches	Primrose Cottage
Bonny Dale	Red, White, and Blue

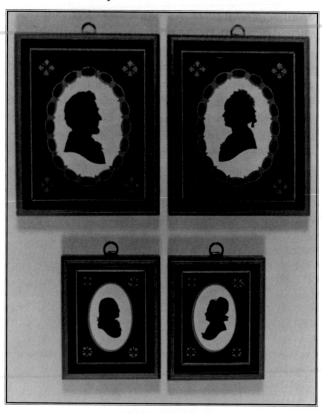

Nutting silhouettes:
Abe & Mary Todd Lincoln and George & Martha Washington.
Est. Value: $75 – 150 pair.

Nutting Collecting Tip:
Process prints were machine-produced prints dating 1938 – 42. The signature was eliminated and the title was moved from the lower left to the lower right corner beneath the picture. Wallace Nutting process prints have minimal interest or value to knowledgeable Nutting collectors.

Wallace Nutting Silhouettes: In 1927, Nutting introduced a series of approximately 40 – 50 different pen-type silhouettes. These were machine-produced silhouettes of original drawings by one of his employees named Ernest John Donnelly. Some Nutting silhouettes are identified with either a WN, an EJD, or both WN and EJD directly on the silhou-ette, while other silhouettes will have a Nutting stamp or label on the back.

Other Wallace Nutting Picture Items: Nutting also produced a series of calendars, holiday and greeting cards, mirrors, and other related items which usually contained a fairly small (1x2" and 3x4") hand-colored Nutting picture positioned somewhere on the item.

1925 Wallace Nutting calendar, Est. Value: $150 – 200.

Mirror with foreign thatched-roof cottage. Est. Value: $175 – 325.

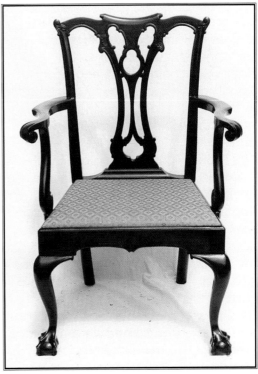

Wallace Nutting books

Greeting card, with Litchfield Minster. Est. Value: $75 – 125.

456 Chippendale mahogany armchair. Est. Value: $1,000 – 1,500.

Wallace Nutting Books & Furniture: Although beyond the scope of this chapter, you should be aware that Wallace Nutting authored nearly 20 books and contributed photographs to several other books. He also reproduced nearly 1,000 different forms of bench-made reproduction furniture which is generally regarded as the best and most desirable reproduction furniture of the early twentieth century.

Reproduction Alert

You should be aware that there have been several generations of Wallace Nutting reproductions and fakes. Most are very easy to detect and all have very minimal value to collectors.

Pirate Prints first appeared in the 1920s when a competing company began machine-reproducing some of Nutting's most popular titles. They even left the original Nutting title under the lower-left corner of the picture, although they removed the Wallace Nutting name from the lower-right corner. Nutting successfully sued in court to stop them, but not until several thousand pirate prints had been released. Small symmetrical dots can be detected on a pirate print with a magnifying glass. Often times unscrupulous individuals have signed the Wallace Nutting name back onto to these prints.

Re-signed Hand-colored Pictures: It is not uncommon for someone to have taken a pencil-signed picture of one of the lesser-known or unknown photographers, erased the original name, and signed the Wallace Nutting name. Not a big problem, but it has occurred.

1970s Photographs of Photographs: In the 1970s a company took photographs of some original Wallace Nutting pictures, and placed them on a matting, adding the title and signature. This series was sold by a popular reproduction house and, because they were photographs, they fail the symmetrical dot test. Typically these reproductions had a glossy photo with a dark tint, thin paper matting, purplish signature, and a new frame. However, over the past 20 years many new frames were replaced by older frames to make them appear original. These are fairly easy to detect once you know what to look for.

Color Laser or Xerox Copies are becoming more prevalent. They are typically shiny, glossy pictures with new mats, and re-signed signatures. The frames are usually old.

Process Prints: Although originally issued by Wallace Nutting, these machine-produced prints are often sold as being hand-colored to unsuspecting buyers. Small symmetrical dots can be detected on a process print with a magnifying glass.

1990s Photographs of Photographs: A new series of fakes appeared on a limited basis in the early 1990s, again photographs of photographs, but this time of very unusual scenes, pictures that fit the title, but pictures that were so unusual that many people assumed them to be Nutting when in fact they were not. These were also very limited in scope.

Calendar Pages: Also in the 1990s several lovely Wallace Nutting calendars appeared, with a different picture for each month. Sometimes you will see these pictures cut down, placed in frames, and sold as original. Small symmetrical dots can be detected on calendar prints with a magnifying glass.

Identifying and Dating Wallace Nutting Pictures

Wallace Nutting hand-colored pictures usually date between 1900 and 1941. You should understand that just because a picture has a copyright marking on the picture (e.g., copyright by Wallace Nutting, 1909 or © W.N. '09) doesn't necessarily mean that the picture dates from 1909. Rather, that year represents only the year that the picture was copyrighted by Wallace Nutting. Your individual picture, although produced from the negative marked "1909," may have been colored and sold anywhere from 1909 to 1941.

However, there are several general guidelines that can help to further identify and date Wallace Nutting pictures:

Pencil Signature: Usually dates the picture as 1910 or earlier.

Pen Signature: Usually dates the picture as 1910 or later.

Nutting Collecting Tip:

Wallace Nutting pictures with pencil signatures usually date the picture as 1910 or earlier. Fewer than 10% of all Nutting pictures will have a pencil signature.

*Most Wallace Nutting pictures will be signed in pen. The specific signature or signature style can help to date the individual picture.

*Wallace Nutting signed relatively few of his pictures. Rather, the Wallace Nutting signature was applied by more than 50 different colorists over a 35+ year period. If the signature is not original and authentic or if the signature has been re-signed at a later date, the value will drop considerably.

*The ability to recognize authentic vs. re-signed pictures is probably the most difficult part of Wallace Nutting collecting and, although beyond the scope of this chapter, it is something that you must be aware of.

Black or Colored Border around the Picture: This was a different matting style introduced by Nutting during the late 1920s – early 1930s in an attempt to rejuvenate declining picture sales. A black border will usually date a picture as circa 1930, and more often than not, a picture with a black border will have an accompanying Wallace Nutting label on the backing.

Nutting Collecting Tips:

*A black border around the picture will usually date it circa 1930.

*A Wallace Nutting label on the picture backing will usually date the picture as circa 1930.

Indented Mats were used throughout the entire 1900 – 1940s period.
Process Print: All process prints will be dated as 1938 or later, as 1938 was the first year that process prints were issued.

Nutting Collecting Tips:

All process prints will be dated as 1938 or later.

Silhouette: Silhouettes will always be dated as 1927 or later. All silhouettes are machine-produced and will be dated as 1927 or later.
Very Bright Colors: The earlier pictures were more subtly colored. Brightly colored pictures represented a different style in coloration and will usually date the picture as 1930 or later.

Understanding the Main Determinants of Value
The value of any Wallace Nutting picture will depend primarily upon three important factors.

Subject Matter: What is the topic or theme of the picture? Exterior, interior, foreign, or miscellaneous unusual scene? How rare is it? How many other people are interested in owning that same picture?
Condition: How pretty is the color? Are there any blemishes to the mat? What is the frame like? Has the matting been cut down or reduced?
Size: How big is the picture? The matting? The frame?

Each of these individual factors must be considered when arriving at an estimated value of a Wallace Nutting picture.

Subject Matter of Wallace Nutting Pictures

There are four primary categories of Wallace Nutting pictures.

A Belle of the Olden Days, 13x16". Est. Value: $100 – 175.

Exterior Scenes: These are the standard outdoor pastoral scenes, including apple blossoms, birches, and other trees, streams, rivers, lakes, ponds, hillsides, and mountains. Exterior scenes account for approximately 85% of

A Welcome Task, 13x16". Est. Value: $250 – 325.

all Wallace Nutting pictures that will be found, and are the most popular type of Wallace Nutting pictures today.

Interior Scenes: These are usually the colonial indoor scenes, typically featuring a woman dressed in a colonial outfit working around a fireplace. Interior scenes account for approximately 10% of all Wallace Nutting pictures.

The Newburyport Church, 13x16" (b&w). Est. Value: $300 — 400.

Old Time Friends, 13x16". Est. Value: $300 — 400.

Foreign Pictures: Wallace Nutting traveled to Europe on three separate occasions and took pictures in 16 different countries, although England, Ireland, and Italy are the counties that will most commonly be found.

Miscellaneous Unusual Scenes: This category includes seascapes, men, children, architectural scenes, florals, snow scenes, pictures with animals, and basically any pictures that do not fit into any of the above three categories. Foreign and miscellaneous unusual scenes combined account for approximately 5% or less of all Wallace Nutting pictures, are generally the most desirable to Wallace Nutting collectors, and usually account for the highest prices paid at auction.

Untitled Pictures: Most Wallace Nutting pictures had titles place under the lower left corner of the picture. On pictures 10x12" or smaller, the title was usually eliminated because it would not easily or tastefully fit beside the Wallace Nutting signature. When

An untitled exterior scene

there is no title next to the signature, the picture is called an *untitled* picture and, as a general rule, is worth less than a comparable picture with a title.

Condition

But more important than rarity and subject matter is condition. Collectors want pieces in excellent condition and blemishes such as water stains, mat tears, foxing, poor coloring, or damaged frames can all significantly reduce value. Over the past five years, Nutting collectors have become increasingly sophisticated regarding condition. Damaged pictures which once sold for top dollar are now bringing less than they did five plus years ago; pictures in very good to excellent condition often bring considerably more than they did five years ago.

A badly damaged picture. Any damage to the picture itself significantly reduces the value.

Purity with a mat burn caused by the original wooden backing

The photograph itself is the most important part of the entire picture and any damage to it, regardless of how major or minor the damage may be, will have a major impact on value.

Confidences with a water stain

The Way It Begins with a severely cut-down mat

An overmat will reduce the value by 50% or more.

The matting upon which the picture is mounted is extremely susceptible to damge, and value will be reduced proportionate to the amount of mat damage. We always equate damage to the matting the same as damage to a piece of glass. Major damage means a major reduction in value. Minor damage is still that — damage.

An attractive and unusual frame can increase the value of a picture by 10 — 25% or more.

Sometimes mat damage can be eliminated by cutting or cropping. Other times it can be concealed by a secondary mat, or overmatting, which hides the damage to the original mat. Either way, once the original matting becomes damaged, blemished, or cropped down, value drops.

Nutting Collecting Tips:

*Always assume that there is damage beneath an overmatting unless you see for yourself that no damage exists. Never pay as much for an overmatted piece as you would pay for a picture with its original matting in very good to excellent condition.

*Whenever you see a picture is backed with an old piece of wood instead of cardboard, remove the wood immediately! The high acidity content of the wood will cause mat and picture damage faster than any original cardboard backing that we have ever seen.

Damage to the frame is the least important thing to be concerned about. A damaged frame can always be replaced with a new or period frame. However, once the picture or matting becomes damaged, value is permanently lost.

Collecting Tip:

The overall condition of a picture, including the picture, matting, and frame, is the most important determinent of value.

Size

Wallace Nutting pictures came in a variety of sizes. Popular images were available in many different sizes, from as small as 1x2" to as large as 20x40", and sometimes larger on custom orders. Less popular images were available in only a single size.

You should understand that mats were very often cropped in size, either originally to fit a specific frame, or more recently to rid a picture of obvious damage.

Some of the More Commonly Found Wallace Nutting Pictures

The following represent Wallace Nutting titles which are quite common and frequently found by collectors. This does not mean that they are not desirable to collectors, but rather that they were sold in large numbers and are among the most commonly found titles today.

* *The Swimming Pool*, the most common Wallace Nutting picture
* *Larkspur*, Nutting's most popular thatch-roofed cottage scene
* *A Garden of Larkspur*, exactly the same as *Larkspur*, but without the lady in the garden
* *Decked as a Bride*, few early twentieth century brides failed to receive one as a wedding or shower gift
* Any Honeymoon picture (*Honeymoon Cottage, Honeymoon Windings, Honeymoon Drive, Honeymoon Blossoms*, etc), these were also very popular wedding gifts and are quite common
* *The Maple Sugar Cupboard*, a popular interior scene taken in Nutting's Southbury house
* *A Sip of Tea*, another popular interior scene taken in Nutting's Southbury house
* *Afternoon Tea*, still another interior taken in Nutting's Southbury house
* *A Barre Brook*, a very popular exterior scene
* *The Coming Out of Rosa*, nearly everybody's favorite Wallace Nutting picture today. Very common, and still very popular with collectors
* *A Little River*, a very popular New Hampshire scene

Some of the More Highly Sought-After Wallace Nutting Pictures

Elizabeth and Her Pets, 14x17". Est. Value: $1,500 – 2,500.

The following represent some very rare and highly desirable Wallace Nutting pictures, or categories of Wallace Nutting pictures, in no particular order. All, in very good to excellent condition, are very desirable to most Wallace Nutting collectors.

* Snow Scenes, most are smaller and untitled.
* Cow & Horse Scenes, titles are preferred, and the larger the better.
* Floral Still-Lifes, are fairly unusual and very popular
* Ocean Seascapes, very popular, with *Sea Ledges* being the most common seascape
* Children, except for *The Coming Out of Rosa* and *Posing*, pictures with children are fairly rare and very desirable.
* Architectural, close-up views of certain (but not all) houses, castles, churches, buildings, etc.
* Men, most pictures with men are quite desirable.
* *Elizabeth and Her Pets*, which features a young girl with her little puppies.

* *On the Shores of the Zuyder Zee*, a rare Holland picture with many children
* *The Meeting Place*, featuring a horse and three cows in a stream
* *The Old Cabinet Maker*, featuring an old man in a woodworking shop, sold at auction for $4,500 in June 1997.
* *The Guardian Mother*, one copy of which still holds the Wallace Nutting auction record price for a single picture at $4,950 (although other copies have sold for less).

The Alphabetical & Numerical Index to Wallace Nutting Pictures

Wallace Nutting sold more than 10,000 different titles between 1900 and his death in 1941, far too many to be listed here. *The Alphabetical & Numerical Index to Wallace Nutting Pictures* is a 310 page book which lists 10,000+ titles alphabetically, and then by studio number. This book includes the location of each picture (where known), some very helpful information on the Wallace Nutting picture process, and can help you to identify untitled pictures by the studio number found on the back of the picture.

To order a copy of this book, see the ordering instructions in the back of this book.

Wallace Nutting Collectors' Club

There is a very active Wallace Nutting Collectors' Club. Founded in 1973, the club's objective is to help members learn more about Wallace Nutting: the man and his works, and is your best way to get in touch with other Wallace Nutting collectors, dealers, events, and special information that will be of interest to all Nutting collectors. The club has an elected slate of officers, holds an annual convention, publishes a semi-annual club newsletter, and provides the complete club membership mailing list to club members.

In 2001 annual dues were $20. Because club officers and trustees change annually, you can contact Mr. Ivankovich to receive current information on how to join the Wallace Nutting Collector's Club.

Wallace Nutting Books and Reference Materials

The Collector's Guide to Wallace Nutting Pictures: Identification & Value, by Michael Ivankovich, is the #1 selling book on Wallace

Nutting pictures, which will help you to place a ballpark value on any Wallace Nutting picture; 160 pages, $18.95.

The Wallace Nutting Expansible Catalog is a reprint of Nutting's 1915 salesman's catalog, featuring nearly 1,000 Wallace Nutting pictures; 160 pages, $14.95.

The Alphabetical & Numerical Index to Wallace Nutting Pictures, by Michael Ivankovich, lists over 10,000 Wallace Nutting picture titles and includes the location where most pictures were taken; 310 pages, out of print.

Wallace Nutting, by Louis MacKeil, includes information on Wallace Nutting's personal background, and his picture and reproduction furniture business, out of print.

To order any of these books, see the ordering instructions in the back of this book.

Wallace Nutting on the Internet

At the time this book went to press, there were two very active Internet web sites devoted to Wallace Nutting:

The Wallace Nutting Gallery (www.wnutting .com) is a web site featuring information on upcoming Wallace Nutting auctions and events, a frequently updated pictures for sale page, Nutting collecting tips, questions and answers, various Nutting trivia, help in obtaining a value on your Nutting pictures, and much more.

The Wallace Nutting Center (www.wallacenutting.com) is another great Wallace Nutting web site.

Where to Go if Looking to Buy or Sell Wallace Nutting Pictures

There are various dealers around the country who specialize in Wallace Nutting pictures, books, furniture, and memorabilia. One obvious reference source would be the author of this book.

If you are interested in either buying or selling Wallace Nutting pictures, or learning more about Wallace Nutting, the man and his works, we highly recommend that you join the Wallace Nutting Collectors' Club. For only $20 per year (1997 dues), you are eligible to enjoy all the benefits the club has to offer. It will also put you in touch with most major Wallace Nutting dealers who are members of the club themselves, and who also send out periodic for sale lists to members. You can contact the author for details on joining this collectors' club.

Other dealers specializing in Wallace Nutting can be found in many of the national and regional antiques and collectibles trade papers.

The generally recognized national center of Wallace Nutting activity is Michael Ivankovich's Wallace Nutting catalog auctions. Held approximately four times per year, generally in the northeastern portion of the country, these auctions provide both collectors and dealers the opportunity to compete for the largest variety of Wallace Nutting pictures, books, furniture, and memorabilia that is available anywhere. These auctions also give sellers the opportunity to place their items in front of the country's leading Wallace Nutting collectors and enthusiasts.

Summary of Wallace Nutting Collecting Tips

* Wallace Nutting pictures come in many different sizes and with a variety of different subject matters.
* All things being the same, i.e., size and condition, interior scenes are often times worth 2 – 3 times as much as a comparable exterior scene.
* Foreign and miscellaneous unusual are generally the most highly sought after pictures.
* It was Nutting's colorists, not Wallace Nutting himself, who signed the Wallace Nutting name to pictures, which accounts for the many and varied Wallace Nutting signatures that will be found on pictures.
* Condition is the primary determinant of value. The rarest picture in poor condition has minimal value; a very common picture in beautiful condition is still a very desirable piece.
* Only the rarest pictures, in the best condition, will sell for top prices. All pictures in less than excellent condition are worth proportionately less.
* Water stains are the most common type of mat damage.
* An overmat place above the original matting is most likely a sign of damage to the original mat and will reduce the value of a picture by 50% or more.
* Wallace Nutting memorabilia, i.e., anything Wallace Nutting outside the scope of pictures, books, and furniture, has become increasingly collectible in recent years.

Wallace Nutting Value Guide

The values listed in this chapter are derived from many different sources, including

* Michael Ivankovich Auction Company auctions
* Other auction houses
* Retail and mail order sales
* Prices observed at antique shows, flea markets, and individual and group antique shops throughout the northeast
* Assorted other reliable sources

Most prices included here represent prices actually paid. In some instances where we were unable to ascertain the final sale price, we have included the dealer asking price if we felt that it was appropriately priced and fell within the acceptable ranges. The sampling of items in this chapter includes titles seen by us, sold by us, or reported to us. Obviously not all titles are included here. This chapter is only intended to provide you with a representative sampling of titles and prices in order to help you to establish a ballpark price on most Wallace Nutting pictures. Significantly more detailed pricing information can be found in *The Collector's Guide to Wallace Nutting Pictures: Identification & Values.*

Title	Size	Type	Rate	Amt.	Date
Accommodating Curves	12x16"	Ext.	4	$320	6/97
Affectionately Yours	14x17"	Int.	4	$190	3/03
After Tea	10x16"	Int.	4	$90	3/97
Afterglow	10x16"	Ext.	3	$20	6/97
Afternoon In Nantucket	14x17"	Misc Un	3	$120	11/03
Afternoon Tea	13x16"	Int.	4	$155	6/97
Afternoon Tea, An	11x14"	Int.	3	$90	6/03
Airing at the Haven, An	14x17"	For.	3	$330	6/97
All the Comforts of Home	13x15"	Cat	4	$300	6/01
All the News	15x18"	Int.	3	$70	3/97
Alstead Drive, An	13x17"	Ext.		$155	6/97
Amalfi	14x17"	For.	4	$635	6/97
Amalfi	13x15"	For.	3	$265	3/97
Ambush for a Redcoat, An	13x15"	Man	4	$770	6/97
Among October Birches	13x16"	Ext.	4	$100	3/97
Among Saffron Sails	11x14"	For.	4	$155	6/97
Among Saffron Sails	14x17"	For.	3	$75	3/97
Among Saffron Sails	8x10"	For.	3	$185	3/97
Among the Ferns	14x17"	Ext.	4	$165	3/97
Ancestral Cradle, The	14x20"	Cat	3.5	$265	3/97
Ancestral Cradle, The	12x20"	Cat	3	$160	3/03
Apple Tree Bend	14x20"	Ext.	3.75	$110	3/97
Arches & Domes	9x15"	For.	3	$465	6/97
At the Well, Sorrento	14x17"	For.	3	$385	6/97
August in the Meadow	12x15"	Ext.	3	$95	3/97
Barre Brook, A	10x16"	Ext.	4	$140	4/97
Barre Brook, A	14x17"	Ext.	4	$120	9/03
Benedict Door, The	11x14"	Misc Un	3	$255	6/97
Berkshire Brook, A	11x14"	Ext.	4	$115	11/03
Berkshire Cross Road, A	14x17"	Ext.	3	$100	6/03
Better than Mowing	16x20"	Man	3	$485	3/97
Between Cloud Crested Hills	12x18"	Ext.	4	$90	3/03
Between the Spruces	10x14"	Ext.	3.5	$130	3/03
Billows of Blossoms	14x17"	Ext.	4	$120	3/97
Birch Approach, A	16x20"	Ext.	3.5	$165	3/97
Birch Grove, A	11x14"	Ext.	4	$65	6/97
Birch Hilltop, A	11x14"	Ext.	4	$120	5/97
Bird in the Hand, A	13x17"	Int.	3.5	$230	3/97
Blacksmith Shoeing White Horse	20x24"	Misc Un	2	$795	3/97
Blossom Landing	11x14"	Ext.	3	$110	3/03
Blossoms at the Bend	10x12"	Ext.	3	$90	9/03
Blossoms that Meet	12x15"	Ext.		$160	11/03
Book by the Window, A	13x17"	Child	4.5	$600	11/00
Book Settle, The	11x17"	Int.		$190	9/03
Braiding a Rag Rug	11x14"	Int.	4	$120	6/03
Braiding a Straw Hat	10x12"	Int.	4.5	$110	9/03
Breezy Call, A	10x16"	Misc Un	3.75	$230	6/03
Bridge and the Elm, The	9x14"	Ext.	3	$70	3/97
Brook Sanctuary, A	13x16"	For.	4	$200	3/97
By the Old Arch	10x12"	For.	4	$240	3/97
By the Sea, Capri	14x15"	For.	3.75	$550	9/03
By the Wayside	11x17"	Sheep	4	$450	6/97
Calendar with Cathedral	4x5"	Misc		$55	6/97
Calendar with Exterior	4x5"	Misc	4	$45	6/97
Calendar, 1932		Misc	4	$185	3/97
California Hilltops	11x14"	Ext.	3.5	$200	11/03
Call at the Window, A	14x16"	Misc Un	3	$125	3/00
Call for More, A	10x13"	Child	3.5	$375	3/03
Call in State, A	10x12"	Misc Un	3	$70	9/03
Call to Liberty, A	11x14"	Int.	4	$100	6/03
Canoeing	8x11"	Man	3	$495	6/97
Canopied Road, A	13x16"	Ext.	3	$100	9/03
Capri Bay	13x15"	For.	3	$190	6/97
Capri from Anacapri	9x15"	For.	4	$470	6/97
Capture of a Redcoat, The	13x16"	Man	4	$220	6/97
Card with snow scene	4x5"	Misc	4	$120	6/97
Cathedral Brook	9x11"	Ext.	4	$80	6/03
Catskill Summit Blooms	11x14"	Ext.	3	$165	3/97
Chair for John, A	12x16"	Int.	4	$150	6/03
Chs Nataniel Vilas Blessing	12x16"	Misc.	3	$30	3/97
Christmas Card, exterior	4x6"	Misc.	3	$45	6/97
Christmas Card, snow	4x5"	Misc	3	$155	6/97
Clougheen Bridge, A	10x14"	For.	3	$155	6/01

Title	Size	Category		Price	Date
Clustered Roses	8x10"	For.	3	$160	11/03
Coachford Bridge, The	13x15"	For.	3	$200	6/97
Colonial Corner, A	13x17"	Int.	4	$175	6/97
Colonial Dames at Tea	14x17"	Int.	3.75	$130	6/03
Colonial Days	12x17"	Misc Un	3	$130	3/97
Colonial Kitchen, A	14x17"	Int.	3	$130	3/97
Comfort and the Cat	14x17"	Cat	3	$445	6/03
Coming Out of Rosa, The	11x14"	Child	4	$175	6/97
Coming Out of Rosa, The	14x17"	Child	4	$170	9/03
Concord Banks	16x20"	Ext.	3.5	$185	3/97
Confidences	16x19"	Int.	2.5	$100	3/97
Corner Cupboard, The	11x17"	Int.	4	$165	6/97
Cottage Garden, The	13x17"	For.	3.5	$140	6/03
Creature Comforts	16x20"	Int.	4	$230	3/97
Cypress Rocks	16x20"	Sea	2.5	$175	6/97
Dainty China	11x14"	Int.	3	$145	6/97
Daughter of Eve, A	3x16"	Int.	3	$95	3/97
Daughter of Eve, A	13x16"	Int.	4	$210	3/00
Decked as a Bride	10x12"	Ext.	4	$100	6/03
Dilatory Escort, The	11x14"	Int.	3	$90	6/97
Dog-On-It	7x11"	Dogs	4	$1,265	6/97
Dog-On-It	7x11"	Dogs	3.75	$3,600	11/00
Donjon, Chenanceau, The,	14x17"	For.	3.75	$670	11/00
Drying Apples	14x17"	Man	4	$350	11/03
Dutch Knitting Lesson, A	10x14"	Child	3.75	$675	6/01
Early June Brides	11x17"	Ext.	4	$75	6/97
Easter Card	5x9"	Misc	4	$200	6/97
Elaborate Dinner, An	14x17"	Ext.	4	$140	6/03
Elm Drapery	15x22"	Ext.	4	$70	11/03
Elm Ford	10x12"	For.	3	$10	3/97
Elmoer Crest	12x15"	Ext.	2.5	$90	3/97
English Door, An	11x14"	For.	3.75	$130	3/97
Enticing Waters	16x20"	Ext.	4	$70	11/03
Evangeline Lane	13x16"	For.	4	$220	9/03
Evening at the River Bend	13x22"	Ext.	3	$75	3/97
Eventful Journey, An	13x16"		3	$1,300	6/03
Exterior in thin metal frame	4x5"	Misc	3	$55	3/97
Exterior in Tray	7x10"	Tray	4	$185	3/97
Face of the Falls, The	13x17"	Ext.	3	$200	6/97
Fairbanks Homestead	6x7"	Snow	3	$230	3/97
Fair Orchard Way, A	11x14"	Ext.	3	$105	6/97
Farm Causeway, The	13x16"	Ext.	3	$50	3/97
Fastidious Taste, A	14x17"	Int.	3	$75	6/97
Favorite Waterside, A	18x22"	Ext.	2.5	$35	6/97
Fine Effect, A	8x10"	Int.	3	$120	6/97
Five O'Clock	15x22"	For.	4	$165	3/97
Final Touch, The	14x17"	Int.	4.5	$340	6/97
First Lesson, The	12x14"	Child	3	$495	6/97
Fleck of Sunshine, A	13x17"	Int.	3.5	$175	9/03
Floral miniature	3x4"	Floral	4	$220	11/03
Floral, large close-framed	16x20"	Floral	4.5	$465	6/97
Floral, close-framed	8x10"	Floral	4	$210	6/97
Floral, close-framed	8x10"	Floral	4	$330	3/97
Florida Sunrise, A	13x17"	Misc Un	4	$715	6/97
Flower Maiden, The	11x17"	Misc Un	4	$415	6/97
Flowery Path, A	13x16"	For.	4	$220	6/03
Flume Falls	12x15"	Ext.	4	$310	6/97
Footbridge by the Ford, The	16x20"	For.	4.5	$350	3/03
Four O'Clock	14x17"	Cows	3.5	$855	3/97
Friendly Reception, A	11x14"	Misc Un	3	$165	6/97
From a Friend	11x15"	Int.	3.5	$100	3/03
Garden Arch, A	13x15"	Misc Un	3	$65	3/97
Garden of Larkspur, A	13x16"	For.	4	$165	3/97
Garden Retreat	9x11"	Misc Un	4	$105	6/97
Garden Running Over, A	12x16"	For.	4	$120	3/03
Gathering a Bouquet	11x17"	Misc Un	3.95	$200	3/00
Genial Stream, The	10x16"	Cows	3	$250	6/97
Gentleman Caller, A	8x12"	Man	4	$210	6/01
Gettysburg Crossing, A	14x17"	Ext.	4	$275	11/03
Gloucester Cloister	16x20"	For.	4.5	$1,100	6/97
Goodman Is Coming, The	11x14"	For.	4	$175	6/01
Grace	16x20"	Ext.	4	$145	6/97
Grace	16x20"	Ext.	3.75	$110	11/03
Grandmother's China	13x22"	Int.	3	$110	3/97
Grandmother's Garden	10x19"	Int.	3	$75	6/97
Grandmother's Hollyhocks	9x11"	Misc Un	4	$395	6/97
Great Grandma's Sewing	10x12"	Int.	4	$200	6/97
Great Wayside Oak, The	14x17"	Ext.	4	$180	3/03
Greeting, A	10x12"	For.	3	$100	3/97
Guardian Mother, The	11x17"	Child	4	$2,800	6/03
Hallway Glimpse, A	10x15"	Int.	3	$175	3/97
Hanging Summer Herbs	13x15"	Int.	4	$230	6/97
Harmony	14x17"	Int.	3	$230	6/03
Hawthorn Cottage	15x20"	For.	3	$120	3/97
Hawthorn Bridge, A	10x12"	For.	4	$350	9/03
Heart Chord, A	13x16"	Man	3.75	$440	6/97
Hearth to Fight For, A	13x15"	Int.	3	$450	3/97
Helping Mother	12x16"	Child	3	$75	6/97
Hesitation	10x16"	Int.	4	$220	6/97
His Rose	12x16"	Int.	4	$90	9/03
Holland Express	10x16"	For.	3.5	$320	6/01
Hollyhock Cottage	14x17"	For.	4	$110	9/03
Hollyhock Cottage	16x20"	For.	3	$185	3/97
Home Room, The	14x17"	Int.	4.5	$230	6/97
Home Sweet Home	14x17"	Misc Un	4	$425	6/01
Honeymoon Cottage	11x17"	Ext.	3	$60	11/03
Honeymoon Drive	13x16"	Ext.	3	$85	4/03
Honeymoon Shore	13x16"	Ext.		$50	6/97
Honeymoon Stroll	11x14"	Ext.	3	$80	9/03
Housatonic Blossoms	11x17"	Ext.	4	$70	6/97
Hurrying Brook, A	10x12"	Ext.	4	$60	6/97
In Tenderleaf	13x20"	Ext.	3.5	$80	6/03

Title	Size	Category	Rating	Price	Date
In the Old Parlor	13x16"	Int.	4	$155	3/00
In Worden	10x16	For.	4	$120	6/01
Informal Call, An	11x14"	Int.	4.5	$210	9/03
Inspiration, An	11x15"	Int.	3	$100	6/97
Interior in thin metal frame	3x4"	Misc	4	$90	6/97
Into the Birchwood	13x16"	Ext.	4.5	$165	3/97
Into the Birchwood	20x30"	Ext.	4	$145	6/97
Italian Cypress Lane	10x12"	For.	3.75	$130	6/97
Ivy and Rose Cloister	13x16"	Misc Un	4	$250	9/03
Jane	9x14"	Misc Un	3	$185	3/97
Joy Path	13x16"	For.	4	$90	3/03
Keene Road, A	13x17"	Ext.	3.5	$165	6/97
Laggard in Love, A	18x22"	Int.	2.5	$200	11/00
Lambs at Rest	11x14"	Sheep	4	$245	11/03
LaMoille Twilight, A	13x15"	Ext.	3.5	$185	3/97
Lane in Norwich Town, A	11x14"	Ext.	4	$145	6/97
Lane in Sorrento, A	10x16"	For.	4	$505	/97
Lane or Highway	13x16"	For.	4	$570	6/97
Langdon Door, The	12x15"	Misc Un	3	$240	3/97
Larkspur	13x16"	For.	4	$110	3/03
Laughing Water	13x16"	Ext.	4	$95	3/97
Life of the Golden Age, The	10x15"	Sheep	4	$275	11/03
Lingering Water	16x20"	Ext.	4	$75	11/03
Litchfield Door, AD 1760	13x16"	Misc Un	3	$220	6/97
Litchfield Minster	10x12"	For.	3.5	$135	9/03
Listless Day, A	11x14"	For.	4	$145	6/97
Little River, A	14x17"	Ext.	4	$90	6/97
Little Washerwomen, Amalfi	13x16"	For.	2.75	$1,500	6/03
Lorna Doone	16x18"	For.	3.5	$495	3/97
Lough Gill Cottage, A	11x14"	Ext.	4	$170	6/03
Main Door, St. Mark's	13x16"	For.	3	$350	6/01
Maine Coast Sky	10x12"	Sea	4	$70	11/03
Manchester Battenkill, The	16x20"	Ext.	3.75	$245	6/97
Many Happy Returns	13x16"	Ext.	4	$70	3/03
Maple-Apple Arch, A	12x16"	Ext.	3	$85	3/97
Maple Sugar Cupboard, The	14x18"	Int.	3	$120	6/03
Maple Sugar Cupboard, The	13x16"	Int.	3.75	$220	6/97
Mary's Little Lamb	4x17"	Sheep	4	$350	11/03
Meadow Blossoms	13x15"	Ext.	3	$90	6/97
Meandering Battenkill, The	10x16"	Ext.	3.5	$155	3/97
Meeting of the Waters, The	16x20"	Ext.	4	$430	6/97
Meeting of the Ways, The	11x14"	Ext.	4	$100	6/03
Mellow Birches	13x16"	Ext.	4	$95	6/97
Melrose on the South	11x14"	For.	4	$275	3/97
Mending	14x17"	Int.	3	$160	3/03
Middlesex Glen	13x15"	Ext.	3.5	$120	6/97
Miniature exterior-birches	4x5"	Mini	4	$65	3/97
Miniature exterior-birches	4x5"	Mini	4	$95	3/97
Miniature exterior-birches	4x5"	Mini	4	$75	3/97
Miniature exterior-blossoms	4x5"	Mini	3	$55	3/97
Miniature exterior-blossoms	4x5"	Ext.	4	$35	6/97
Miniature exterior-blossoms	4x5"	Ext.	4	$65	6/97
Miniature exterior-hilltops	4x5"	Mini	4	$70	3/97
Miniature exterior-mountain	4x5"	Mini	4	$55	3/97
Miniature exterior-pond	4x5"	Mini	4	$55	3/97
Miniature exterior-pond	4x5"	Mini	4	$70	3/97
Miniature exterior-river	4x5"	Mini	4	$65	3/97
Miniature exterior-river	4x5"	Mini	4	$50	6/97
Miniature exterior-stream	4x5"	Mini	3	$60	3/97
Miniature exterior-stream	4x5"	Mini	4	$60	3/97
Miniature exterior-stream	4x5"	Mini	4	$55	6/97
Miniature garden scene	4x5"	Mini	5	$80	6/97
Miniature interior-girl cupboard by	4x5"	Mini	4	$80	3/97
Miniature interior-girl by fire	4x5"	Mini	4	$80	3/97
Miniature interior-girl by fire	4x5"	Mini	4	$80	3/97
Miniature interior-girl in bedroom	4x5"	Mini	3.75	$75	3/97
Morning Duties	14x17"	Int.	4	$170	11/03
Morning Mail, The	11x14"	Int.	3	$165	6/97
Mossy Stair, A	18x22"	Ext.	4	$155	6/97
Mountain Born	10x12"	Ext.	4	$165	3/97
Narcissa	11x17"	Int.	4	$325	3/00
Nest Foreign, The	9x11"		3.5	$105	3/97
New England Shore, A	10x12"	Sea	2.5	$65	3/97
Newburyport Church, The	12x16"	Misc Un	3.75	$185	3/97
NH Roadside, A	10x16"	Ext.	3	$90	6/97
Not One of the 400	14x17"	Sheep	3	$110	6/97
Nutting Garden Corner, The	9x11"	Misc Un	4	$290	11/00
Nuttinghame, A Nook	13x16"	Int.	4	$235	6/03
Old Cabinet Maker, The	12x14"	Man	3	$4,510	3/97
Old Chamber, Suffield, An	8x10"	Misc	4	$55	3/97
Old Colony Kitchen, An	14x17"	Int.	3	$100	3/97
Old Framlingham	13x16"	For.	4	$300	3/97
Old Italy	18x22"	For.	3	$155	3/97
Old Italy	18x22"	For.	3	$165	6/01
Old Parlor Idyll, An	13x16"	Man	3.5	$400	3/03
Old Stage Road, The	16x20"	Misc Un	4	$285	3/97
Old Story, The	11x14"	Int.	3.5	$90	6/97
Old Time Friends	13x16"	For.	4	$220	6/97
Old Tune Melody, An	13x17"	Int.	4	$220	6/97
Old Tune Revived, An	10x12"	Man	3	$165	3/97
Old Venice	13x17"	For.	4	$685	6/97
Olden Time	11x17	Misc Un	4	$185	6/97
On Either Hand	11x14"	Ext.	3.5	$70	6/97
On the Antietam	13x16"	Misc	3.75	$230	6/01
On the Heights	10x16"	For.	3	$100	6/97
On the Slope	13x17"	Sheep	4	$220	6/03
On Worcester Hills	13x15"	Ext.		$110	3/97
Orchard Heights	16x20"	Ext.	4	$110	11/03

Title	Size	Category	Grade	Price	Date
Orta in Blossom time	11x14"	For.	3.5	$110	6/97
Ovaca's Colleens	12x16"	For.	3	$210	6/97
Overflowing Cup, An	13x16"	Ext.	3.25	$100	9/03
Palmetto Grace	13x17"	Misc Un	4	$465	6/97
Parlor Mantel, Keim House	13x16"	Int.	4.75	$1,500	11/00
Parting at the Gate	10x14"	Man	3	$550	3/97
Pasture at Muckross, The	9x16"	Sheep	3	$330	6/03
Peasant's Palace, A	14x17"	For.	3.75	$460	3/97
Pennsylvania Stream, A	13x16"	Ext.	3.5	$375	9/03
Pergola, Amalfi, The	14x17"	For.	3.75	$165	3/97
Pergola, Amalfi, The	14x17"	For.	3	$250	6/03
Perkiomen October, A	9x11"	Ext.	4	$255	11/03
Petal Brown, A	14x17"	Ext.	3.5	$95	3/97
Petunias Run Wild	13x16"	Misc Un	4	$715	6/97
Pin Donegal, A	13x16"	For.	4	$395	6/97
Picture Library, A	14x17"	Int.	3.5	$190	3/97
Pilgrim Fireside, A	11x14"	Int.	4	$130	3/97
Pink, Blue & Green	11x14"	Ext.	3.5	$70	6/03
Pool, The	10x12"	Ext.		$90	9/03
Porch Door, The	16x20"	For.	3.5	$285	3/97
Pride of the Lane, The	13x17"	Ext.	3	$165	6/97
Pomfret Waters	10x12"	Ext.	3.75	$60	3/97
Ponti Fabrico	10x12"	For.	3	$170	11/00
Porta Della Carta	7x9"	For.	3	$250	6/01
Preparing an "At Home"	13x22"	Int.	4	$265	6/97
Priscilla's Cottage	14x17"	For.	3.75	$360	3/97
Process print — A Barre Brook	12x15"	Process	4	$45	1/97
Process print — A Garden of Larkspur	12x15"	Process	3.5	$15	1/97
Process print — All Sunshine	16x20"	Process	4	$55	5/97
Process print — Decked as a Bride	16x20"	Process	4	$20	4/97
Process print — October Glories	16x20"	Process	3	$15	6/97
Process print — Primrose Cottage	16x20"	Process	4	$20	2/97
Process print — Red, White, And Blue	16x20"	Process	3	$10	8/97
Providence Pond	10x12"	Ext.	4	$240	3/97
Prudence Drawing Tea	11x14"	Int.	3	$165	6/97
Purity	13x22"	Ext.	3.5	$170	11/03
Quilting Party, The	13x15"	Int.	3.5	$145	6/97
Red Square House, The	12x14"	Misc Un	3	$425	6/01
Red, White, and Blue	13x16"	Ext.	4	$65	6/97
Returning from a Walk	14x17"	Int.	3	$140	9/03
Returning from a Walk	11x17"	Int.	3	$130	6/97
Rheinstein	13x16"	For.	4	$800	6/01
Rising Tide	13x22"	Ext.	3	$40	6/97
Rising Tide, The	13x22"	Sea	3.5	$175	6/01
River at Williamstown, The	13x16"	Misc	4	$260	6/01
River Farm, The	10x12"	Ext.	3.5	$175	3/97
River Meadow, The	8x10"	For.	2	$160	11/03
Roadside Brook, A	9x15"	Ext.	3	$70	6/97
Roanoke Sycamores	16x20"	Ext.	3	$65	3/97
Rocks Off Portland	11x14"	Sea	3.5	$230	6/97
Rocks Off Portland	11x14"	Sea	3	$130	11/00
Rose Gate	10x12"	For.	3.75	$130	6/97
Roses and a Bud				$350	6/03
Royal Palm Border, A	11x14"	Misc Un	3.75	$220	6/97
Russet and Gold	16x20"	Ext.	4	$90	11/03
Russet and Gold oil painting	20x26"	Misc	4	$190	3/97
Sallying of Sally, The	14x17"	Misc Un	3	$130	9/03
Sea Capn's Daughter, The	13x15"	Misc Un	4	$375	11/00
Sea Ledges	11x1"	7	Sea	$230	3/03
Sea Ledges, North Shore	15x18"	Sea	3	$255	3/97
Sea Ledges of New England, The	13x15"	Sea	3.5	$220	6/97
Seeking the Shade	11x14"	Sheep	4	$360	3/97
Settle Nook, The	11x14"	Int.	3	$75	6/97
Shadows in the Dell	16x20"	Ext.	4	$55	3/97
Sharon Bridge	12x16"	Misc Un	3.75	$160	9/03
Sheffield Basket, A	13x16"	Floral	3.5	$1,400	6/03
Shore of Delight, A	9x11"	Ext.	4.5	$100	3/97
Silent Forest, The	15x18"	Ext.	3	$40	3/97
Silhouette-calendar		Misc	4	$220	6/97
Silhouette-folding greeting card		misc	4	$70	1/97
Silhouette-girl & little lamb	7x8"	Silhouette	4	$60	6/97
Silhouette-girl at desk	7x8"	Silhouette	4	$55	1/97
Silhouette-girl by mirror	4x4"	Silhouette	4	$30	6/97
Silhouette-girl by urn	4x4"	Silhouette	4	$45	2/97
Silhouette-girl in rocker	4x4"	Silhouette	4	$50	4/97
Silhouette-girl snips flowers	4x4"	Silhouette	4	$20	4/97
Silhouettes, George & Martha Washington	3x4"	Silhouette	4	$25	11/03
Sip of Tea, A	12x16"	Int.	3.5	$155	6/97
Sip of Tea, A	13x15"	Int.	3	$150	6/03
Sleeping Canal	10x15"	For.	3.5	$230	3/97
Snow Road, A	8x10"	Snow	5	$1,730	6/97
Snow scene (untitled)	7x9"	Snow	4	$195	6/97
Southern Colonial Room, A	13x17"	Int.		$240	6/97
Spinnet Corner	10x12"	Int.	3.5	$25	3/03
Spinnet Corner, The	13x15"	Int.	3	$170	3/03
Spring Basket	8x10"	Floral	4	$415	3/97
Stepping Stones to Bolton Abbey	11x14"	For.	4	$330	3/97
Stitch in Time, A	10x12"	Int.	4	$110	6/03
Stony Brook Bridge	13x15"	Ext.	3	$255	3/97
Stourhead Church Path	13x16"	For.	4	$210	6/97
Summer Wind	13x16"	Ext.	4	$100	3/97
Summer Wind	18x22"	Ext.	3.5	$100	6/97

Title	Size	Cat.		Price	Date
Sun-Kissed Way, A	16x19"	Ext.	4	$105	3/97
Sunneyside (Washington Irving Home)	13x16"	Misc Un	3	$330	3/97
Sunshine and Music	13x16"	Int.	4	$140	9/03
Sweet Pastures	10x16"	Sheep	3	$200	6/97
Swimming Pool, The	15x19"	Ext.	3	$65	6/97
Swimming Pool, The	14x17"	Ext.	4	$100	6/97
Swimming Pool, The	14x17"	Ext.	3.75	$85	11/03
Swimming Pool, The	10x16"	Ext.	4	$80	3/97
Swimming Pool, The	11x17"	Ext.	3	$50	6/97
Swimming Pool, The	20x30"	Ext.	4.5	$100	3/97
Tabitha	14x16"	Int.	3.75	$225	3/00
Tangled Skein, The	11x14"	Int.	3	$125	6/01
Tea for Two	10x12"	Int.	4	$110	3/97
Tea Maid, The	13x16"	Int.	2	$170	11/03
There's Rosemary!	11x14"	Misc Un	3	$450	3/03
Three Chums	8x10"	Cat	3	$230	9/03
Tiger Lilies and Elder	11x14"	Misc Un	3	$110	3/97
Touching Tale, A	11x14"	Int.	4	$165	6/97
Toward Slumberland	13x17"	Child	4	$770	6/97
Toward Slumberland	11x14"	Child	3.5	$240	3/97
Tray with interior scene	8x12"	Misc	4	$145	3/97
Treasure Bag, The	11x14"	Int.	3	$140	3/03
Treasure Bag, The	11x14"	Int.	3.75	$175	6/97
Trumpets	8x10"	Floral	4	$575	3/97
Turn, The	12x20"	Ext.	3	$30	3/97
Twin Miniatures	11x14"	Int.	4	$175	6/97
Two b & w floral glossies		Misc	4	$55	6/97
Two Lilies	9x11"	Floral	4	$160	11/03
Unbroken Flow, The	16x20"	Ext.	3.5	$90	3/97
Uncle Sam Taking Leave	12x15"	Man	3	$385	6/97
Under the Pine	11x17"	Ext.	3.5	$75	3/97
Undulating Reflections	9x15"	Misc Un	3.5	$210	3/03
Untitled -All Sunshine	6x8"	For.	3	$105	3/97
Untitled -amalfi	12x14"	For.	3	$65	3/97
Untitled castle	7x9"	For.	4	$330	3/97
Untitled exterior-birches	10x12"	Ext.	4	$90	6/97
Untitled exterior-birches	10x12"	Int.	3	$75	3/97
Untitled exterior-birches	7x9"	Ext.	4	$145	6/97
Untitled exterior-birches	7x11"	Ext.	3	$35	6/97
Untitled exterior-birches	10x12"	Ext.	3	$45	6/97
Untitled exterior-birches	6x8"	Ext.	4	$45	6/97
Untitled exterior-blossoms	7x9"	Ext.	3	$40	3/97
Untitled exterior-blossoms	7x11"	Ext.	4	$55	6/97
Untitled exterior-blossoms	7x9"	Ext.	3.5	$40	6/97
Untitled exterior-blossoms	20x40"	Ext.	4	$75	6/97
Untitled exterior-blossoms	6x8"	Ext.	4	$60	3/97
Untitled exterior-blossoms	7x11"	For.	3.5	$45	3/97
Untitled exterior-hills	6x8"	Ext.	4	$50	6/97
Untitled exterior-hills	8x10"	Ext.	4	$60	6/97
Untitled exterior-mountains	7x9"	Ext.	4	$30	6/97
Untitled exterior-mountains	7x9"	Ext.	4	$30	6/97
Untitled exterior-pond	7x9"	Ext.	4	$35	3/97
Untitled exterior-pond	5x7"	Ext.	4	$65	3/97
Untitled exterior-pond	6x8"	Ext.	4	$40	3/97
Untitled exterior-pond	5x7"	Int.	3	$35	6/97
Untitled exterior-stream	6x8"	Ext.	4	$70	3/97
Untitled exterior-stream	6x8"	Ext.	4	$60	3/97
Untitled exterior-stream	8x12"	Ext.	4	$45	6/97
Untitled exterior-stream	9x12"	Misc Un	3	$25	3/97
Untitled floral	6x8"	Floral	4	$175	3/97
Untitled floral	6x8"	Floral	3	$176	6/97
Untitled floral	6x8"	Floral	3	$220	3/97
Untitled floral	6x8"	Floral	4	$330	3/97
Untitled garden scene	6x8"	Misc Un	3.5	$95	3/97
Untitled garden scene	7x9"	Misc Un	4	$70	6/97
Untitled girl by window	5x7"	Child	4	$130	3/97
Untitled girls by house	5x7"	Misc Un	3.5	$70	6/97
Untitled girls by house	5x7"	Misc Un	4	$165	6/97
Untitled hilltop house	11x15"	Misc Un	3	$240	6/97
Untitled house	7x9"	Misc Un	3.75	$100	3/97
Untitled interior-girl by cupboard	4x6"	Int.	3	$90	6/97
Untitled interior-girl by fire	8x12"	Int.	3	$60	3/97
Untitled interior-girl by fire	7x9"	Int.	3	$90	3/97
Untitled interior-girl in bedroom	5x7"	Int.	4	$70	3/97
Untitled interior-girl in bedroom	11x15"	Misc Un	3	$55	6/97
Untitled interior-girl in rocker	7x9"	Int.	3.5	$85	3/97
Untitled interior-girl sewing	8x12"	Int.	3	$80	6/97
Untitled man in red jacket	5x7"	Man	4	$240	6/97
Untitled seascape	7x11"	Sea	4	$100	6/97
Untitled sepia exterior	5x7"	Misc	4	$90	6/97
Untitled swans	7x10"	For.	3	$110	3/97
Untitled vilas farm driveway	12x16"	Misc	3.5	$165	3/97
Untitled-at the fender	13x15"	Int.	3	$45	6/97
Untitled-Caherlough	7x11"	For.	4	$145	6/97
Untitled-Evangeline Lane	6x8"	For.	4	$100	3/97
Untitled-joy path	5x6"	For.	3	$65	6/97
Untitled-our neighbor	7x9"	Misc Un	4	$210	6/97
Untitled-posing	7x9"	child	3.95	$65	6/97
Untitled-posing	7x9"	child	4	$80	6/97
Untitled-Rheinstein	7x9"	For.	4	$410	6/97
Untitled-spinning	13x15"	Misc Un	4	$470	6/97
Vale of the Derwent, The	11x14"	For.	3	$70	6/97
Venice Afar	11x14"	For.	4	$1,200	11/03
Venice's Chief Glory	14x17"	For.	3.75	$575	3/97
Venice's Chief Glory	14x17"	For.	3.5	$1,350	11/00
Venice's Chief Glory	16x20"	For.	3	$255	6/97
Village Dale, The	8x10"	Ext.	3	$95	6/97
Village Elm, A	16x20"	Misc Un	4	$460	6/97

Village End	14x20"	For	3.75	$500	11/00	Wayside Inn Corner	13x17"	Misc Un	4	$240	6/03
Village Spires	10x12"	Ext.	4	$115	6/03	Wayside Inn from Highway	13x16"	Misc Un	4	$220	3/97
Vico Equisnè	13x17"	For.	3	$185	6/97	Westmore Drive	13x22"	Ext.	3	$85	6/03
Virginia Reel, A	20x24"	Int.	3	$130	11/03	Westmore Drive	11x14"	Ext.	4	$55	6/97
Waiting Bucket, The	9x11"	Misc Un	3	$100	6/97	Westport Garden, A	13x16"	For.	4	$310	6/97
Wall Shadows	13x15"	Ext.	3.5	$110	3/03	Where Grandma was Wed	16x20"	Misc Un	4	$385	6/97
Wandering Among Roses	9x11"	Misc Un	4	$220	6/97	Where Grandma was Wed	14x17"	Misc Un	4	$190	6/03
Warm Spring Day, A	10x17"	Sheep	3	$220	11/03	Where Trout Lie	11x14"	Ext.	3	$45	6/97
Warm Spring Day, A	13x22"	Sheep	4	$200	3/97	Wealth of October, The	15x22"	Ext.	4	$90	3/97
Warm Spring Day, A	13x17"	Sheep	3.75	$155	3/97	Whirling Candlestand, The	11x14"	Child	3.5	$130	3/97
Warm Spring Day, A	14x17"	Sheep	3	$285	6/97	White Mountain Twins	10x16"	Ext.	4	$95	6/97
Warm Spring Day, A	9x17"	Sheep	3	$220	3/97	Whitsunday	9x16"	Ext.	3.5	$70	9/03
Warm Spring Day, A	10x16"	Sheep	4	$320	6/97	Wig Wag Churning	13x16	Int.	3.75	$250	3/00
Watching for Papa	12x16"	Child	2	$110	6/97	Wilkes-Barre Brook, A	7x9"	Ext.	3	$290	9/03
Watching for Papa	13x17"	Child	4	$1,600	6/01	Willow Pastoral, A	13x16"	Sheep	3	$80	6/03
Water Gambols	13x16"	Ext.	4	$130	6/97	Wilton Waters	13x16"	Ext.	3.75	$155	3/97
Water Garden in Venice, A	10x12"	For.	4	$360	6/97	Winding an Old Tall Clock	14x17"	Int.	3.75	$230	3/03
Water Garden in Venice, A	10x12"	For.	4	$325	11/03	Windings in Holland	13x15"	For.	3	$190	6/03
Water Garden in Venice, A	16x20"	For.	3.75	$300	6/01	Windsor Blossoms	14x20"	Ext.	3	$70	6/97
Water Maples	9x15"	Ext.	3	$110	3/97	Winslow Water	14x17"	Ext.	3.5	$130	6/03
Water Maples	14x17"	Ext.	3	$110	6/97	Wiscasset Terrace, A	13x16"	Misc Un	4	$300	3/97
Water Path, A	14x17"	For.	4	$155	3/97	Wissahickon Decorations	13x16"	Ext.	4	$395	11/00
Way Down in Dixie	14x17"	Misc Un	3.75	$200	9/03	Witching Hour, The	11x14"	Ext.	3	$45	3/97
Way It Begins, The	13x16"	Man	4	$465	3/97	Work Basket, The	11x14"	Int.	4	$70	11/03
Way It Begins, The	13x16"	Man	3	$220	6/97	Woodland Cathedral, A	13x17"	Ext.	3.5	$80	3/97
Wayside Inn Approach	11x14"	Misc Un	4	$120	6/97	Youth of the Saco, The	13x16"	Ext.		$90	6/97
Wayside Inn Approach	8x10"	Misc Un	3	$110	3/97	Zinnias	13x16"	Floral	3.25	$1,400	11/03

A Florida Sunrise. Est. Value: $715.

A Gettysburg Crossing. Est. Value: $375.

A Hallway Glimpse.
Est. Value: $175.

A Little River. Est. Value: $105.

A Perkiomen October. Est. Value: $275.

A Royal Palm Border. Est. Value: $425.

A Sheffield Basket. Est. Value: $580.

A Village Elm. Est. Value: $460.

A Water Garden in Venice. Est. Value: $360.

A Wiscasset Terrace. Est. Value: $300.

Afternoon in Nantucket. Est. Value: $450.

Amalfi. Est. Value: $635.

An Old Parlor Idyll. Est. Value: $330.

At the Well, Sorrento. Est. Value: $385.

Blacksmith Shoeing White Horse. Est. Value: $795.

Braiding a Straw Hat. Est. Value: $300.

Dog-On-It.
Est. Value: $1,750.

Four O'Clock. Est. Value: $855.

Hanging Summer Herbs. Est. Value: $375.

Harmony. Est. Value: $325.

Jane. Est. Value: $350.

Litchfield Door, AD 1760. Est. Value: $325.

Litchfield Minster. Est. Value: $250.

Maine Coast Sky. Est. Value: $375.

Mary's Little Lamb. Est. Value: $325.

Palmetto Grace. Est. Value: $465.

Rose Gate. Est. Value: $275.

Sea Ledges, North Shore. Est. Value: $255.

Sunneyside (Washington Irving Home).
Est. Value: $330.

Seeking the Shade. Est. Value: $360.

The Coming Out of Rosa. Est. Value: $450.

Sharon Bridge. Est. Value: $200.

The Old Cabinet Maker. Est. Value: $4,510.

The Old Stage Road. Est. Value: $285.

The Way It Begins. Est. Value: $745.

Untitled Exterior-Blossoms. Est. Value: $75.

Three Chums. Est. Value: $375.

Way Down in Dixie. Est. Value: $375.

Venice's Chief Glory. Est. Value: $575.

Wayside Inn From Highway. Est. Value: $325.

Untitled Vilas Farm Driveway.
Est. Value: $275.

Wayside Inn Approach. Est. Value: $325.

Chapter 8

David Davidson (1881 – 1967)

David Davidson, circa 1940

up in Providence and attended local schools there. In 1901 he entered Brown University, majoring in civil engineering. Davidson was not born to a family of great means and he had to work his way through college. While attending Brown he worked four separate newspaper routes simultaneously to help raise money for tuition and books, living at home to reduce his education expenses.

Union Congregational Church, circa 1910
(Jan Liberatore Collection)

Her House in Order interior scene

"...Hardly a New England wedding went by where the bride didn't receive a David Davidson picture..."

An Introduction to David Davidson Pictures

David Davidson was born on February 24, 1881, in Providence, Rhode Island. With his parents John H. and Adelaide P. Davidson, he grew

While a student at Brown, Davidson also attended the Union Congregational Church, in Providence. As luck would have it, the pastor at the Union Congregational Church just happened to be Wallace Nutting. Apparently the Reverend Nutting was looking for an assistant to work with him in various aspects of his growing photography hobby/business and Davidson was only too eager to help. Davidson, then 20, developed a friendship with the 40-year-old Nutting, and began working with Nutting on a part-time basis in his photography studio which was located in the Edgewood-Cranston area of Rhode Island. Nutting was happy to find a younger man willing to carry his camera equipment, work in his dark room, handle much of his matting and framing, and do many other related jobs that Nutting didn't really have time to do. And David Davidson was eager to learn the fine art of commercial photography from Wallace Nutting.

Although there has been speculation for many years about whether Nutting taught Davidson the art of photography or vice versa, it's quite clear that although Wallace Nutting was still learning and developing his photographic skills at the turn of the century, Nutting was the teacher and Davidson was the student and they eventually worked together for several years.

They shot many pictures together, trying new techniques and experimenting with different cameras, negatives, lighting, angles, and photographic papers. The most obvious example of their mutual work is evidenced by a series of sheep pictures that were taken outside of Providence. Nutting's most commercially successful sheep pictures over the years were *A Warm Spring Day*, *On the Slope*, and *Not One of the 400*. Each of these pictures featured several dozen sheep grazing beside a colorful blue, tree-lined pond.

David Davidson's Beside Still Water

the number and location of the sheep, and the time of day, it would seem safe to conclude that both pictures were taken on the same day. Whether both men shared one camera, or whether each used his own equipment, there is no denying the similarity of the two pictures.

In 1904, Wallace Nutting decided to retire from the ministry due to ill health. He left Providence and opened a small photography studio in New York City. Shortly thereafter, he moved to Southbury, Connecticut, where he opened a small studio and continued to develop and refine his photographic process. Over the next 35 years Wallace Nutting went on to become one of the twentieth century's most famous photographers.

After Nutting left Providence in 1904, Davidson continued his education, graduating from Brown University in 1905. Upon graduation he took a full-time position with Providence Steel & Iron as a civil engineer, the career that he trained for in college. Davidson worked for PS&I for two years, while continuing to work with photography as his hobby. Apparently engineering didn't suit him as much as he expected and he found himself increasingly drawn to photography.

Also in 1905 David Davidson married his college sweetheart, Louise (Whitcher) Davidson, who had graduated from the Pembroke College of Brown University that same year with a degree in English. She worked for several years as a teacher at the Peace Street grammar school in Providence.

In 1907, David and Louise Davidson jointly decided to leave their engineering and teaching careers and together they opened the David Davidson Studios at 57 Whitemarsh St. in Providence. The studio was located in a large third floor wood frame building. The first floor

Wallace Nutting's A Warm Spring Day

Davidson's most commercially successful sheep picture was titled *Beside Still Waters*. If you look at a comparison between Nutting's *A Warm Spring Day* and Davidson's *Beside Still Waters*, you'll see the similarity between the two pictures. Based upon the foliage on the trees,

Louise Davidson, circa 1940

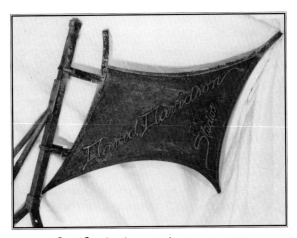

David Davidson bronze studio sign, circa 1925

used for storing boxes, picture frames, cardboard, glass, and wood shavings packing material. Nearly all aspects of the business were conducted at the Whitemarsh Street studio and the building remained standing until 1967 when it was demolished to make room for an additional parking lot for a nearby hospital.

David Davidson's original studio camera

Davidson's work, although significantly smaller than Nutting's in both diversity and total volume, was higher than all other hand-colored photographers of the early twentieth century except for Wallace Nutting. He also used a very similar photographic process to the other photographers. In the early years, a box camera on tripod stand, glass negatives, platinum paper, proper sizing and coloring, indented matting, and a lower-left title/lower right signature, all paralleled the work of Wallace Nutting. Pencil signatures were used in early years (1907–1915), pen signatures in the later years (1915 and later) as volume increased. Louise Davidson applied most of the titles and signatures and, according to Davidson's son Donald, many picture titles

included a picture showroom, and was where the framing, backing, labeling, boxing, packing, and shipping were handled. The second floor included the sales and accounting office and is where pictures were signed and titled. The dark room was on the third floor and is where pictures were developed, dried, enlarged, colored, and mounted. The cellar, which could be entered from both inside and outside the building, was

originated during meal-time discussions in the Davidson household.

Davidson Collecting Tip:

David Davidson sold more hand-colored photographs during the early twentieth century than all of his contemporaries except Wallace Nutting.

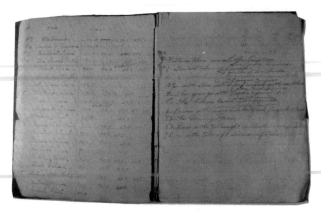

Davidson's original studio number book

Over a 40-year period, Davidson produced more than 1,000 picture titles. Some titles sold literally thousands of copies each while other titles were very poor sellers and resulted in minimal sales. As each new picture title was assigned, it was entered into Davidson's studio number book. A listing of most known Davidson picture titles can be found in The Alphabetical Index to David Davidson Pictures section of this chapter.

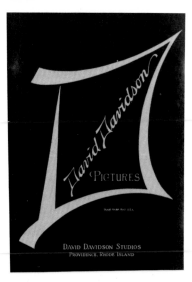

1917 and 1925 picture catalogs

Each picture was assigned an individual number which was used to identify loose pic-

tures within the studio and to facilitate picture orders. Subsequently Davidson produced various salesman's picture catalogs which were given to his salesman and department stores, and pictures were ordered by either the title or studio number. To date we have seen four separate catalogs (1909, 1911, 1917, and 1925). Each catalog grew in size, indicating that the size of both Davidson's business and picture inventory was growing.

Davidson Collecting Tip:

Davidson picture catalogs are difficult to find and are quite desirable to most collectors.

Davidson's business was small in comparison to Nutting's. At its peak he employed a staff of fewer than 12 people (compared to Nutting's 200+ employees). He became best known for his exterior pictures of Rhode Island, Roger Williams Park, colonial Kingston, Vermont, and New Hampshire's White Mountains, and hardly a wedding event in the Rhode Island area went by where the bride didn't receive at least one Davidson picture as a wedding or shower gift. When Donald and Alice Davidson were married, even they received a Davidson picture as a gift from an acquaintance who didn't realize that David was Donald's father.

Davidson pictures were generally sold in department stores and gift shops. The Shepperd Company in Providence had an entire David Davidson room where Davidson pictures were displayed, framed, and sold. He employed two traveling salesmen who sold his pictures to stores throughout New England and New York, and it was not uncommon for Davidson himself to call on a new prospective client and walk out with a picture order in hand.

David Davidson Studio Staff (circa 1930s)

* Chief Photographer: David Davidson
* Darkroom Processor: Harry James — handling the printing, enlarging, and drying of prints
* Colorists: Nellie Horner, Scituate, Rhode Island — colored both in the studio and at home
Jennie Richards, Pawtuxet, Rhode Island — colored mostly at home

Margaret Schurman, Warwick, Rhode Island — colored both in the studio and at home
Millie Goldsworthy, Edgewood, Rhode Island — colored mostly at home
Sue Morgan, Block Island, Rhode Island — colored mainly at home. Living on Block Island, she returned to the mainland only every two months or so to pick up food and provisions with her husband. On each trip she would drop off completed work and pick up new pictures for coloring.
Vera Davidson, Providence, Rhode Island — colored mostly in the studio. She was David Davidson's sister-in-law and only lived five houses away from the studio.

* Picture Titles & Signatures: Louise and David Davidson
* Mounting & Framing: Howard Tyler
* Housekeeping and Studio Chores: George Davidson (David Davidson's oldest brother); David and Donald Davidson, sons of David Davidson
* Bookkeeper: Carolyn Cady, Cranston Rhode Island (Louise Davidson's aunt)
* Salesmen: Oscar Perry, handled New Hampshire and upper New England
Bert Huff, handled New York and lower New England

In the Making (Note that Louise Davidson is the model who also made the costume and flag.)

Davidson produced many colonial interior scenes, with Mrs. Davidson posing in many of them. Although his interiors were very well done and quite colorful and charming, they generally did not equal Nutting's interiors in terms of quality

and variety of the antique furniture and accessories used, or in the manner the room was decorated. Nutting possessed a knowledge of antiques that was unparalleled by any other photographer of his day, and this, along with Nutting's extensive personal collection of antiques and his knowledge of where to borrow those pieces that he didn't already own, enabled Nutting to put together colonial settings that were unsurpassed by any other photographer.

Davidson Collecting Tip:
Although Davidson sold many colonial interior scenes, they were generally not as historically accurate as Wallace Nutting's, with most furniture featured in the pictures being significantly more common than that used in Nutting's interior scenes.

Davidson calendar. Est. Value: $100 – 150.

As his business grew, Davidson began to expand beyond basic framed pictures into calendars, greeting cards, and other more unusual items. These helped him to increase sales and they are quite desirable to collectors today.

As a businessman, Davidson learned to change with the times. Early pictures were more subtly colored than the more brightly colored pictures of the 1930s. Although most were mounted on indented matboards, he also pro-

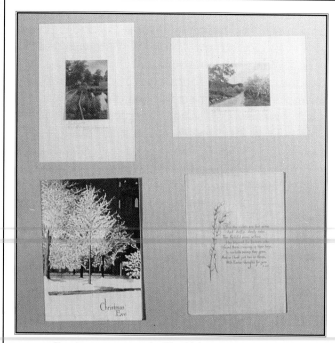

Davidson greeting cards. Est. Value: $100 — 150 each.

Davidson triple grouping. Est. Value: $150 — 275.

Brightly colored close-framed picture in box. Est. Value: $75 — 150.

Pair of exterior scenes with gold foil matting (Ed Moody Collection). Est. Value: $75 — 100 each.

duced close–framed pictures and even pictures mounted on gold foil mattings. Davidson also resorted to machine produced four-color process prints (which he called *facsimile* prints) as expenses increased and sales declined.

During World War I David Davidson made the change to motion pictures, producing *The Rhode Island Weekly*, a motion picture news-reel which brought actual World War I film footage back to the home front. His weekly war newsreels became a regular feature at local movie theaters during the war. Also during World War I, David Davidson worked as an instructor for enlisted men, teaching them the fine art of photography.

In 1918, Davidson was appointed to the Rhode Island War Photographs Committee by then-Governor Beeckman. His objective was to collect and preserve a photographic history of Rhode Island's activities during World War I. This not only included actual war footage from the front, but also included back-home activities such as mobilization, parades, demonstrations of support, industrial contributions, and the like. He completed this assignment with much praise for his precision and accuracy.

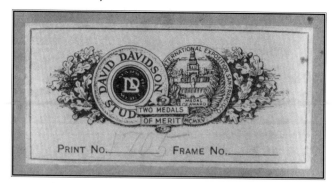

International Exposition Medal of Merit label.

But as far as collectors of hand-colored photography are concerned, Davidson was well recognized for the high quality of his pictures. In 1915, at the Panama Pacific Exposition in San Francisco, he was awarded the bronze medal for his hand-colored photography.

After more than 30 years of rising picture sales, the public began to lose interest in hand-colored photographs, including David Davidson's pictures, and eventually his orders began to decline. Davidson continued selling hand-colored photographs into the early 1950s, but on a significantly smaller scale than in the 1910 – 1940 peak period. America's constantly changing tastes and the invention of color photography led to a gradual decline in business, with sales of his hand-colored photographs slowing to a trickle after the Depression of the 1930s. Much of Davidson's later business included color photography and commercial and private commissions and assignments.

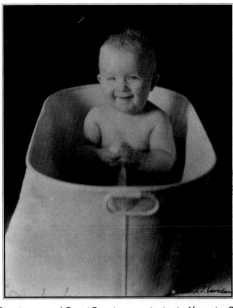

Donald Davidson, son of David Davidson, in a bathtub. Note the Smilemaker title and signature on the picture (Donald & Alice Davidson Collection).

(Author's Note: Special thanks to Donald and Alice Davidson for sharing many of their family's memories and mementos.)

The Collecting Cycle of David Davidson Pictures

Phase I. Initial Production and Peak Period: Initially sold between 1907 and the 1950s, the peak period for David Davidson pictures was 1915 – 1930s. Although sales were lower than Wallace Nutting's, David Davidson sold more hand-colored pictures than any other photographer except for Wallace Nutting.

Phase II. Gradual Market Decline: Interest gradually declined after the 1930s, with relatively few new titles being introduced after the late 1920s.

Phase III. Renewed Collectibility: By the mid to late 1970s, collectors began rediscovering David Davidson pictures. Generally collectors of Wallace Nutting pictures also sought out David Davidson pictures because of their similarity in style, subject matter, and price.

Phase IV. Current Market: As the price of Wallace Nutting pictures has soared over the past 10 years, an increasing number of collectors have shifted their search to David Davidson pictures, with many individual collectors now specifically collecting David Davidson pictures, making them either the exclusive or primary focus of their collection.

David Davidson, circa 1955

Davidson retired in 1955, after spending more than 50 years in the photography business.

David and Louise Davidson had two sons, David Lymen Davidson, born June 7, 1910, and Donald James Davidson, born April 2, 1924. Both still reside in Rhode Island.

David Davidson died on February 3, 1967, at the age of 85, at the Gray Rock rest home in Cumberland, Rhode Island.

Louise Davidson, died on February 16, 1983 at the age of 100, at the Diamond Hill nursing home in Cumberland, Rhode Island.

However, the number of collectors specializing either exclusively or primarily in David Davidson is significantly smaller than Wallace Nutting, although this number is on the rise.

David Davidson Pictures: What Are They?

Hand-Colored Photographs: The vast majority of David Davidson pictures are hand-colored black and white photographs. The early pictures were produced on a platinum paper while later pictures were produced on paper with a higher silver concentration. All colors were hand applied by individual colorists.

Facsimile Prints: A very limited number of David Davidson titles are machine-produced facsimile prints. If you see the word *facsimile* on the picture label, it means that it was machine produced and it has minimal value. Collectors generally prize the hand-colored pictures and have extremely little interest in the machine-produced pictures. If in doubt, inspect the picture with a 15x magnifying glass. If you see a series of small symmetrical dots, it is a machine-produced print.

Davidson Collecting Tip:

All Davidson facsimile prints are exterior scenes and each are easily detectable with a 15x magnifying glass. There are only four different facsimile print titles.

Sunset Point facsimile print

The Mayflowers of Plymouth, a colonial print

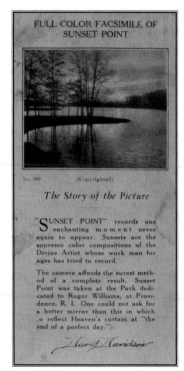

A Davidson facsimile print label

Making of the Flag, another colonial print

Hand-Colored Drawings/Prints: A very limited number of Davidson colonial scenes are actually machine-produced prints rather than hand-colored photographs. Apparently Davidson sold some colonial prints in addition to his hand-colored photographs. Although extremely rare, these are not very desirable to collectors.

Miscellaneous Items: Davidson also produced a series of calendars and greeting cards, most of which contained a smaller hand-colored picture.

Reproduction Alert

At the time this book went to press, we were unaware of any current or previous David Davidson reproductions on the market.

Identifying and Dating David Davidson Pictures

David Davidson close-framed interior

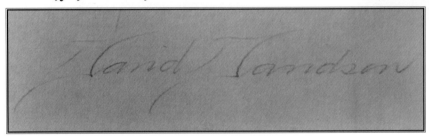

Pencil signature

> ### Davidson Collecting Tip:
> Davidson's earliest pictures were signed in pencil (1907 – 1915). His later pictures (1915 and later) were signed in pen.

Pen signature on picture

> ### Davidson Collecting Tip:
> Many Davidson pen signatures have severely faded. Beware that a faded signature will significantly reduce the value of a picture, perhaps by 50% or more.

> ### Davidson Collecting Tips:
> Pictures framed without a matting are called close-framed pictures and typically date the picture as 1930 or later.
> An original label on the picture backing can help you to date the picture and can add 10 – 15% to the value of a picture.

Subject Matter of David Davidson Pictures

Exterior Scenes: The most common form of Davidson pictures — blossoms, birches, streams, etc. — were the most popular pictures, sold in the highest quantities, and are most readily available today. Approximately 90% of the David Davidson pictures you will find will be exterior scenes.

Interior Scenes are fairly common. Davidson colonial interiors with women dressed in colonial costumes, working around a fire, were the most common. However, a fair number of Davidson pictures have no people in them. Davidson interiors also typically included furniture of no special significance (e.g., country rush-seated chairs vs. carved

David Davidson labels (top, circa 1925; bottom, circa 1910)

David Davidson label, circa 1930

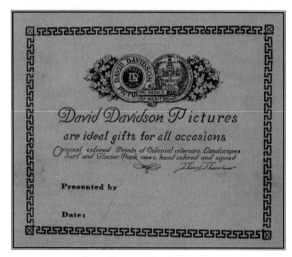

David Davidson label, circa 1930

Chippendale mahogany chairs, spinning and flax wheels vs. high-style Chippendale, Queen Anne, Hepplewhite, Federal, Sheraton, or other more expensive furniture).

Foreign and Miscellaneous Unusual Pictures: Aside from a few pictures taken in the Canadian Rockies, Davidson produced no foreign scenes. Overall, Davidson produced the same variety of miscellaneous unusual pictures as did Nutting, however in far fewer numbers, and he did not produce any florals or colonial interior pictures with men that we are aware of.

David Davidson pictorial labels

The type of label on the backing paper can also help to date the picture.

Size

The size of David Davidson pictures will vary from 1x2" to 16x20". Rarely will you see a David Davidson larger then 16x20".

Condition

The same condition guide that applies to Wallace Nutting pictures also applies to David Davidson pictures.

Some of the More Commonly Found David Davidson Pictures

The following titles represent some David Davidson titles which are quite common and frequently found by collectors. This does not mean that they are not desirable to collectors, but rather that they were originally sold in large numbers and are more commonly found today.

A Berkshire Sunset, an evening lakeside sunset

A Comfy Corner, an interior scene with no people

Diadem Aisle, a common garden scene

Feathery Aisle, a common outdoor scene

Grandmother's Garden, girl standing in house garden

Her House in Order, another interior with no people

Porch Beautiful, girl on front porch

Sunset Point, another evening lakeside sunset

The Four Friends, four birches by a lake

The Lamb's May Feast, sheep by a pond

Some of the Rarest and Most Highly Sought-After David Davidson Pictures

The following represent some of the rare and more highly sought-after David Davidson pictures or categories of Davidson pictures, in no particular order. All, in very good to excellent condition, are very desirable to most Davidson collectors:

Western United States American Indian pictures (extremely rare)

Glacier National Park pictures (Montana)

Canadian Rockies pictures (including Lake Louise)

Hand-colored drawings of colonial scenes (vs. hand-colored photographs. Note that although these are extremely unusual, they are not highly prized by most collectors.)

Southern and Florida Landscapes (often Daytona, Florida)

The Seine Reel (fishing pier)

The Midday Rest (cows)

The Last Load (oxen)

Any David Davidson picture catalog (1909, 1911, 1917, and 1925)

David Davidson Collectors' Club

There is presently no collectors' club devoted exclusively to David Davidson pictures. However, the Wallace Nutting Collectors' Club would be the best place to go for further information on David Davidson pictures. We also write a column for the Wallace Nutting Collectors' Club newsletter which sometimes focuses on David Davidson pictures. You can obtain more information from the author.

David Davidson Books and Reference Material

At the time this book went to press, we were aware of no other books or reference material devoted to David Davidson. Much of the David Davidson material found in *The Guide to Wallace Nutting-like Photographers of the Early Twentieth Century* has been included in this chapter.

David Davidson on the Internet

Information on David Davidson can be found in the Wallace Nutting-like photographers section of The Wallace Nutting Gallery at www.wnutting.com.

Where to Go If Looking to Buy or Sell David Davidson Pictures

There are various dealers around the country, including Michael Ivankovich, who specialize in hand-colored photography of the early twentieth century, including David Davidson. Most such dealers are members of the Wallace Nutting Collectors' Club.

One obvious reference source would be The Michael Ivankovich Antiques and Auction Co. Several times per year the The Michael Ivankovich Auction Company conducts separate auctions of Wallace Nutting-like pictures which are typically held on the same weekend as the Wallace Nutting catalog auction. Many Davidson pictures are usually included in these auctions. You can contact Michael Ivankovich at P.O. Box 2458, Doylestown, PA 18901 (215)345-6094, fax (215)345-6692, via e-mail: wnutting@comcat.com, or visit his website at: www.wnutting.com.

Summary of David Davidson Collecting Tips

* David Davidson worked for Wallace Nutting during the 1899–1904 period while Nutting lived in Providence, Rhode Island.

* David Davidson ranked #2 in total output, selling more hand-colored pictures than any other early twentieth century photographer, except Wallace Nutting.

* Davidson exterior scenes are significantly more common than Davidson interior scenes.

* David Davidson interior scenes may or may not include people. Furniture used in Davidson interior scenes was typically of the more common variety (spinning wheels, rushed chairs, etc.) and rarely did a Davidson interior include the best examples of Chippendale, Hepplewhite, Queen Anne, and other higher style furnishings.

* Davidson produced no foreign scenes aside from a limited number of pictures taken in the Canadian Rockies. Davidson visited Montana's Glacier National Park and the Canadian Rockies in 1914, and shot a considerable number of pictures there. They were very poor sellers and, as a result, are considered quite rare today.

* Titles and signatures were applied in both pencil (1907–1915) and pen (1915 and later).

* The early pictures (1905 – 25) were very subtly colored; later pictures (1925 – 30s) included somewhat brighter coloring.

* Most Davidson pictures had indented mats, although in later years, some close-framed pictures were also sold. Matted pictures are generally more desirable than close-framed pictures without mats.

* During the Depression years Davidson, like Nutting, turned to machine-produced prints in an attempt to lower production costs. Although these facsimile prints are very limited in number, you should be certain that the David Davidson you are buying is actually a hand-colored photograph, not a machine-produced print.

* A David Davidson backing label can increase the value by 10 – 15%.

* David Davidson sold a variety of smaller novelty items which included calendars, greeting cards, triple grouping pictures, etc.

David Davidson Value Guide

The values listed in this chapter are derived from many different sources, including

* Michael Ivankovich Auction Co. auctions
* Other auction houses
* Retail and mail order sales
* Prices observed at antique shows, flea markets, and individual and group antique shops throughout the northeast
* Assorted other reliable sources

Most prices included here represent prices actually paid. In some instances where we were unable to ascertain the final sale price, we have included the dealer asking price if we felt that it was appropriately priced and fell within the acceptable ranges. The sampling of items included in this chapter includes titles seen by us, sold by us, or reported by us. Obviously not all titles are included here. This chapter is only intended to provide you with a representative sampling of titles and prices in order to help you to establish a ballpark price on most David Davidson pictures.

Title	Size	Type	Price	Rating	Date
3 Brothers, Dixville Notch	12x15"	Ext.	$15	4	10/94
Afternoon Call, The	7x9"	Misc. Un.	$65	4	11/03
Alluring Trail, An	13x16"	Ext.	$72	3	9/96
Angler, The	10x12"	Boy	$90	4	6/03
Antlered Elm, The	12x15"	Ext.	$50	4	4/95
Artist's Ideal, The	10x12"	Ext.	$22	3.75	9/96
Banjo Clock, The	5x12"	Int.	$40	3	3/03
Barefoot Boy, The	13x16"	Child	$99	3.5	10/94
Barefoot Boy, The	14x17"	Child	$135	4	11/96
Breaker's Victim, The	12x15"	Sea	$60	3.5	3/96
Apple Blossoms	8x10"	Ext.	$140	3.5	11/03
Arboretum Jewels	13x16"	Misc. Un.	$50	3.5	4/95
Bald Mt., Mohawk Trail	12x15"	Ext.	$39	4	9/96
Berkshire Bride	13x16"	Ext.	$75	4	5/95
Berkshire Jewel, A	10x12"	Ext.	$145	4	6/01
Berkshire Sunset	11x14"	Ext.	$40	4	9/03
Berkshire Sunset	5x7"	Ext.	$130	4	11/00
Berkshire Sunset	8x10"	Ext.	$60	4	4/97
Beside Still Water	11x14"	Sheep	$150	4	7/96
Beside Still Water	13x16"	Sheep	$140	4	8/96
Beside Still Water	9x15"	Sheep	$50	4	4/95
Birch Bower	7x9"	Ext.	$25	3	3/96
Birch Sentinels	7x9"	Ext.	$17	3	9/96
Boyhood Joys	8x14"	Child	$88	4	9/96
Bridal Aisle	12x16"	Ext.	$40	4	9/03
Bride and Bridesmaid	8x10"	Ext.	$45	4	4/97
By the Mohawk Trail	10x12"	Ext.	$45	4	11/03

Title	Size	Type	Price		Date
Calendar with Snow Bound Brook	6x9"	Calendar	$22	3	11/95
Charming Youth	4x5"	Mini	$28	4	10/94
Chimney Cupboard	7x9"	Int.	$50	4	3/96
Chippendale Reflection	5x7"	Int.	$39	4	11/95
Christmas Eve	10x12"	Snow	$160	4	3/03
Christmas Eve	11x14"	Snow	$120	3	4/95
Christmas Eve, card	6x8"	Snow	$90	4	11/00
Cleft Falls	13x16"	Misc. Un.	$100	4	4/95
Close-famed exterior	16x20"	Ext.	$66	5	10/94
Close-framed exterior	12x16"	Ext.	$30	4	11/95
Close-framed exterior	12x16"	Ext.	$45	4	3/96
Close-framed exterior	12x16"	Ext.	$40	4	3/96
Close-framed exterior	8x10"	Int.	$28	4	3/96
Close-framed house	12x16"	Misc. Un.	$77	4	10/94
Close-framed interior	12x16"	Int.	$50	4	11/95
Close-framed interior	13x16"	Int.	$20	4	3/97
Close-framed interior	13x16"	Int.	$55	4	10/94
Close-framed seascape	12x16"	Sea	$50	4	3/96
Close-framed seascape	8x10"	Sea	$40	4	3/96
Comfy Corner, A	10x12"	Int.	$65	4	10/95
Comfy Corner, A	13x16"	Int.	$135	4	5/95
Comfy Corner, A	4x5"	Mini	$28	4	10/94
Connoseur, The	8x14"	Child	$63	3	3/96
Contemporary Masterpieces	13x16"	Int.	$125	4	10/96
Contemporary Masterpieces	14x17"	Int.	$195	4	12/96
Contemporary Masterpieces	5x7"	Int.	$28	3.5	3/97
Convalescent, The	10x16"	Int.	$80	4	3/96
Dancing Gypsies	10x12"	Ext.	$65	4	5/95
Daughter of Sheffield, A	12x14"	Int.	$30	3.5	11/03
Daughter of Sheffield, A	13x16"	Int.	$250	4.5	3/96
December Greeting, A	10x12"	Snow	$61	4	10/94
Diadem Aisle	10x12"	Ext.	$43	4	3/96
Diadem Aisle	12x15"	Ext.	$43	3	4/95
Diadem Aisle	13x16"	Ext.	$40	4	3/03
Diadem Aisle	13x16"	Ext.	$95	4	1/96
Diadem Aisle	8x10"	Ext.	$35	4	2/96
Dorothy Perkins	13x15"	Misc. Un.	$135	4	5/96
Dorothy Perkins	13x16"	Misc. Un.	$125	4	4/96
Dorothy Perkins	7x9"	Misc. Un.	$39	3	9/96
Dorothy Perkins	8x12"	Misc. Un.	$45	3	4/95
Driving Home the Cows	13x16"	Cow	$80	4	9/03
Driving Home the Cows	5x7"	Cows	$120	4	3/97
Dropt Stitch, The	5x7"	Int.	$80	4	3/03
Early Arrival	6x9"	Misc. Un.	$25	4	4/95
Easter Bonnet	7x9"	Int.	$20	3	11/03
Ebbing Tide, The	5x7"	Sea	$25	3.75	3/97
Echo Lake	10x12"	Ext.	$45	4	10/96
Echo Lake	7x9"	Ext.	$35	4	12/96
Echo Lake	8x10"	Ext.	$60	4	3/96
Echo Lake Drive	13x16"	Ext.	$35	4	11/03
Elbow Pine	9x16"	Ext.	$75	4.5	3/96
Escaping Waters	12x15"	Ext.	$61	4	11/95
Ever Winding Mohawk Trail	9x12"	Ext.	$35	4	4/96
Fairyland Wall	5x7"	Ext.	$28	4	4/95
Feathery Aisle	10x12"	Ext.	$22	4	9/96
Feathery Aisle	11x14"	Ext.	$65	4	6/96
Feathery Aisle	8x10"	Ext.	$35	4	5/96
Feathery Aisle, A	13x16"	Ext.	$65	4	7/96
Feathery Aisle, A	7x11"	Ext.	$33	3.5	3/96
Feathery Birch, A	11x14"	Ext.	$65	4	5/96
Feathery Birch	12x16"	Ext.	$39	4	10/94
Feathery Birch	13x17"	Ext.	$43	3.5	4/95
Fortune in Tea, A	10x12"	Int.	$50	4	10/94
Four O'Clock Tea	13x16"	Int.	$33	4	10/94
Franconia Mirror	11x14"	Ext.	$45	4	9/95
Franconia Notch	11x14"	Ext.	$120	4	3/03
Frosted Banks	9x14"	Snow	$140	4	6/03
Frozen Valley Brook	12x16"	Ext.	$115	4	11/00
Gay Head	7x9"	Misc. Un.	$100	4	11/00
Glacier Park	16x20"	Misc. Un.	$176	3.5	9/96
Golden Sunset	13x16"	Ext.	$30	4	3/03
Golf Green, The	5x7"	Ext.	$25	4	3/97
Golf Green, The	7x9"	Ext.	$38	4	4/95
Grandmother's Garden	12x15"	Misc. Un.	$80	5	3/03
Grandmother's Garden	5x7"	Misc. Un.	$55	3	11/95
Grandmother's Garden	7x9"	Misc. Un.	$35	4	3/97
Grandpa's Marguerites	11x17"	Child	$275	4	10/94
Greeting card with ext.	5x7"	Misc	$60	4	11/95
Greeting card with ext.	5x7"	Misc	$45	4	11/96
Greeting card with int.	5x7"	Misc	$75	4	12/95
Hearthside Comforts	13x16"	Int.	$55	3.5	3/97
Heirloom, The	13x16"	Int.	$99	4	9/96
Heirloom, The	13x16"	Int.	$88	4	10/94
Her House in Order	11x14"	Int.	$125	4	2/96
Her House in Order	12x16"	Int.	$40	4	3/96
Her House in Order	13x16"	Int.	$55	4	11/03
Her House in Order	14x17"	Int.	$160	4	12/95
Historic Homestead, A	12x15"	Misc. Un.	$85	4	4/95
Home of the Lorelei	10x12"	Sea	$90	3	6/03
Home of the Lorelei	11x14"	Sea	$70	4	11/03
Homestead, The	8x10"	Misc. Un.	$110	3	11/95
House in Order, The	12x15"	Int.	$33	3.5	3/96
In Pineland	12x16"	Ext.	$55	4	12/95
In the Making	7x9"	Int.	$105	4	9/96
Jack Frost Palette	10x12"	Snow	$20	3.5	3/96
Jack Frost Palette	9x12"	Snow	$38	3	3/96
Knock at the Squire's Door, A	13x16"	Misc. Un.	$165	4	8/96

Title	Size	Type	Price		Date
Ladies of the Lake	10x12"	Ext.	$28	4	9/96
Ladies of the Lake	11x13"	Tray	$17	3	11/95
Lake Onata	10x12"	Ext.	$25	4	3/96
Lake Placid	12x15"	Man	$65	3	3/96
Lamb's May Feast, The	10x12"	Sheep	$55	3	9/96
Lamb's May Feast, The	5x7"	Sheep	$75	4	11/01
Lamb's May Feast, The	11x14"	Sheep	$60	3	9/03
Lamb's May Feast, The	11x14"	Sheep	$55	3	3/97
Lamb's May Feast, The	13x16"	Sheep	$72	4	11/95
Lamb's May Feast, The	14x17"	Sheep	$55	4	3/96
Lamb's May Feast, The	16x20"	Sheep	$150	4	5/01
Land of Dreams, The	13x16"	Child	$165	4	10/94
Land of Dreams, The	13x16"	Child	$187	4	11/95
Last Load, The	6x10"	Men	$85	3.75	3/97
Life Long Friends	10x12"	Ext.	$25	4	3/97
Life Long Friends	11x14"	Ext.	$55	4	1/96
Life Long Friends — process print	12x16"	Process	$10	4	1/96
Lover's Lane	13x16"	Ext.	$23	4	3/97
Lover's Lane	9x16"	Ext.	$85	3	11/00
Mass O'Bloom	12x16"	Ext.	$50	4	11/03
Match Makers	8x10"	Int.	$225	4	11/03
Match Maker, The	13x16"	Misc. Un.	$143	4	11/95
Mayflowers of Plymouth, The	13x16"	Misc	$55	4	4/95
Mayflowers of Plymouth, The	14x17"	Misc	$60	4	4/95
Maytime Fragrance	14x17"	Misc. Un.	$95	3.5	11/03
Merry Blossom, A	11x14"	Child	$110	3.5	11/95
Mighty Fortress, A	13x16"	Sea	$143	4	10/94
Mill Pond	7x9"	Misc. Un.	$63	4	11/95
Mill Pond	8x10"	Misc. Un.	$75	4	12/96
Mill Pond	9x12"	Misc. Un.	$20	4	9/03
Miniature exterior	4x5"	Mini	$10	4	3/96
Miniature interior	4x5"	Mini	$55	3.5	3/97
Mirror Cove	13x16"	Misc. Un.	$61	3.5	11/95
Mirror with interior scene	3x9"	Mirror	$58	4	11/95
Mountain Mirror, A	13x15"	Ext.	$94	4	11/95
My Father's Cot	9x15"	Misc. Un.	$39	3.75	11/95
Nantucket Mill	5x7"		$180	4	11/00
Neighbors	10x13"		$250	4	3/03
Ocean Symphony	11x14"	Sea	$75	4	11/96
October Mantle	3x15"	Ext.	$110	3.75	9/96
October Sunset	5x7"	Ext.	$20	4	11/03
Old Ironsides	11x14"	Sea	$61	4	11/95
Old Ironsides	16x20"	Sea	$170	4.25	3/97
Old Ironsides	16x20"	Sea	$68	3	3/96
Old Ironsides	16x20"	Sea	$45	3	11/03
Old Mill	13x16"	Misc. Un.	$125	4	5/95
Old Mill, The	13x16"	Misc. Un.	$90	4	6/03
Old Mill, The	12x15"	Misc. Un.	$130	4	6/01
Old Mill Pond, The	12x15"	Misc. Un.	$55	3	3/96
Old Mill Pond, The	13x16"	Misc. Un.	$95	3.5	3/96
Olde Oaken Bucket, The	14x17"	Man	$231	4	10/94
Old Spanish Sugar Mill, An	14x17"	Misc. Un.	$231	4.5	9/96
On a News Hunt	14x17"	Misc. Un.	$45	3	3/96
On Moonlit Seas	5x7"	Misc. Un.	$25	4	9/96
Over the Hills	14x16"	Ext.	$55	4	4/95
Pasture Pool, The	13x16"	Cow	$143	4	10/94
Pasture Pool, The	7x9"	Cow	$22	3	11/95
Pawtuxet Falls	9x15"	Ext.	$20	4	3/03
Pawtuxet Falls	5x7"	Ext.	$28	4	9/96
Paying Calls	14x17"	Misc. Un.	$143	4.5	11/95
Plymouth Elm	10x16"	Ext.	20	3	3/97
Plymouth Elm	9x12"	Ext.	$45	4	4/96
Pool, The	13x17"	Ext.	$39	4	11/95
Porch Beautiful, The	9x15"	Misc. Un.	$20	4	11/03
Porch Beautiful	10x12"	Misc. Un.	$110	4	11/01
Porch Beautiful	10x16"	Misc. Un.	$165	4	3/96
Porch Beautiful	11x14"	Misc. Un.	$125	4	7/95
Porch Beautiful	7x9"	Misc. Un.	$40	4	3/97
Porch Beautiful	9x14"	Misc. Un.	$60	4	3/97
Portland Head Light	11x14"	Sea	$65	3	11/03
Portland Head Light	20x28"	Sea	$175	4	6/01
Portland Head Light	7x9"	Sea	$66	4	9/96
Pres. Coolidge's Father's Home	10x12"	Misc. Un.	$65	4	11/95
Pres. Coolidge's Father's Home	11x14"	Misc. Un.	$77	4	11/95
Pres. Coolidge's Father's Home	13x16"	Man	$225	4	11/03
Primping	11x14"	Int.	$75	4	7/95
Primping	7x9"	Int.	$22	4	11/95
Prize Pewter	12x15"	Int.	$28	2	11/95
Prize Pewter	12x16"	Int.	$40	4	3/96
Prize Pewter	12x16"	Int.	$90	4	4/95
Prize Pewter	13x16"	Int.	$60	3	11/03
Prize Pewter	8x10"	Int.	$120	5	4/95
Prize Pewter, The	7x9"	Int.	$28	4	3/96
Promise of Harvest, A	13x16"	Sheep	$140	4	4/95
Promise of Harvest, A	14x17"	Sheep	$110	4	7/95
Puritan Lady, A	10x12"	Int.	$75	4	8/96
Puritan Lady, A	12x16"	Int.	$65	3	3/96
Puritan Lady, A	13x15"	Int.	$80	4	3/96
Puritan Lady, A	13x16"	Int.	$115	4	9/96
Rambler Rose	10x16"	Misc. Un.	$10	4	11/03
Rambler Rose	13x20"	Misc. Un.	$72	4	11/95
Rambler Rose	6x8"	Misc. Un.	$77	4	9/96
Rambler Rose, The	14x17"	Misc. Un.	$110	4	11/03
Real D.A.R., A	12x15"	Int.	$200	5	4/95
Real D.A.R., A	14x17"	Int.	$72	4	11/95
Road Home	6x8"	Ext.	$85	4	11/03

Road Home, The	9x12"	Ext.	$58	3.5	3/96
Roadside Spring	7x9"	Ext.	$35	4	4/95
Rows of Peace	14x22"	Ext.	$33	3.75	9/96
San Juan Harbor	10x12"	Ships	$45	3	3/96
Seine Reel, The	13x16"	Misc. Un.	$190		3/97
Seine Reel, Maine, The	14x17"	Man	$330	4	10/94
Sewing Circle Gossip	13x16"	Misc. Un.	$176	4	10/94
Shattered Waves	12x15"	Sea	$100	4	4/95
Shattered Waves	13x16"	Sea	$190	4	5/96
Shattered Waves	8x10"	Sea	$45	4	8/96
Shattered Wave, The	10x12"	Sea	$41	4	11/95
Shattered Wave, The	12x15"	Sea	$45	4	3/96
Shattered Wave, The	14x17"	Sea	$110	4	3/01
Shattered Wave, The	5x7"	Sea	$28	3	11/95
Siesta, The	10x12"	Cows	$170	3	3/96
Silent Wave, The	13x16"	Sea	$260	3	6/03
Skirmish Line, The	12x16"	Sea	$140	4	3/96
Skirmish Line, The	16x20"	Sea	$130	3	3/96
Skirmish Line, The	11x14"	Sea	$75	3	3/96
Skirmish Line, The	16x20"	Sea	$175	3	7/96
Small Handled Tray	3x4"	Tray	$70	4	4/95
Snow Basin	12x14"	Ext.	$140	3	3/96
Snowbound Brook	13x16"	Snow	$90	3.75	4/95
Snowbound Brook	13x16"	Snow	$145	3.5	11/03
Snowbound Brook	14x17"	Snow	$110	3	11/95
Song Trees	12x15"	Ext.	$44	4	11/95
Spent Wave, The	8x14"	Misc. Un.	$44	4	10/94
Spring Delights	13x16"	Sheep	$130	4	4/95
Spring Delights	8x12"	Sheep	$45	4	4/95
Spring Invitation, A	13x16"	Ext.	$10	4	9/03
Spring Symphony, A	13x16"	Ext.	$60	4	10/95
Spring Thoughts	13x17"	Ext.	$39	4	9/96
Steps to Glory	13x16"	Ext.	$52	4	11/95
Summer Dream, A	9x16"	Ext.	$30	3	3/96
Sunset Point	10x12"	Ext.	$17	4	11/95
Sunset Point	10x12"	Ext.	$60	4	10/96
Sunset Point	12x16"	Process	$19	4	9/96
Sunset Point	6x8"	Ext.	$35	3	11/03
Sunset Point	7x9"	Ext.	$35	4	12/96
Sunset Point — process print	12x16"	Process	$5	4	3/96
Sunset Point — process print	12x16"	Process	$14	4	10/94
Thoughtful Hostess, A	13x16"	Int.	$72	5	10/94
Three Arched Mohawk Trail	10x12"	Ext.	$50	4	10/94
To the Beach	13x16"	Ext.	$36	3	11/95
Treasure Scarf	13x16"	Int.	$39	4	10/94
Treasure Scarf, The	12x16"	Int.	$30	5	3/03
Treasured Scarf	10x12"	Int.	$52	4	11/95
Tribute to Raphael, A	13x16"	Int.	$70	4	11/03

Tribute to Raphael, A	5x7"	Int.	$65	4	11/00
Trio, The	10x12"	Geese	$143	3.5	10/94
Tulip Aisle	8x10"	Ext.	$35	4	7/95
Tumult, The	13x16"	Sea	$40	3.5	9/03
Untitled Seascape	10x12"	Sea	$45	4	3/97
Vanity	13x16"	Int.	$70	3	3/97
Vanity	14x17"	Int.	$35	4	3/03
Vanity	5x10"	Int.	$55	4	9/96
Village Maiden, The	13x15"	Misc. Un.	$66	3.75	10/94
Village Maiden, The	13x16"	Misc. Un.	$125	4	8/96
Village Prattlers, The	11x14"	Misc. Un.	$130	4	3/03
Village Prattlers, The	13x16"	Misc. Un.	$160	4	3/97
Welcome Guest	4x5"	Misc. Un.	$30	3	3/03
Welcome Guest	8x14"	Misc. Un.	$39	3	11/95
White Mountains	12x16"	Ext.	$14	4	11/95
Wisteria	13x16"	Misc. Un.	$85	4	3/96
Wisteria	14x17"	Ext.	$90	4	11/03
Wisteria	14x17"	Misc. Un.	$175	4	11/00
Wisteria	9x16"	Misc. Un.	$60	3	3/96
Woodland Magic	12x15"	Ext.	$30	3.75	3/96
Woods in Spring	12x15"	Ext.	$85	5	4/95
Ye Olden Tyme	13x16"	Interior	$80	4.5	9/03

A Merry Blossom. Est. Value: $110.

A Puritan Lady. Est. Value: $115.

Berkshire Sunset. Est. Value: $75.

An Old Spanish Sugar Mill. Est. Value: $231.

Christmas Eve. Est. Value: $308.

Diadem Aisle. Est. Value: $110.

Driving Home the Cows. Est. Value: $187.

Dorothy Perkins. Est. Value: $135.

Feathery Aisle. Est. Value: $65.

Life Long Friends. Est. Value: $55.

Grandmother's Garden. Est. Value: $200.

In the Making, est. value: $105, shown on page 183.

Old Ironsides. Est. Value: $170.

Porch Beautiful.
Est. Value: $165.

Rambler Rose. Est. Value: $121.

Snow Basin. Est. Value: $140.

Snowbound Brook. Est. Value: $125.

The Heirloom. Est. Value: $125.

The Lamb's May Feast. Est. Value: $100.

The Seine Reel. Est. Value: $225.

The Last Load. Est. Value: $275.

The Skirmish Line. Est. Value: $175.

Vanity. Est. Value: $160.

Wisteria. Est. Value: $100.

Ye Olden Tyme. Est. Value: $280.

Prize Pewter. Est. Value: $95.

Alphabetical and Numerical Index to David Davidson Pictures

The following represents basically all of the nearly 1,000 David Davidson titles that we have been able to compile to date. Most have been gathered from Davidson salesman's picture catalogs, or from titles we have either seen in our travels or sold through our auctions, and represent most of his known titles as of 1930. Please note that this serves as a cross-referencing guide, with the entire left column listing the picture titles alphabetically (with corresponding studio numbers), whereas the entire right column lists the studio numbers in numerical order (with corresponding titles).

Chapter 9

Sawyer Pictures

Charles Henry Sawyer
(Courtesy of Carol Begley Gray)

Harold Boardman Sawyer
(Courtesy of Carol Begley Gray)

Sawyer's Mt. Washington

"...Sawyer pictures are known throughout New England..."

An Introduction to Sawyer Pictures

It was said that the hand-colored photographs of Charles H. Sawyer did more to publicize the beautiful New England scenery than all New Hampshire state promotional materials and resort hotel literature combined. That statement may very well be true because the Sawyer Picture Company operated significantly longer than the businesses of Wallace Nutting, David Davidson, or Fred Thompson.

Charles H. Sawyer formed the Sawyer Picture Company in 1903, beginning in his family home of Norridgewock, Maine. Prior to that he had been a crayon portrait artist in, of all places, Providence, Rhode Island — the lifelong home of David Davidson, and the home of Wallace Nutting between 1894 and 1904.

After a short stay there, he moved to Farmington, Maine, in 1904, where he did much of his earlier work.

During the earliest years of the business, Charles Sawyer did all of the work himself. He was not only the photographer, but the dark room man, colorist, framer, and salesman. As he expanded over the next several years, he began adding to staff.

Echo Lake, Sawyer's bestselling and most famous picture

By 1912, business had grown to where he needed new and different views to increase the size of his picture inventory. Thanks in part to the recently invented automobile, Sawyer began traveling to the White Mountains of New Hampshire. By 1915 he had photographed such famous White Mountain locations as Franconia Notch, The Flume, The Old Man in the Mountains, and perhaps his most famous, Echo Lake. With his business continuing to grow over the next several years, in 1920 Sawyer decided to move to larger quarters in Concord, New Hampshire. This not only moved him closer to his primary source of pictures, the White Mountains, but also closer to the large and commercially important Boston market.

Also in 1920, Sawyer hired Gladys Towle, a colorist who eventually worked with him for over the next 50 years. In order to ease the transition from Maine to New Hampshire, Sawyer had temporarily brought several colorists with him from Farmington to help train his new colorists in Concord. It was the Farmington colorists that initially trained Gladys Towle.

The peak period for the Sawyer Art Company seems to have been during the 1920s. At this time he had a staff of 11 colorists, along with an additional staff of framers, dark room men, and associated office personnel. In the earlier and later years, Sawyer's staff was considerably smaller.

Just as we have been able to establish a definite connection between Wallace Nutting, David Davidson, and Fred Thompson, we have also found that Charles Sawyer had actually worked with Nutting for about one year. Although we have been unable to determine the exact date, it would appear that Sawyer possibly worked for Nutting around 1902 – 03, while in Providence, and before he went into business for himself.

Sawyer's The Original Dennison Plant at Brunswick, Maine

Nutting's Original Dennison Plant, Brunswick, Maine

One early Nutting Maine picture was entitled *Original Dennison Plant, Brunswick, Maine.* Sawyer was also selling the exact same picture, with a slightly different title. One story had it that Sawyer stole the negative while he was working for Nutting and took it with him when he struck out on his own. Knowing Nutting's tendency to sue through the courts when he felt he was wronged (e.g., the pirated prints), I doubt that Nutting would have let someone steal one of his pictures, commercially market it, and get away with it.

Another story had it that Sawyer took the Dennison Plant picture while working for Nutting and sold it under the Nutting name while employed by Nutting. Then, when he left, Sawyer was allowed to take all of his own negatives with him, along with the right to continue marketing them.

Whatever the correct story, there is no doubt that both Nutting and Sawyer were marketing the same picture with slightly different titles. And to complicate matters further with this title, we have also seen this Dennison Plant title sold over the David Davidson signature as well.

Sawyer also marketed various other pictures that looked remarkably similar to Nutting's. For example, we have seen this Sawyer exterior scene which looks almost exactly like one of Nutting's bestselling New Hampshire exterior scenes, *A Little River.*

However, despite certain similarities in styles, subject matter, and titles, we have never seen anything to contradict the belief that Nutting and Sawyer were anything more than friendly competitors.

A Sawyer San Juan Capistrano California scene

Close-framed Sawyer exterior scene

Nutting's A Little River

Sawyer's Lake Louise, Canadian Rockies

In later years, Charles H. Sawyer was joined by his son, Harold B. Sawyer, who continued to oper-

Portland Head Light on the Maine seacoast

Groveton Birches, a Sawyer lacquered print, framed without glass

ate the business. They frequently traveled together, taking pictures throughout New England, New York, California, Washington State, and several national parks in the American West and Canadian Rockies.

Sawyer used a similar process to Nutting's in the early years, but altered it in later years as styles and tastes changed. Platinum paper was eventually replaced by substitute paper called *Satista*, which contained mostly silver and very little platinum. Subsequently that was replaced by a gelatine-coated paper made by Eastman & Defender. Coloring grew significantly brighter in later years.

Sawyer Collecting Tip:
Sawyer pictures have a distinctive coloring, which accentuate the oranges and browns.

It is important to note that the Sawyers focused almost exclusively on exterior scenes. In nearly 20 years of buying, selling, and seeking out Sawyer pictures, we have only seen one colonial interior title, *Pilgrim Mothers*, and we have only seen several examples of that particular title, indicating to us that Sawyer sold very few interior scenes.

Sawyer Collecting Tip:
Sawyer interior scenes are extremely rare and are especially desirable to Sawyer collectors. The only Sawyer interior scene we have seen is *Pilgrim Mothers* which features two ladies sitting near a fire.

By the 1950s, White Mountain pictures were still being sold to tourists by the Sawyer Art Company. The early matted, hand-colored platinum pictures, mounted under glass, were replaced by colored pictures which were covered with a special lacquer, and framed without glass.

Sawyer Collecting Tip:
Sawyer lacquered pictures, without glass, are later pictures dating from the 1950s to the 1970s and are not very popular with collectors.

The primary outlets for Sawyer pictures were gift shops, hotels, stationary, and jewelry stores — in that order. The gift shops and hotels were primarily seasonal, catering to the tourist trade. The stationary and jewelry stores were year-round, with local New Hampshire residents the primary customers. Pretty much anyone having a birthday, shower, wedding, or other special event was a prime candidate to receive a Sawyer picture as a gift.

Miniature prints (top: Echo Lake; bottom: Mt. Lafayette)

Triple White Mountain grouping

Assorted Sawyer tourist novelty items, including a mirror, miniature triple grouping, greeting cards, and an Echo Lake wooden trivet

Because the Sawyer Pictures Company catered to the increasing White Mountain area tourist trade, they developed a series of items designed to appeal exclusively to them. Greeting cards, mirrors, calendars, miniature picture postcard packs, even wooden trivets, all focusing upon a beautiful Sawyer White Mountains picture were produced.

Sawyer Collecting Tip:
Although Sawyer pictures are popular in most areas, New Hampshire is the heart of Sawyer pictures and is where Sawyer pictures are currently the hottest.

The Sawyer Pictures Company finally closed its doors in the 1970s, after nearly 70 years of selling its hand-colored pictures to the American public. Gladys Trowle passed away in 1997.

The Collecting Cycle of Sawyer Pictures

Phase I. Initial Production and Peak Period: Initially sold between 1904 and the 1970s, Sawyer pictures were sold longer than any other hand-colored photographs. Like the other photographers, the peak period for Sawyer pictures was 1915 – 1930.

Phase II. Gradual Market Decline: With the stock market crash of 1929 and the onset of the Depression, picture sales were significantly diminished. Although the business remained in operation until the late 1970s, sales never regained their original height of the 1915 – 1930 period.

Phase III. Renewed Collectibility: By the mid–late 1970s, collectors began rediscovering Sawyer pictures. Collectors of Wallace Nutting pictures also sought out Sawyer pictures because of their similarity in style, subject matter, and price.

Phase IV. Current Market: As the price of Wallace Nutting pictures has soared over the past 10 years, an increasing number of collectors have shifted their search to Sawyer pictures, making them either the primary or exclusive focus of their collection. With the 1995 publication of Carol Gray's excellent book, *The History of the Sawyer Pictures*, awareness in Sawyer pictures increased and prices have shot up, especially in New Hampshire. However, the number of collectors specializing in Sawyer pictures is significantly lower than Wallace Nutting, although this number is on the rise.

Sawyer Pictures: What Are They?
Hand-Colored Photographs:
Sawyer pictures are hand-colored black and white photographs. All colors were hand-applied by individual Sawyer colorists.

Lacquered Prints:
Lacquered pictures which are framed without glass, are also hand colored, although they date from the 1950s – 1970s era. There is minimal interest in lacquered prints by collectors.

Novelty Items:
Sawyer also produced a series of novelty-type items which included calendars, greeting cards, small mirrors, photo packs, wooden trivets, and other assorted items, all of which featured a Sawyer hand-colored or black and white picture. These are quite desirable and highly sought after by Sawyer collectors.

We have never seen any Sawyer process or facsimile prints.

Reproduction Alert
At the time this book went to press, we were unaware of any hand-colored Sawyer pictures being reproduced.

However, in recent years we have seen an increasing number of original Sawyer pictures which have been either remounted and re-signed, or signed on the picture in white ink (note that 99% of white ink signatures are authentic, however we have seen a limited number of recently signed pictures with newer white ink applied). Apparently a significant volume of loose, unmounted, and unframed Sawyer pictures came into the market during the mid-1990s. As these loose pictures have become dispersed through Sawyer collectors and the antique trade, certain individuals have starting remounting, re-signing, and framing some of these pictures, frequently signing the matting with a signature that looks very much like the authentic Sawyer signature. Sometimes these pictures are sold as being re-signed; sometimes no mention is made of the recently applied signature. This is not a major widespread problem but it is something you should be aware of. We have also seen some black and white Sawyer reproductions recently, usually of rarer scenes, which apparently were reproduced from original Sawyer glass negatives. We know of some antique dealers who unknowingly purchased them as original.

Sawyer Collecting Tip:

Beware that there are some original Sawyer pictures which have been remounted and re-signed. This is not a major problem, but it is something that collectors should be aware of.

Identifying and Dating Sawyer Pictures

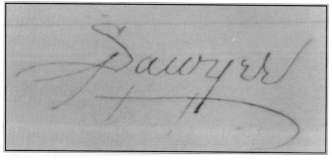

A Sawyer pencil signature

Unlike Wallace Nutting pictures which had many different signature styles, most Sawyer pictures will bear a consistent and distinctive Sawyer signature. Earlier pictures were signed in pencil, later pictures in pen. Like Wallace Nutting pictures, Sawyer pictures were mounted upon a light colored matting, titled lower-left, and signed lower right, below the picture, and within an indented platemark.

An early Sawyer picture with a colored border

In addition to the pencil signatures, the earliest Sawyer pictures were mounted upon a colored paper, which provided a ¼" border around the entire picture, which was then mounted upon a non-indented mat. The title and signature were applied to the matting below the picture border. These pictures are usually considered to be early pre-1910 Farmington, Maine, pictures.

A Sawyer white ink signature, applied directly to the picture

Sawyer also sold a fair number of close-framed pictures, without a mat, which were signed in white ink directly upon the picture. Close-framed pictures are usually later, dating 1925 or later.

Most Sawyer pictures originally included a Sawyer identification label on the backing. However, as time goes on and the backing paper becomes increasingly brittle, more and more labels are being lost as the backings are removed or fall off of pictures. On a few occasions we have seen labels which related to specific picture titles. Newfound Lake and Lake Louise, Canadian Rockies, are two specific examples. These picture specific labels are quite unusual and can increase the value of certain pictures by 10 – 15%.

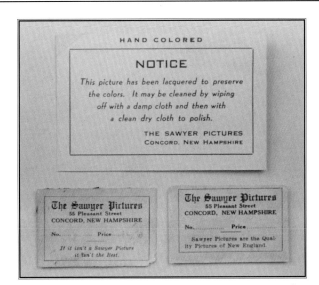

Assorted Sawyer backing labels. Top: Lacquered picture label (1950s – 1970s); bottom: early 1910 – 1920 picture labels, each with a different sales tag line.

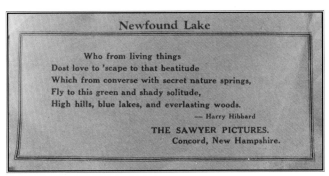

1920s – 1930s Sawyer backing label

Sawyer picture label, offering sales copy for a specific picture

Sawyer Collecting Tip:

As the paper backing on Sawyer pictures becomes increasing brittle, damaged, and lost, original Sawyer backing labels are becoming increasingly scarce. A Sawyer backing label can sometimes add 5 – 10% to the value of a picture.

Sawyer Collecting Tip:

Picture specific labels are quite rare and can add 10 – 15% to the value of a picture.

Subject Matter of Sawyer Pictures

Exterior Scenes: The most common type of Sawyer pictures, with the vast majority of Sawyer pictures being taken in New Hampshire and northern New England.

Interior Scenes: We are only aware of one Sawyer interior scene, *Pilgrim Mothers*, of which we have only seen on several occasions.

Foreign Scenes: Aside from a limited few pictures taken in the Canadian Rockies, we are aware of no Sawyer foreign pictures.

Miscellaneous Unusual Scenes: As with the other photographers, these represent some of Sawyer's most desirable pictures. Seascapes, snow scenes, and pictures with animals are all quite desirable. Aside from a relatively few titles, Sawyer pictures rarely include people.

Some of the More Commonly Found Sawyer Pictures

The following titles and classifications represent some of the most common Sawyer pictures. This does not mean that they are not desirable to collectors, but rather that they were originally sold in larger numbers and are more commonly found today.

* *Echo Lake*, far and away the most common of all Sawyer pictures
* *Echo Lake, Franconia Notch*, very common
* *Mount Chocoroa*, there are five different Mt. Chocoroa scenes
* *The Old Man of the Mountain*, again, very common
* *Surf at Pinnacle Rock*, a seascape
* *Which Way?*, the only Sawyer title ending with a question mark
* *To Join the Brimming Water*, common exterior
* Smaller 5x7" and 7x9" exterior scenes

Some of the More Highly Sought-After Sawyer Pictures

The following represent some of the rarer and more highly sought-after Sawyer pictures or categories of Sawyer pictures, in no particular order. All, in very good to excellent condition, are very desirable to most Sawyer collectors.

* *The Sea*, a rare picture featuring a close-up of a sea gull
* *Pilgrim Mothers*, he only Sawyer interior scene we are aware of
* *Joseph Lincoln's Garden, Cape Cod*, colorful garden
* *A Rock Garden, Cape Cod*, colorful garden
* *Among New England Hills*
* *A New England Sugar Birth*, snow and oxen
* *Sugar Hill Drive*
* *The Last Load*, rare oxen
* Many early Farmington, Maine, pictures with a pencil signature and a colored border around the picture

Alphabetical Index to Sawyer Pictures

The best alphabetical listing for Sawyer picture titles would include the Sawyer Price List which concludes this chapter, and the titles found in Carol Begley Gray's *The History of the Sawyer Pictures* book.

Sawyer Collectors' Club

There is presently no collectors' club devoted exclusively to Sawyer pictures. However, the Wallace Nutting Collectors' Club would be the best place to go for further information on Sawyer pictures. You can obtain the address of this club from the author.

Sawyer Books and Reference Material

Gray, Carol Begley. *The History of The Sawyer Pictures*. 1995.

Sawyer on the Internet

Information on Sawyer and other early twentieth century hand-colored photographers can be found in the Wallace Nutting-like Photographers section of The Wallace Nutting Gallery Internet web site at www.wnutting.com.

Where to Go If Looking to Buy or Sell Sawyer Pictures

There are various dealers around the country who specialize in hand-colored photographs of the early twentieth century, including Sawyer.

One obvious reference source would be Michael Ivankovich. Another would be Carol Gray, author of *The History of the Sawyer Pictures* book. Most others belong to the Wallace Nutting Collectors' Club.

The generally recognized center of Sawyer activity would be Michael Ivankovich's Wallace Nutting-like Photographers catalog auctions. Held two times per year, generally in the northeastern portion of the country, these auctions provide both collectors and dealers the opportunity to compete for the largest variety of Nutting-like pictures, including many Sawyer pictures, available anywhere in the country. These auctions also give sellers the opportunity to place their items in front of the country's leading Sawyer collectors and enthusiasts.

Summary of Key Collecting Points

* There were actually two Sawyers, Charles H. Sawyer, the father, and Harold B. Sawyer, the son.
* Most Sawyer pictures were taken in New Hampshire, although the earliest pictures were taken in Maine.
* Sawyer briefly worked with Wallace Nutting, circa 1903, in Farmington, Maine.
* Sawyer's bestselling pictures were *Echo Lake* and *Echo Lake, Franconia Notch*, both from the White Mountains of New Hampshire.
* Sawyer interiors are extremely rare, with only one known.
* Lacquered prints with no glass were still sold in the 1960s – 70s and are not very desirable to collectors.
* Sawyer pictures are presently the hottest in New England.
* Sawyer pictures were signed both in pencil and pen.
* An original label can sometimes add 10 – 15% to the value of the picture.
* There are a limited number of Sawyer pictures that have been recently re-signed, which greatly decreases the value.

Sawyer Pictures Value Guide

The values listed in this chapter are derived from many different sources, including:

* Michael Ivankovich Auction Company auctions

* Other auction houses
* Retail and mail order sales
* Prices observed at antique shows, flea markets, and individual and group antique shops throughout the northeast
* Assorted other reliable sources

Most prices included here represent prices actually paid. In some instances where we were unable to ascertain the final sale price, we have included the dealer asking price if we felt that it was appropriately priced and fell within the acceptable ranges. The sampling of items in this chapter includes titles seen by us, sold by us, or reported to us. Obviously not all titles are included here. This chapter is only intended to provide you with a representative sampling of titles and prices in order to help you to establish a ballpark price on most Sawyer pictures.

Title	Size	Type	Price	Rating	Date
Afterglow, The	13x16"	Ext.	$70	4	3/97
Afterglow, The	11x14"	Ext.	$50	4	3/03
Advertising Sign	8x12"	Misc.	$61	4.5	9/96
Advertising Sign	8x12"	Misc.	$125	4	11/96
Along the Deerfield					
River	8x10"	Ext.	$70	4	7/01
Among the Frost					
Flowers	11x13"	Ext.	$41	3.5	11/95
Among the New					
England Hills	8x15"	Misc. Un.	$61	3.5	10/94
Among the New					
England Hills	10x16"	Misc. Un.	$95	4	2/97
Apple Blossom Lane	13x16"	Sawyer	$120	4	9/03
At the Bend of					
the Road	8x10"	Ext.	$65	4	7/01
At the Water's Edge	15x20"	Ext.	$121	4	9/96
Ausable Chasm	11x14"	Ext.	$85	4	4/97
Ausable Chasm	6x8"	Ext.	$105	4	11/00
Ausable Chasm	8x10"	Ext.	$65	4	4/01
Ausable Chasm	13x16"	Ext.	$140	4	3/03
Autumnal Glory	8x10"	Ext.	$65	4	8/01
Autumnal Glory	13x16"	Ext.	$70	4	11/03
Back Cove,					
Pennaquid	10x13"	Misc. Un.	$70	4	8/01
Beside Still Water	10x16"	Misc. Un.	$110	4	6/01
Beside Still Water	7x9"	Misc. Un.	$75	4	3/97
Beside Still Water	13x16"	Misc. Un.	$125	4	3/96
Breaking on the					
Rocks	9x11"	Sea	$39	3.5	11/95

Bridge of Flowers	10x13"	Misc Un.	$90	4	11/03
Bridge of Flowers Pin		Misc	$220	4	
Bridge of Gold, A	10x12"	Sea	$75	4	10/00
Camel's Hump	13x16"	Ext.	$60	4	11/03
Camel's Hump on					
Winooski	8x10"	Ext.	$60	4	5/96
Camel's Hump in					
Winooski	13x16"	Ext.	$125	4	1/97
Canaan Valley Brook	13x16"	Ext.	$55	4	3/96
Canadian Rockies	13x22"	Misc. Un.	$308	4.5	9/96
Cathedral in the					
Pines	8x10"	Ext.	$6	4	11/95
Cathedral Spires-					
Yosemite	13x16"	Ext.	$80	3.5	3/96
Cathedral Woods,					
Intervale	14x16"	Ext.	$94	3.5	9/96
Chapel, San Juan					
Capistrano	13x16"	Misc. Un.	$140	4	3/96
Cloisters San Juan					
Capistrano	16x20"	Misc. Un.	$120	4	3/01
Close-framed Echo					
Lake	10x13"	Ext.	$15	2	4/95
Close-framed ext.	8x10"	Ext.	$30	4	3/97
Close-framed ext.	9x12"	Ext.	$72	4	9/96
Close-framed ext.	10x13"	Ext.	$22	4	10/94
Close-framed ext.	8x10"	Ext.	$33	3.5	9/96
Close-framed ext.	7x9"	Ext.	$17	4	11/95
Close-framed ext.	10x24"	Ext.	$25	4	3/96
Close-framed ext.	9x14"	Ext.	$39	4	9/96
Close-framed rocky					
stream	8x10"	Ext.	$22	4	10/94
Close-framed sea.	11x14"	Sea	$40	3	3/97
Close-framed					
"Flume Bridge"	4x"6	Ext.	$22	4	11/95
Cypress Point	11x14"	Sea	$140	4	3/03
Cypress Point	13x16"	Sea	$175	4	2/97
Cypress Rocks	11x14"	Sea	$90	4	10/96
Dublin Lake, Mt.					
Monadnock, A	10x13"	Ext.	$39	4	9/96
Echo Lake	10x13"	Ext.	$90	4	11/03
Echo Lake	8x10"	Ext.	$35	4	1/97
Echo Lake	7x9"	Ext.	$45	4	7/97
Echo Lake	13x16"	Ext.	$85	3.5	11/96
Echo Lake	11x14"	Ext.	$75	4	12/96
Echo Lake	4x5"	Mini.	$40	4	4/95
Echo Lake,					
Franconia Notch	14x17"	Ext.	$80	4	11/03
Echo Lake,					
Franconia Notch	13x16"	Ext.	$125	4.5	12/96
Echo Lake,					
Franconia Notch	11x14"	Ext.	$95	4	9/96

Title	Size	Type	Price		Date
Echo Lake, Franconia Notch	8x10"	Ext.	$75	4	2/01
Elephant's Head	13x16"	Ext.	$85	4	7/96
Elephant's Head	7x9"	Ext.	$60	4	3/01
Everlasting Hills, The	10x15"	Ext.	$121	4	9/96
February Morning, A	13x16"	Snow	$160	4	3/03
Flume Falls	11x14"	Ext.	$85	4	9/96
Flume Falls	8x10"	Ext.	$45	3.5	12/96
Flume Falls, Franconia Notch	9x12"	Ext.	$44	3.5	11/95
Flume, The	11x14"	Ext.	$45	4	11/03
Flume, The	13x16"	Ext.	$85	4	2/97
Flume, The	8x10"	Ext.	$50	4	10/96
Flume, The	4x5"	Mini.	$60	4	12/00
Gateway to the Adirondacks	13x20"	Ext.	$140	4	3/96
Glimpse of the Sea, A	13x15"	Ext.	$61	4	11/95
Greeting card- Nubble Light	4x5"	Misc.	$50	5	9/96
Greeting card-ext.	4x5"	Misc.	$39	4	9/96
Greeting card-ext.	4x5"	Misc.	$50	3.5	9/96
Greeting card - Dixville Notch	4x5"	Card	$65	4	12/00
Greeting card - Mt. Washington	4x5"	Card	$65	4	12/00
Housatonic River, Lover's Leap	13x16"	Ext.	$88	4	9/96
In the Intervale	7x11"	Sheep	$52	4	11/95
Indian Summer	12x20"	Ext.	$125	4	11/00
Joseph Lincoln's Garden	16x20"	Misc. Un.	$230	5	6/03
Joseph Lincoln's Garden	13x16"	Misc. Un.	$135	4	3/97
Kimball's Castle, Lake Winnip.	10x16"	Misc. Un.	$110	3	9/96
Lafayette Slides	13x15"	Ext.	$80	4	3/96
Lafayette Slides	8x10"	Ext.	$40	4	11/96
Lake Champlain	9x15"	Misc. Un.	$160	4	4/95
Lake Champlain	8x10"	Misc. Un.	$85	4	9/96
Lake Louise	10x13"	Snow	$135	4	11/03
Lake Mohonk	11x14"	Ext.	$132	3.5	9/96
Lake Placid	12x16"	Ext.	$100	4	3/96
Ledges, Ilion Gorge	13x16"	Ext.	$75	4	3/96
Lonesome Lake, Franconia, NH	13x22"	Ext.	$176	4.5	9/96
Majestic Nature	12x14"	Ext.	$55	4	3/97
Melody	10x12"	Ext.	$80	3	9/01
Moonlight Lake George	16x20"	Ext.	$95	4	3/96
Mount Chocoroa	8x10"	Ext.	$110	4	9/01
Mount Chocoroa	7x9"	Ext.	$65	4	3/01
Mount Chocoroa	10x12"	Ext.	$65	4	11/96
Mount Chocoroa	13x16"	Ext.	$135	4	12/96
Mount Ranier	10x13"	Snow	$125	4	11/96
Mt. Abram & the Sandy River	12x16"	Ext.	$60	4	12/00
Mt. Chocorua, NH	4x6"	Ext.	$45	4	11/01
Mt. Chocorua	11x14"	Ext.	$75	3.5	1/97
Mt. Chocorua	8x10"	Ext.	$60	4	4/01
Mt. Chocorua	7x9"	Ext.	$45	4	7/96
Mt. Chocorua	13x16"	Ext.	$135	4	11/96
Mt. Lafayette	4x5"	Mini.	$80	4	3/03
Mt. Lafayette & Gale River	10x12"	Ext.	$35	3	4/95
Mt. Lafayette & Gale River	7x9"	Ext.	$45	4	12/96
Mt. Washington	8x10"	Ext.	$35	4	11/03
Mt. Washington	13x16"	Ext.	$125	4	9/96
Mt. Washington	4x5"	Mini.	$45	4	3/97
Mt. Washington & the Saco River	11x15"	Ext.	$85	4	3/96
Mt. Washington and the Ammonpossic River	8x10"	Ext.	$70	4	8/01
Newfound Lake	10x13"	Ext.	$75	4.5	3/97
Newfound Lake-mini.	4x5"	Ext.	$55	4	7/97
New England Sugar Birth, A	16x20"	Oxen	$300	3	3/97
Notecard	4x6"	Misc.	$65	4	4/95
Nubble Light-mini.	4x5"	Sea	$75	4	4/95
Nubble Light, York	12x20"	Sea	$121	4.5	11/95
N.H. Franconia Lonesome Lake	7x14"	Ext.	$61	4.5	9/96
October's Golden Harvest	10x14"	Misc. Un.	$210	3	4/95
Old Man of the Mountains.	4x5"	Mini.	$38	4	3/97
Old Man of the Mountains	7x9"	Ext.	$270	4	9/03
Old Man of the Mountains	8x10"	Ext.	$55	4	7/97
Old Man of the Mountains	13x16"	Ext.	$90	4	7/97
Old Man of the Mountains, The	11x14"	Ext.	$260	4.5	6/03
Old Man of the Mountains, The	5x7"	Ext.	$25	4	1/97
Old Montgomery Bridge	8x10"	Misc. Un.	$132	5	9/96
Original Dennison Plant	13x16"	Misc. Un.	$100	4	3/97
Overlooking Dixville Notch	13x16"	Ext.	$77	4	11/95

Philbrook Farm	10x17"	Misc. Un.	$53	3	3/96
Pool, The	10x12"	Ext.	$80	4	10/01
Pool, Ausable Chasm, The	6x8"	Ext.	$40	4	9/96
Pool, Ausable Chasm, The	8x10"	Ext.	$55	3.5	12/96
Pool, Ausable Chasm, The	13x16"	Ext.	$95	4	1/97
Pulpit Rock	7x8"	Sea	$35	3	4/95
Rainbow Falls	7x9"	Ext.	$30	3	11/03
Ramona's Garden	7x9"	Misc. Un.	$120	5	3/96
Receipt, Sawyer Business (framed)	8x10"	Misc.	$22	4	9/96
Rock Garden, Cape Cod, A	10x13"	Misc. Un.	$250	3.5	3/01
Rock Garden, Cape Cod, A	16x20"	Misc. Un.	$275	4.5	1/97
San Gabriel Mission	15x19"	Misc. Un.	$154	5	9/96
San Juan Capistrano Chapel	7x9"	Misc. Un.	$40	3.75	4/95
San Juan, Capistrano Mission	4x6"	Misc. Un.	$200	4	11/03
San Juan, Capistrano Mission	16x20"	Misc. Un.	$165	4	7/97
Sap Time	13x16"	Ext.	$110	3	9/96
Sea Gull, The	11x14"	Sea	$220	3.75	10/94
Silver Birches	10x16"	Ext.	$120	4	11/03
Silvery Spray	14x17"	Sea	$88	3	11/95
Spring's Greeting	6x10"	Ext.	$50	3	9/96
Storm King Highway	16x20"	Ext.	$100	4	3/03
Storm King Highway	11x14"	Ext.	$65	4	7/97
Storm King Highway at the Highlands	13x16"	Ext.	$80	5	4/95
Summer Greeting	7x9"	Ext.	$55	4	11/95
Sunset on the Kennebec	10x16"	Ext.	$160	4	11/03
Sunset on the Kennebec	12x20"	Ext.	$175	4.5	7/97
Surf at Pinnacle Rock	13x20"	Sea	$80	3.5	3/96
Surf at Pinnacle Rock	13x16"	Sea	$150	4	9/96
Surf at Pinnacle Rock	7x9"	Sea	$85	4	3/01
Thru the Birch Woods	17x21"	Ext.	$40	3.5	4/95
Thru the Birch Woods	13x16"	Ext.	$75	4	11/96
Thru the Birches	11x18"	Ext.	$75	4	7/01
To Join the Brimming River	13x16"	Ext.	$66	4	9/96
To Join the Brimming River	7x9"	Ext.	$35	4	11/96
Tumbledown Mt. & Webb Lake	8x10"	Ext.	$28	5	9/96
Untitled Canoe	7x9"	Ext.	$36	3	11/95
Untitled Church	7x9"	Misc. Un.	$66	4	11/95
Untitled ext.-Birches	7x11"	Ext.	$35	4	3/97
Untitled ext.-Blossoms	7x9"	Ext.	$25	4	4/95
Untitled ext.-Stream	5x7"	Ext.	$25	4	4/95
Waramaug Lake	8x15"	Ext.	$45	3.5	4/95
Which Way?	13x16"	Ext.	$70	4	11/03
Wizard Island, Crater Lake	13x16"	Ext.	$165	4.5	9/96
Wooden Trivet, Echo Lake	6x6"	Misc.	$83	5	11/95

A February Morning. Est. Value: $175.

A New England Sugar Birth. Est. Value: $300.

A Rock Garden, Cape Cod. Est. Value: $275.

Among the New England Hills. Est. Value: $275.

Cathedral Spires, Yosemite. Est. Value: $250.

Cypress Rocks. Est. Value: $150.

Elephant's Head. Est. Value: $85.

Lake Champlain. Est. Value: $160.

Majestic Nature. Est. Value: $55.

Moonlight Lake George. Est. Value: $95.

Mount Rainier. Est. Value: $275.

Nubble Light. Est. Value: $75.

October's Golden Harvest. Est. Value: $210.

Overlooking Dixville Notch. Est. Value: $175.

San Juan Capistrano. Est. Value: $165.

Silver Birches. Est. Value: $85.

Storm King at the Highlands. Est. Value: $80.

Surf at Pinnacle Rock. Est. Value: $150.

The Afterglow. Est. Value: $85.

The Sea Gull. Est. Value: $220.

Chapter 10

Fred Thompson (1844 – 1923)

Frederick H. Thompson (1844 – 1923) . . . the only known photo

Lombardy Poplar, one of Thompson's most popular exterior scenes

"…If you vacationed in Maine after the turn of the century, you probably took home a Fred Thompson picture…"

An Introduction to Fred Thompson Pictures

Frederick H. Thompson was another of New England's most popular photographers in the early 1900s. Born on Stevens Avenue in Deering Center, Maine (known today as Westbrook), on March 17, 1844, Frederick H. Thompson was 17 years older than Wallace Nutting.

The son of the Reverend Zenas and Leonora Thompson, he attended local schools, including Bethel Academy, where his father also preached. Frederick H. Thompson had been married for many years, although we were unable to learn his wife's name. She died in 1904 of unknown causes.

Like Wallace Nutting, Frederick H. Thompson was a versatile businessman. In 1888 he became a member of Zenas Thompson and Brother, a manufacturer of carriages in Portland, Maine. Zenas was his brother, not his father, as he did have an older brother by that name.

Their original carriage factory was located on Union Street in Portland but was destroyed by fire and later moved to Elm Street, also in Portland. This firm was sold in 1906, presumably due to competition from the growing automobile trade.

In 1907, he purchased the Daisy Lunch Room in Portland, a small local restaurant, and changed its name to Thompson Spa.

Frederick H. Thompson was also an avid amateur photographer and soon became a prominent member of both the Portland Camera Club and the Portland Society of Natural History. Like Wallace Nutting, his hobby soon became an overwhelming compulsion and eventually turned into a business.

Somewhere around 1908, Frederick H. Thompson opened the Thompson Art Company, or TACO as it was called on many of his picture labels. Using a process very similar to Wallace Nutting's, Thompson traveled throughout Maine, New Hampshire, and northern Massachusetts taking what he referred to as *nature pictures*. These consisted of blossoms, birches, mountains, streams, and whatever else in the outdoors caught his eye.

A Thompson Art Company TACO label

Thompson Collecting Tip:
"TACO" represented the abbreviated name of the Thompson Art CO.

similar in style and quality to Nutting's. Catchy titles were then applied.

There is no doubt that despite the fact that Frederick H. Thompson was significantly older than Wallace Nutting, Nutting was the innovator and Thompson was the follower. Just as we have seen a definite link between Nutting and David Davidson, there is also a connection between Nutting and Frederick H. Thompson. Although we have found nothing in writing connecting the two, it is obvious that Thompson visited Nutting on at least one occasion.

A typical Wallace Nutting interior scene, filled with quality antique furniture

A typical Fred Thompson interior scene, with minimal antique furniture

In addition to his scenic outdoor views, the Thompson Art Company also became well known for its colonial interior scenes. Using a formula similar to Nutting's, Thompson would locate the appropriate room setting, decorate it with period furniture and antique accessories, provide a female model with the typical long dress and bonnet, and photograph interior views

Thompson's Fireside Fancy Work

Nutting's An Elaborate Dinner

If you look closely at Thompson's *Fireside Fancy Work* and Nutting's *An Elaborate Dinner*, there is no doubt that both pictures were taken in the same room. Knowing that *An Elaborate Dinner* was taken in Nuttinghame, Nutting's Southbury home during the 1905 – 12 period, *Fireside Fancy Work* would seem to confirm that Thompson visited Nutting at least once and, since Nutting allowed him to shoot that picture within his home, would seem to suggest that perhaps Nutting was providing photographic guidance to Thompson. Also knowing that Nutting removed the ceiling in this room around 1907 in order to expose the beams, and knowing that Fred Thompson died in 1909, this would seem to isolate the Nutting-Thompson meeting in Southbury to the 1907 – 1909 time period.

Neath the Blossoms sheep scene

Thompson Collecting Tip:

Frederick H. Thompson collaborated with Wallace Nutting between 1907 and 1909 to improve his hand-colored photographic process.

On the whole Thompson's interior scenes, although very good when compared to other photographers of that period, never surpassed Wallace Nutting's in terms of quality of furnishings and decorative authenticity. As we said earlier, Nutting's knowledge of fine antiques and his access to them enabled him to put together room settings that far surpassed those of his contemporaries.

And, like Nutting, Thompson expanded into other miscellaneous unusual areas as well. After his picture inventory became complete with blossoms, birches, country lanes, stream, hillsides, and colonial interior scenes, Thompson began taking pictures of the Maine coastline, animals in the country, children scenes designed to appeal to a mothers, men in colonial outfits, and other miscellaneous unusual scenes.

Interior scene with child

Two Roses featuring a man

Portland Head, one of Thompson's bestselling pictures

The Old Pilot, a very rare Thompson

Brook in Doubt winter snow scene

Some subjects worked quite well for Thompson. For example, Portland Head, which features Portland's very famous seacoast lighthouse, sold very well for Thompson. During the early twentieth century the beautiful Maine coastline was a popular tourist destination and nearly anyone who visited it wanted to take home a remembrance of it, and quite often they took home a Fred Thompson picture. Some of his sheep scenes also were good sellers.

Thompson Collecting Tip:
Portland, Maine's Portland Head lighthouse was one of Thompson's most popular and bestselling pictures.

Toiler of the Sea, another very rare Thompson

Although Maine tourists loved Thompson's *Portland Head* lighthouse picture, they apparently failed to fall in love with Thompson Old Fisherman pictures. From our perspective, *The Old Pilot* and *Toiler of the Sea* represent two of Thompson's very best and most unique photographs. The subject matter was wonderful, and the clarity and detail were as good as any other hand-colored photographs we have seen. Yet, judging by the fact that these are two of the rarest Thompson pictures known, they apparently weren't very popular with Maine tourists and failed to sell many copies.

Other of Thompson's pictures did not sell very well. Just as Nutting experienced, the typical New Englander simply didn't want pictures of snow, men, cows, and horses, and someone else's children hanging on the walls of their houses. Thompson tried them, they didn't sell, and today are considered to be collector's rarities.

But Fred Thompson also pursued several different areas that were rarely sold by other photographers. One example would be close-up pictures of schooners or sailing ships. As previously mentioned, Thompson catered to the visiting Maine tourists and he learned that the photogenic tall-masted ships found in many Maine coastal ports became good sellers. They typified Maine to the tourists and many wanted such a picture to take home with them. Thompson photographed literally dozens of these sailing ships and today they are probably the most popular Thompson pictures with collectors, rarely selling for less than $100.

A sampling of Fred Thompson sailing ship pictures

Thompson Collecting Tip:
Fred Thompson pictures of sailing ships and schooners are very popular with collectors, and rarely sell for less than $100 today.

Girl sewing American flag

Spinning Days

Thompson Collecting Tip:
Hand-colored photographs featuring the American flag are fairly unusual, and Thompson seemed to sell more flag scenes than any other early twentieth century photographer.

Knitting for the Boys

Another subject that Thompson pursued was an area seemingly avoided by most other photographers: the American flag. America's 1917 – 18 participation in World War I occurred during the peak period of early twentieth century hand-colored photography and, with patriotism at a fever pitch, you would have thought that most photographers would have tried to capitalize on it. Yet aside from Thompson, few did.

Thompson miniature in thin metal frame. Probably at one time had a calendar attached below on thin ribbons.

Assorted oddities including ship, mirror, and glass paperweight

Two-handled tray with interior scene

Thompson triple exterior grouping, with Thompson stamp on backing

And still another area that Thompson pursued more so than his competitors was in the area of *oddities*. Thompson coined the term oddities to cover all his non-framed picture items, including calendars, small mirrors, tiny two-handled trays, glass paperweights, etc., each having a Fred Thompson hand-colored picture included as part of the item.

> *Thompson Collecting Tip:*
> Fred Thompson sold a variety of oddities which are highly prized by collectors today.

Thompson pictures were long regarded as some of the best pictures available and became known throughout the country, although their primary market was New England. The main marketing outlets, in addition to selling directly from the studio, were through gifts shops and department stores throughout southern and central Maine, especially along the seacoast. Fred Thompson pictures made excellent gifts and provided pleasant memories for the increasing number of vacationers traveling to Maine due to the advent of the automobile.

What may come as a surprise to many people is that Frederick H. Thompson died a sudden, tragic, and unnatural death. On November 16, 1909, he was found dead in his studio. His death was ruled a suicide as a result of his ingesting cyanide. Worry over business matters is believed to have been the cause of his suicide. He died at the age of 65.

The Thompson Art Company didn't end there, however. His son, Frederick M. Thompson, took control of the business upon his father's death and continued it until 1923. Therefore, the Fred Thompson name that appears on so many hand-colored photographs actually referred to two Fred Thompsons...Frederick H. Thompson, the father, and Frederick M.Thompson, the son.

> *Thompson Collecting Tip:*
> There were actually two Fred Thompsons. Frederick H. Thompson, the father, died in 1909. Frederick M. Thompson, the son, died in 1923.

Frederick M. Thompson had attended Tufts University and didn't enter the Thompson Art Company until shortly before his father's death. Prior to his joining the family business, Frederick M. had worked in Cuba on an engineering project.

Although he knew little about photography prior to joining it, he quickly became known as an expert in the business of nature prints. Not only did he continue selling his father's pictures, he added many new pictures to the Thompson Art Company line.

Throughout the next several years, he acquired several smaller studios in the Portland area (along with their complete line of pictures), including the Lamson Nature Print Company, the Owen Perry Company, and the Lyman Nelson Company.

Frederick M. Thompson died on November 24, 1923, at the age of 47. With his death, the doors of the Thompson Art Company were closed and no more Thompson pictures were sold.

The Collecting Cycle of Fred Thompson Pictures

Phase I. Initial Production and Peak Period: Initially sold between 1908 and 1923, the peak period for Fred Thompson pictures was 1910 – 1920. Although sales were lower than Wallace Nutting, David Davidson, and the Sawyer Picture Company, Thompson sold more hand-colored pictures than any other photographer. And when you consider that Nutting and Davidson sold pictures into the 1940s while Sawyer sold pictures into the 1970s, Thompson's sales volume was quite significant for the very limited amount of time the Thompson Art Co. was in business.

Phase II. Gradual Market Decline: With the death of Frederick M. Thompson in 1923, the Thompson Art Company came to an immediate halt.

Phase III. Renewed Collectibility: By the mid to late 1970s, collectors began rediscovering Fred Thompson pictures. Generally collectors of Wallace Nutting pictures also sought out Fred Thompson pictures because of their similarity in style, subject matter, and price.

Phase IV. Current Market: As the price of Wallace Nutting pictures has soared over the past 10 years, an increasing number of collectors have shifted their search to Fred Thompson pictures, with many individual collectors now specifically collecting Fred Thompson pictures, making them either the primary or exclusive focus of their collection. However, the number of collectors specializing in Fred Thompson is significantly lower than Wallace Nutting, although this number is on the rise.

Fred Thompson Pictures: What Are They?

Hand-colored Photographs:

Fred Thompson pictures are hand-colored black and white photographs. All colors were hand applied by individual Thompson colorists and are found in smaller numbers than Wallace Nutting, David Davidson, and Sawyer pictures.

Oddities:

Thompson also produced a series of oddities which included calendars, greeting cards, small mirrors, paperweights, handled trays, and other assorted items, all of which featured a Fred Thompson hand-colored picture.

We have never seen any Fred Thompson process prints or facsimile prints.

Reproduction Alert

At the time this book went to press, we were unaware of any Fred Thompson pictures being reproduced, faked, or forged.

Identifying and Dating Fred Thompson Pictures

Unlike Wallace Nutting pictures which had many different signature styles, most Fred Thompson pictures used only one single and distinctive pencil signature. Thompson's pictures were mounted upon a light colored matting and although some were placed upon the more common Nutting and Davidson-style matboard, most pictures were mounted upon a matting with a linen texture. Generally pictures were titled under the lower left corner, with the Fred Thompson name appearing under the lower right picture corner. The Fred Thompson signature was almost always printed with a distinctive block pencil lettering, although we have seen a very few with either a block rubber stamp lettering stamped onto the signature portion of the matting, with the signature written directly onto the picture itself, or impressed directly into the picture.

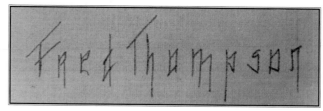

Fred Thompson signature

However, the vast majority of Fred Thompson pictures are easily identified by the distinctive Fred Thompson pencil signature directly under the lower-right corner of the picture.

Thompson Collecting Tip:
The vast majority of Thompson's pictures were signed in pencil using his distinctive block pencil signature.

Fred Thompson stamp signature

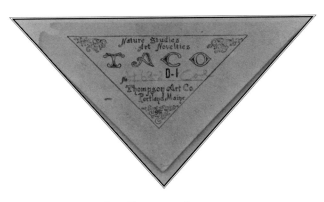

Fred Thompson backing stamps

Stamped Labels:

Often times the backing paper on a Fred Thompson picture carried a back stamp which identified the picture as a Fred Thompson. Because the paper is now old and brittle, many backs have subsequently fallen off. Those remaining original backs with the Fred Thompson/TACO stamp are therefore very desirable to collectors.

Subject Matter of Fred Thompson Pictures

Exterior Scenes: The most common form of Fred Thompson pictures—birches, blossoms, streams, etc.—were the most popular pictures, sold in the highest quantities, and are the most readily available today. Approximately 90% of all Fred Thompson pictures you will find will be exterior scenes.

Interior Scenes are fairly common. Thompson interior scenes with women dressed in colonial costumes, working around a fire, are most common. Many Thompson interiors have only a minimal amount of furniture.

Foreign and Miscellaneous Unusual Pictures: Fred Thompson produced no foreign scenes himself that we are aware of. However, he did sell several foreign scenes that he had acquired when he purchased a local Portland photography studio. Thompson did sell various miscellaneous unusual scenes, including seascapes, men, children, and snow scenes. He sold no floral still-lifes that we are aware of.

Silhouettes: We have recently come across several Fred Thompson silhouettes, the first we have ever seen. These silhouettes predate Nutting's silhouettes so they were not an attempt to compete with Wallace Nutting.

Size

Most framed pictures seem to be of the smaller size, ranging from 5x7" to 16x20". Although we have seen a few very tiny Thompsons (e.g., 1x2" – 4x5"), we have never seen pictures comparable in size to Nutting's largest (e.g., 20x30" – 20x40").

Some of the More Commonly Found Fred Thompson Pictures

The following titles and classifications represent what we have found to be some of the most commonly found Fred Thompson pictures. This does not mean that they are not desirable to collectors but rather that they were originally sold in larger numbers and are more commonly found today.

* most blossom scenes are fairly common
* most birch scenes are fairly common
* Smaller Thompson untitled exterior scenes (5x7", 7x9", and 8x10") are generally very common
* *Lombardy Poplar*, very common
* *The Old Toll Bridge*, also very common
* *Fireside Fancy Work*, is Thompson's most common interior scene
* Smaller Thompson untitled interior scenes (5x7", 7x9", and 8x10") are generally quite common
* *Portland Head*, common seascape

Some of the More Highly Sought-After Fred Thompson Pictures

The following represent some of the rarest and most highly sought-after Fred Thompson pictures. All, in very good to excellent condition, are very desirable to most Thompson collectors.

* Ships and schooners
* Pictures with children
* Pictures with men
* Pictures with snow
* Glass paperweights
* Calendars
* Small mirrors and trays
* Triple groupings, especially seascapes
* We have even seen one very rare Thompson grocery list

Alphabetical Index to Fred Thompson Pictures

There is no complete alphabetical listing of Fred Thompson pictures available of which we are aware. We have never seen any Fred Thompson salesman's picture catalogs, studio number log books, studio records, or anything else that would provide this information. Therefore, the best alphabetical listing source for Fred Thompson picture titles still in existence would be the Fred Thompson Price List at the end of this chapter.

Fred Thompson Collectors' Club

There is presently no collector's club devoted exclusively to Fred Thompson pictures. However, the Wallace Nutting Collectors' Club would be the best place to go for further information on Fred Thompson pictures. You can obtain the address of this club from the author.

Fred Thompson Books and Reference Material

At the time this book went to press, we were aware of no other books or reference material devoted to Fred Thompson. Even contact with the Portland Public Library and the Maine Historical Society revealed nothing substantial or new relating to Fred Thompson. Much of the Fred Thompson material found in *The Guide to Wallace Nutting-Like Photographers of the Early Twentieth Century* is included in this chapter.

Fred Thompson on the Internet

Information on Fred Thompson and other early twentieth century hand-colored photographers can be found in the Wallace Nutting-like photographers section of The Wallace Nutting Gallery at www.wnutting.com.

Where to Go If Looking to Buy or Sell Fred Thompson Pictures

There are various dealers around the country who specialize in hand-colored photographs of the early twentieth century, including Fred Thompson. One obvious reference source would be Michael Ivankovich Antiques. Most Thompson collectors also belong to the Wallace Nutting Collectors' Club.

The generally recognized national center of Fred Thompson activity would be Michael Ivankovich's Wallace Nutting-like photographers catalog auctions. Held two times per year, generally in the northeastern portion of the country, these auctions provide both collectors and dealers the opportunity to compete for the largest variety of Nutting-like pictures, including many Fred Thompson pictures, available anywhere in the country. These auctions also give sellers the opportunity to place their items in front of the country's leading Fred Thompson collectors and enthusiasts.

Summary of Fred Thompson Collecting Tips

* There were actually two Fred Thompsons — Frederick H. Thompson, the father, and Frederick M. Thompson, the son.
* Thompson's pictures ranked fourth in total output behind Wallace Nutting, David Davidson, and Sawyer.
* The most common Fred Thompson pictures include blossoms, birches, and colonial interior scenes.
* Oddities represent non-picture items including calendars, glass paperweights, tiny mirrors, tiny two-handled trays, etc.
* TACO was an abbreviation for the Thompson Art Co.
* Thompson picture sales came to an abrupt end in 1923 with the death of Frederick M. Thompson.
* Fred Thompson always signed his name, Fred Thompson. Pictures signed Thompson in pencil script are usually pictures by Florence Thompson.
* An original paper backing carrying the original TACO stamp can add 10 – 15% to the value of a picture.

Fred Thompson Value Guide

The values listed in this chapter are derived from many different sources, including:
* Michael Ivankovich Auction Company auctions
* Other auction houses
* Retail and mail order sales
* Prices observed at antique shows, flea markets, and individual and group antique shops throughout the northeast
* Assorted other reliable sources

Most prices included here represent prices actually paid. In some instances where we were unable to ascertain the final sales price, we have included the dealer asking price if we felt that it was appropriately priced and fell within the acceptable ranges. The sampling of items included in this chapter includes titles seen by us, sold by us, or reported to us. Obviously not all titles are included here. This chapter is only intended to provide you with a representative sampling of titles and prices in order to help you to establish a ballpark price on most Fred Thompson pictures.

Title	Size	Type	Gross	Rate	Date
Apple Blossoms	10x16"	Ext.	$50	4	2/96
Apple Blossoms	14x17"	Ext.	$65	4	3/96
Apple Blossoms in May	9x14"	Ext.	$60	4	3/96
Apple Tree Bend	7x9"	Ext.	$65	4	10/00
Apple Tree Bloom	9x12"	Ext.	$30	4	3/97
Apple Tree Road	13x17"	Ext.	$45	3	3/97
Apple Tree Road	11x14"	Ext.	$50	4	3/03
Bend in the Road, A	11x14"	Ext.	$65	4	7/95
Birch Bank	10x16"	Ext.	$55	4	6/96
Birch Landing	5x7"	Ext.	$50	4	10/00
Birch Landing	7x9"	Ext.	$25	3.5	10/96
Birch Lane	11x14"	Ext.	$47	3.75	11/95
Birch Lane	7x9"	Ext.	$60	4	9/01
Birch Road	11x17"	Ext.	$45	4	3/01
Birch Road	13x16"	Ext.	$38	4	4/95
Birch Road	10x16"	Ext.	$55	4	8/96
Birthday Card	3x5"	Misc	$28	4	11/95
Birthday Verse Collection	4x4"	Misc	$61	4.5	9/96
Blossom Dale	13x16"	Ext.	$75	4	3/97
Blossom Time	10x16"	Ext.	$60	4	4/97
Blossom Time	14x17"	Ext.	$85	4	8/96
Blossoms Beautiful	7x9"	Ext.	$18	3	3/96
Bridesmaid, The	14x17"	Int.	$105	4	10/94
Brook of Winter	13x16"	Snow	$525	4	11/03
Brook in Winter	14x17"	Snow	$155	4	6/96
Calendar in original box	3x4"	Calendar	$39	4	9/96
Calendar with Sailing Ship	1x2"	Calendar	$88	4	9/96
Calendar, 1927	4x5"	Calendar	$286	4	11/95
Calm of Fall	10x16"	Ext.	$75	4	8/95
Close-framed Sailing Ship	8x10"	Ship	$165	4	6/96
Close-framed Sailing Ship	8x10"	Ship	$150	4	4/95
Close-framed Sailing Ship	8x10"	Ship	$125	4	5/95
Close-framed Sailing Ship	8x14"	Ship	$225	4	1/96
Colonial Baby	13x15"	Child	$77	4	10/94
Colonial Garden	11x16"	Misc Un	$83	3.75	9/96
Country Birch, A	10x16"	Ext.	$45	3	8/96
Country Lane, A	9x15"	Ext.	$65	4	4/96
Country Road, A	10x16"	Ext.	$50	4	5/96
Cradle Days	16x20"	Int.	$65	3	3/97
Day is Done, The	14x17"	Snow	$132	3	9/96
Deep Hole Brook	10x15"	Ext.	$75	4	

Title	Size	Category	Price		Date
Drifting	10x16"	Ship	$209	4	11/95
Elms and Apple Blossoms	15x19"	Ext.	$20	3	3/97
Exterior in metal frame	3x4"	Misc	$50	4	3/97
Exterior in thin metal frame	3x4"	Misc	$44	4	9/96
Exterior in thin metal frame	3x4"	Misc	$41	4	11/95
Fernbank	9x15"	Ext.	$55	4	4/95
Fernbank	10x16"	Ext.	$85	4	6/96
Fernbank	10x12"	Ext.	$70	4	6/01
Fireside Dreams	16x20"	Int.	$65	4	11/03
Fireside Fancy Work	8x10"	Int.	$85	4	4/96
Fireside Fancy Work	14x17"	Int.	$50	4	3/03
Fireside Fancy Work	7x9"	Int.	$45	4	1/96
Gamecock	8x14"	Ship	$165	4	11/95
Gay Head	13x16"	Sea	$250	4	9/03
Glass Negative	11x14"	Misc.	$40	4	3/96
Glorious Autumn	10x16"	Ext.	$65	4	4/95
Glorious Autumn	7x9"	Ext.	$25	3	2/96
Glorious Fall	9x12"	Ext.	$35	4	4/95
Glorious Ocean	8x14"	Sea	$75	4	7/96
Golden Trail	7x9"	Ext.	$75	4	11/03
Gossips, The	7x9"	Int.	$80	4	3/97
Gossips, The	11x14"	Int.	$125	4	2/97
Grocery List	3x6"	Misc	$44	3.75	9/96
Hazy Morn	11x14"	Ship	$209	4	10/94
High and Dry	7x9"	Ext.	$55	4	10/94
Lake Champlain	11x14"	Ext.	$75	4	10/96
Lake Side	10x18"	Ext.	$23	3	3/96
Lakeside Drive	13x16"	Ext.	$60	4	3/97
Lakeside Elm, A	7x9"	Ext.	$45	4	10/95
Lane Blossoms	8x14"	Ext.	$55	4	4/95
Laneside Blossoms	9x16"	Ext.	$75	4	6/96
Lombardy Poplar	14x17"	Ext.	$100	3	3/97
Lombardy Poplar	11x14"	Ext.	$75	4	3/96
Lombardy Poplar	10x16"	Ext.	$65	3.5	3/97
Longfellow's Dining Room	14x17"	Int.	$110		6/01
Longfellow Statue	8x10"	Misc. Un.	$55	4	3/96
Maiden Reveries	7x9"	Int.	$33	3	3/96
Majestic Waves	10x16"	Sea	$85	4	1/97
Midsummer	7x11"	Misc Un	$55	3	4/95
Midsummer	7x9"	Misc Un	$75	4	1/97
Milady's Desk	10x16"	Int.	$33	3	10/94
Miniature interior	4x5"	Miniature	$55	4	5/95
Miniature interior	4x5"	Miniature	$35	4	1/96
Miniature interior	4x5"	Miniature	$45	4	7/96
Miniature interior	4x5"	Miniature	$75	4	12/95
Mini. Sailing Ship	2x3"	Misc	$88	4	9/96
Mirror with Seascape Scene	5x14"	Mirror	$66	3	9/96
Mother's Joy	8x12"	Child	$100	3	3/97
Mother's Joy	11x14"	Child	$175	4	1/97
Mother's Reveries	13x16"	Int.	$50	4	10/94
Neath the Blossoms	7x9"	Sheep	$95	4	3/97
Neath the Blossoms	11x14"	Sheep	$165	4	2/97
Neath the Blossoms	14x17"	Sheep	$185	4	10/96
Ocean Spray	11x16"	Sea	$28	3	3/96
October Woods	11x14"	Ext.	$30	4	11/95
Old Fashioned Flowers	7x14"	Int.	$110	3.5	9/96
Old Grist Mill, The	11x14"	Misc Un	$125	4	7/95
Old Grist Mill, The	7x9"	Misc Un	$85	4	3/97
Old Homestead, The	9x17"	Ext.	$40	3.75	4/95
Old Oaken Bucket	11x13"	Misc. Un.	$110	3	10/94
Old Timer, An	6x13"	Ship	$198	4	10/94
Old Toll Bridge	10x16"	Ext.	$50	3	3/97
Old Toll Bridge	11x17"	Ext.	$75	4	1/97
Old Toll Bridge	14x17"	Ext.	$50	4	6/03
Olde Toll Bridge, The	14x17"	Ext.	$115	4	2/97
Olde Toll Bridge, The	10x16"	Ext.	$85	4	12/96
Old Toll Bridge, The	7x11"	Ext.	$65	4	1/97
Old Toll Bridge, The	11x14"	Ext.	$220	3.5	9/03
Outlet, The	7x9"	Ext.	$17	3	11/95
Paring Apples	10x14"	Int.	$80	4	11/03
Paring Apples	7x9"	Int.	$55	4	7/96
Peace River	11x14"	Ext.	$75	4	1/97
Pendexter Brook	16x19"	Ext.	$44	3	9/96
Pine Grove	8x10"	Ext.	$65	4	8/01
Portland Head	18x22"	Sea	$240	4	3/97
Portland Head	14x17"	Sea	$195	4	2/96
Portland Head	11x14"	Sea	$125	3.5	3/97
Roasting Apples	7x9"	Int.	$44	4	10/94
Roasting Apples	11x14"	Int.	$110	4	12/96
Rocky Point	7x9"	Sea	$55	4	9/96
Roses and Reading	9x15"	Misc Un	$125	3.5	12/96
Roller, The	8x14"	Sea	$130	3	11/03
Roller, The	10x16"	Sea	$125	4	3/97
Saco Drive	8x10"	Ext.	$60	4	6/96
Saco Lake	8x10"	Ext.	$45	4	4/96
Sailing Ship	2x3"	Ship	$105	4	11/95
Schooner Lawrence	15x18"	Ship	$260	3.5	3/97
Sea Foam	7x11"	Sea	$40	3	3/96
Setting Grandfather's Clock	14x17"	Int.	$39	4	11/95
Small mirror w/ interior scene	3x8"	Mirror	$44	4	9/96

Small mirror w/ interior scene	3x9"	Mirror	$61	4	10/94
Small mirror w/ interior scene	3x9"	Mirror	$66	4	10/94
Small tray w/ flag scene	3x4"	Tray	$55	4	3/00
Small tray w/ interior scene	3x4"	Misc.	$70	4	3/96
Small tray w/ interior scene	3x4"	Misc	$48	4	4/95
Small tray w/ interior scene	3x4"	Tray	$70	4	4/95
Small tray w/ interior scene	3x4"	Tray	$99	4	10/94
Small tray w/ interior scene	4x6"	Tray	$80	4	4/95
Small triple grouping	3x8"	Misc	$110	4	3/97
Spinning Days	7x9"	Int.	$94	4	10/94
Spinning Days	14x17"	Int.	$145	4	7/96
Spring Flowers	10x16"	Ext.	$55	4	2/97
Spring Flowers	7x9"	Ext.	$30	3	7/96
Still Valleys	10x13"	Ext.	$39	4	10/94
Still Valleys	7x9"	Ext.	$35	3.5	2/96
Stony Brook	14x17"	Ext.	$70	4	4/95
Sunset on Fore River	11x17"	Ext.	$25	3	3/97
Sunset on the Suwanee	11x14"	Ext.	$35	3.5	4/95
Sunset on the Suwanee	10x16"	Ext.	$65	4	12/96
Tea Time	7x10"	Int.	$110	3	7/01
Tea Time	7x9"	Int.	$65	4	3/97
Three Tiny Framed Pictures	2x3"	Ext.	$116	4	11/95
Thru Autumn Woods	14x16"	Ext.	$170	3	11/03
Tired of Spinning	7x9"	Int.	$45	4	11/03
Tired of Spinning	14x17"	Int.	$110	4	6/97
Touch of Autumn, A	11x20"	Ext.	$8	2	11/95
Tray with int. scene	5x7"	Tray	$77	4	11/95
Tray with int. scene	10x16"	Tray	$175	4	1/97
Triple ext. grouping	3x8"	Misc	$39	4	9/96
Triple ext. grouping	5x12"	Misc	$99	4	11/95
Triple ocean grouping	5x13"	Misc Un	$121	4	9/96
Triple ocean grouping	5x13"	Misc Un	$150	4	4/97
Twilight	5x7"	Ext.	$33	4	10/94
Twixt Apple Trees	13x15"	Ext.	$33	3	9/96
Twixt Apple Trees	10x16"	Ext.	$65	4	4/95
Two Master	10x16"	Ship	$150	4	9/96
Two Roses	10x14"	Man	$85	3	3/96
Under the Birches	14x17"	Ext.	$125	4.5	12/95
Untitled birches	8x14"	Ext.	$40	3	3/96
Untitled exterior	7x9"	Ext.	$25	3	12/96
Untitled exterior	7x9"	Ext.	$60	4	10/95
Untitled exterior	7x9"	Ext.	$40	4	1/97
Untitled exterior	7x9"	Ext.	$35	4	2/97
Untitled interior	4x5"	Int.	$58	3.5	9/96
Untitled interior	7x9"	Int.	$35	3.5	5/96
Untitled interior	7x9"	Int.	$55	4.5	1/96
Untitled interior	7x9"	Int.	$45	4	10/95
Untitled interior	7x9"	Int.	$75	4.5	4/96
Untitled sailing ship	7x9"	Ship	$55	3	8/96
Untitled sailing ship	7x9"	Ship	$60	4	4/95
Untitled sailing ship	8x10"	Ship	$75	4	12/96
Untitled sailing ship	8x10"	Ship	$115	4	7/95
Untitled sailing ship	8x14"	Ship	$175	4	12/96
Vale of splendor	7x9"	Ext.	$30	3	4/95
Waiting	7x9"	Int.	$28	3	4/95
Wharf Scene	8x10"	Misc Un	$20	3	3/97
White Head	8x15"	Sea	$65	4	3/96
White Head	10x16"	Sea	$135	4	6/97
Woodland Symphony	9x12"	Ext.	$80	4	3/01
Woodland Symphony	11x14"	Ext.	$75	4	6/97

Apple Tree Bloom. Est. Value: $65.

Birch Bank. Est. Value: $65.

Blossom Dale. Est. Value: $75.

Blossoms Beautiful. Est. Value: $55.

Glorious Autumn. Est. Value: $65.

Midsummer. Est. Value: $75.

Mother's Joy. Est. Value: $175.

Portland Head. Est. Value: $240.

Roses and Reading. Est. Value: $125.

The Old Toll Bridge. Est. Value: $115.

Under the Birches. Est. Value: $125.

Wharf Scene. Est. Value: $175.

White Head. Est. Value: $135.

Chapter 11

Lesser Known & Unknown Early Twentieth Century Hand-Colored Photographers

The following list represents those photographers we have been able to accumulate over the past several years. This list is fairly extensive, but certainly not complete. You should realize that no other photographers were as successful as Nutting, Davidson, Sawyer, or Thompson. Many of the photographers selling hand-colored pictures at this time were amateur photographers selling their pictures on a part-time, seasonal, or on a very limited basis, while others were professional photographers whose businesses simply did not last more than a year or two.

The values listed in this chapter are derived from many different sources, including:
  * Michael Ivankovich Auction Company auctions
  * Other auction houses
  * Retail and mail order sales
  * Prices observed at antique shows, flea markets, and individual and group antique shops throughout the northeast
  * Assorted other reliable sources

Most prices included here represent prices actually paid. In some instances where we were unable to ascertain the final sales price, we have included the dealer asking price if we felt that it was appropriately priced and fell within the acceptable ranges. The sampling of items in this chapter includes titles seen by us, sold by us, or reported to us. Obviously not all titles are included here. This chapter is only intended to provide you with a representative sampling of titles and prices in order to help you to establish a ballpark price on most lesser-known and unknown photographers.

ATKINSON (first name not known)
  * Probably New England
  * Recent Sale Prices:

Old Man of the Mountains, NH	6x8"	Misc. Un.	$25	5	10/94

AUSTIN, I.
  * No other information available
  * Recent Sale Prices:

Close-framed Pool	18x10"	Ext.	$6	4	10/94

BABCOCK (first name not known)
  * No other information available
  * Recent Sale Prices:

Untitled exterior	8x10"	Ext.	$18	4	11/95

BAKER, FLORIAN A.
  * No other information available
  * Recent Sale Prices:

Autumn by the Lake	14x17"	Ext.	$28	4	3/97
Inland Beauty	14x17"	Ext.	$35	4	3/97
Rushing Waters	14x17"	Ext.	$50	4	3/97

A Bicknell picture label

Bicknell's Porcupine Island, $55.

BICKNELL, J. CARLETON (also J.C.BICKNELL and BICKNELL)

* Bicknell Mfg. Co., 16 Pitt Street, Portland, ME
* Typically worked in Maine and northern New England
* Typically shot exterior scenes
* We have never seen a Bicknell colonial interior scene
* Recent Sale Prices:

Across the Intervale	10x12"	Ext.	$47	4	11/95
Apple Blossoms	7x10"	Ext.	$35	4	3/97
Cathedral Ledge	16x20"	Ext.	$55	4	4/95
Close-framed exterior	4x7"	Ext.	$11	4	11/95
Close-framed exterior	6x8"	Ext.	$5	4	3/96
Close-framed lake	12x16"	Ext.	$30	4	3/96
Close-framed lighthouse	12x16"	Sea	$100	4	3/96
Country Road, A	14x22"	Ext.	$80	4	3/97
Glen Ellis Falls	10x14"	Ext.	$15	4	3/97
High Surf	13x15"	Sea	$50	4	4/95
Ledges, The	14x22"	Ext.	$55	4	11/95
Lone Apple Tree, The	10x14"	Ext.	$28	3.75	3/97
Lovejoy Bridge	14x17"	Ext.	$44	4	9/96
Masonic Temple	9x12"	Misc. Un.	$30	4	3/96
Meadow Elms	14x22"	Ext.	$40	3	3/97
Old Red Home, The	8x12"	Ext.	$53	4	Mar'97
Old Wooden Bridge, The	8x12"	Ext.	$45	4	3/97
Parsacouauay Mountain	8x10"	Ext.	$52	4	11/95
Porcupine Island	11x13"	Ext.	$55	4	3/97
Porcupines from Nupert	8x11"	Ext.	$45	4	3/97
Quiet Stream, The	8x14"	Ext.	$36	3	9/96
Salmon Pool, The	18x26"	Misc. Un.	$55	3.5	3/97
Shepherd River	10x12"	Ext.	$25	4	3/97
Valley Farm	13x15"	Ext.	$30	4	3/96
Vermont Card	5x8"	Card	$28	3.5	11/95

BLAIR, S.L.

* No other information available

BLOOD, RALPH

* Probably Maine or New England
* The Portland Head Light 1791 picture we sold was as nice as any we have seen by a major photographer
* Recent Sale Prices:

Portland Head Light 1791	14x20"	Sea	$77	3.5	9/96

BRAGG, E.A.

* No other information available

BREHMER, BILL

* Rutland, VT

BROOKS (first name not known)

* New Hampshire, probably Weare

Burrowes, The Intervale, $50.

BURROWES (first name not known)

* Probably Vermont
* Recent Sale Prices:

Homeward	12x15"	Misc. Un.	$110	4	11/95
Intervale ,The	10x12"	Cows	$50	3.75	11/95
Natural Bridge of Virginia	14x17"	Misc. Un.	$40	4	3/97
Spring Charms	10x12"	Ext.	$48	4	4/95
Winter Time	7x9"	Snow	$35	3	3/96

BUSCH, L.A.

* No other information available

CACCIOLA, PEDRO

* Massachusetts
* Worked for Wallace Nutting
* Recent Sales Prices:

A Golden Path	13x16"	Misc. Un.	$58	4	11/95

CARLOCK (first name not known)

* Have only seen Washington DC scenes by Carlock
* Recent Sales Prices:

Japanese Cherry Blossoms	8x10"	Misc. Un.	$28	3	3/96
Lincoln Memorial	8x10"	Misc. Un.	$35	4	6/97

CROFT (first name not known)

* No other information available

CURRIER, C.D.

* Franklin, Vermont

DEREK (first name not known)

* Probably Vermont

DOWLY (first name not known)

* No other information available

Dupue Bros., The Straggler, $70.

DUPUE BROS.
* No other information available
* Recent Sales Prices:

The Straggler	10x12"	Misc. Un.	$70	3	3/96

EDDY (first name not known)
* No other information available
* Recent Sales Prices:

Cotton Picking Time	16x20"	Misc. Un.	$260	5	3/96
Southern Pines	12x18"	Misc. Un.	$55	3	6/97

EDSON, NORMAN
* No other information available
* Recent Sales Prices:

The Knoll, Bolton Pass	8x10"	Ext.	$14	3	10/94

FARINI, MAY
* Not a photographer, but an artist. Her pictures are prints, not photographs, and are frequently confused with hand-colored photographs because of the colonial interior subject matter.
* Was primarily known as a postcard artist
* Created a series of colonial interior scenes in an attempt to compete with Wallace Nutting
* Recent Sales Prices:

An Old Sweet Song	11x14"	Misc. Un.	$19	3	11/95
Au Revoir	11x14"	Misc. Un.	$28	4	9/96
Days of Old	11x14"	Int.	$22	4	9/96
In the Garden	7x9"	Misc. Un.	$17	4	9/96

FOREST, GEO.
* No other information available
* Recent Sales Prices:

New Divinity, The	8x10"	Int.	$10	3	9/96

GANDARA (first name not known)
* No other information available

GARDINER, H. MARSHALL
* A photographer who primarily did postcards
* Bermuda and Florida scenes are his most common
* Nantucket scenes are the most desirable pictures
* His Nantucket postcards identified as "Published by H. Marshall Gardiner, Nantucket Mass" are highly collectible in their own right
* A book titled *H. Marshall Gardiner's Nantucket Postcards, 1910 – 1940* was published in 1995 by his daughter, Geraldine Gardiner Salisbury
* 1884–1942
* Recent Sales Prices:

Bermuda	11x14"	Sea	$72	4	9/96
Hawthorne Lane, Nantucket	10x12"		$330	4	11/01

GARDINER, W.H.
* The father of H. Marshall Gardiner
* Also shot photographs in Florida, Bermuda, and Nantucket
* Recent Sale Prices:

A Florida River Scene	9x13"	Ext.	$25	3	11/95
Giant Staircase, Mackinal	10x16"	Ext.	$35	3.5	6/97
Tomoka River, Florida	13x15"	Ext.	$65	4	6/97

Garrison's Desert Verbanas & Primroses, $75.

GARRISON, J.M.
* Southwestern United States
* Recent Sale Prices:

Desert Verbanas & Primroses	8x10"	Misc. Un.	$75	4	6/01

GIBSON (first name not known)
* Location unknown, although we believe some pictures were shot in Pennsylvania

Gibson's Lover's Road, $35.

* Typically exterior scenes; we have never seen a Gibson colonial interior scene.
* Pencil titles and signatures are the most common.
* Pre-printed titles and signatures are sometimes found.
* Recent Sales Prices:

Afterglow, The	7x10"	Ext.	$11	4	11/95
Beacon Light	9x12"	Misc. Un.	$30	3	4/95
Bending Tree, The	11x14"	Ext.	$11	4	9/96
Country Road	10x12"	Ext.	$30	4	11/95
Peaceful Brook	10x13"	Ext.	$18	3	3/96
Lover's Road	11x14"	Ext.	$35	4	11/96
Two Birches, The	7x9"	Ext.	$13	3	3/96
Waterfall im Autumn	9x11"	Ext.	$30	4	11/95
Weeping Willow	11x14"	Ext.	$18	4	3/97

GIDEON (first name not known)
* No other information available

Gunn's Lake Worth, Florida, $15.

GUNN (first name not known)
* No other information available
* Recent Sale Prices:

Lake Worth, Florida	9x12"	Ext.	$15	4	7/97

GUTMANN
* This was actually Bessie Pease Gutmann, the noted infant/child artist
* Colonial interior scenes only

* These were produced by Bessie Pease Gutmann in an unsuccessful attempt to compete with Wallace Nutting's colonial interior scenes.
* Relatively few were sold.
* Note that these are hand-colored prints of drawings, not hand-colored photographs.
* See Chapter 3 for more information on Bessie Pease Gutmann.
* Recent Sale Prices:

Lavendar and Old Lace	11x14"	Int.	$83	4	9/96
Candle Making	7x9"	Int.	$75	4	7/97

GUY, EDWARD
* Massachusetts
* Worked as Wallace Nutting's iron master at the Saugus Iron Works
* Recent Sale Prices:

Untitled stone church	7x9"	Misc. Un.	$11	3	10/94

HANNUM, H.S.
* No other information available
* Recent Sale Prices:

Untitled rocky stream	12x18"	Ext.	$25	3.5	11/95

Harris's Garden, Oldest School House, St. Augustine, Florida, $30.

HARRIS (first name not known)
* New York, New England, and Florida pictures
* Often Harris's work was lovely and brightly colored.
* Typically exterior scenes; we have never seen a colonial interior scene.
* Recent Sale Prices:

Falls, The, Clifton, NJ	11x14"	Misc. Un.	$43	3	3/96
From Black Bear Mt, Inley, NY	12x21"	Ext.	$95	4	3/97
Garden, Oldest School House	11x14"	Misc	$110	4	7/01
Mt. Whiteface, Lake Placid	11x14"	Ext.	$33	3	3/96
Old City Gates	11x14"	Misc. Un.	$58	3.5	9/96

Oldest School House,					
St. Augustine	7x9"	Misc	$75	4	11/00
Patio, Oldest House,					
St. Augustine	11x12"	Misc. Un.	$125	4	3/01
Peace River, Florida	6x10"	Ext.	$60	4	3/01
River Palms, Florida	11x21"	Ext.	$47	4	11/95
Untitled country road	4x9"	Ext.	$50	4	11/00

HAYNES (first name not known)
* St. Paul, Minnesota
* Did a Yellowstone Park series
* Recent Sale Prices:

Hot Springs	8x10"	Misc. Un.	$28	4	9/96
Jupiter Terrace,					
Monmouth Springs	8x10"	Misc. Un.	$22	3.75	9/96

HAZEN, C
* No other information available
* Recent Sale Prices:

Sunken Garden	7x9"	Misc. Un.	$6	3	9/96

HENNESSEY, MARGARET
* Massachusetts
* Worked for Wallace Nutting

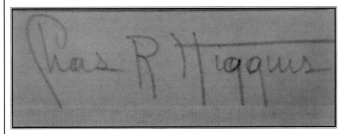

The distinctive Higgins signature

HIGGINS, CHAS. R. (also CHARLES R. HIGGINS and HIGGINS)

Charles Higgins is another New England photographer who did some very nice work. Born in 1867 in Dedham, Massachusetts, his father, John C. Higgins, was also a well-known professional Maine photographer whose early photographs of ship launchings have hung in The Maine Maritime Museum in Bath, Maine.

Not surprisingly, Charles Higgins received much of his early photographic training from his father. While living in Bath, Higgins studied many photographic techniques as a child and eventually joined his father in his photography business. After his father passed away, Higgins continued operating the business on his own. Initially working in his father's studio, he later moved to 138 Front St., and eventually to Allen's Lane, both in Bath.

Higgins's Going Shopping, $70.

The photographic process used by Charles Higgins was also comparable to that used by Wallace Nutting. Traveling around with his box camera and tripod, Higgins would photograph scenes that caught his attention throughout Maine — blossoms, birches, mountains, and winter scenes. He also photographed interior scenes with and without people, exterior views of houses, seascapes, children, and the like. Glass negatives were used to develop black and white pictures onto the much-preferred platinum paper.

Although Charles Higgins took all photographs, most were colored by Carrie Doherty, Higgins' primary colorist. She used the same Windsor and Newton moist water colors that were used by Wallace Nutting and she would highlight those portions of the pictures that she wanted to accentuate. In later years, the platinum paper was replaced with a substitute paper when platinum became unobtainable.

The scope of Charles Higgins's business was considerably smaller than Nutting's, even at its peak. Whereas Wallace Nutting employed nearly 200 people as colorists, framers, salesmen, and administrative office personnel, Higgins staff numbered less than 10 at its peak in the 1920s. Some of Higgins's staff performed several duties. For example, Carrie Doherty, the colorist, was also the primary model used in the interior scenes. When a second model was needed, Higgins used his bookkeeper, Mary Spear.

As with most other photographers selling hand-colored pictures of colonial interior scenes at that time, none of Higgins interior settings appeared as authentic or detailed as Wallace Nutting's interior pictures. The furniture used by Charles Higgins was not of the finest form or design, the rooms were not as precisely decorated as the finest rooms of the day would have been, and the models were not always dressed in the correct attire. For exam-

Fireside Reflections, $75.

through the mail. There is no doubt that a Charles Higgins hand-colored platinotype picture provided many fond memories of family vacations to far-away Maine in the early twentieth century.

A 1919 advertisement in the Bath, Maine, business directory summed up the work of the Charles Higgins Studios this way:

The most appreciated gift for any occasion is one of
HIGGINS'S HAND COLORED PLATINUMS
These pictures are from artistic bits of nature's best scenery, and colonial studies.
Write for illustrated catalog and prices.
The Higgins Pictures Studios
Allen's Lane, Bath, Maine

---

ple, Carrie Doherty and Mary Spear frequently had to make their own costumes as those provided by Higgins did not always fit.

Most pictures were mounted upon an indented, linen-type mat. Titles were signed in the lower left corner under the picture, the Charles Higgins name was placed under the lower right side of the picture. Most titles and signatures were applied by Carrie Doherty.

Higgins framed pictures came in a variety of sizes, with mats ranging from 5x7" to 15x22", the largest I have seen. Many seem to be approximately 10x16". Frames were generally a thin gold or brown wood frame, again very similar to the style used by Wallace Nutting.

Although we found no direct link between Nutting and Charles Higgins, Nutting's influence is evident throughout Higgins work, from the types of exterior and colonial interior scenes sold, to the title and signature placement, framing, and type of matting used.

Charles Higgins also offered a line of what he called novelties. These were hand-colored pictures that were small enough to decorate the top of a cork stopper, match boxes, or wrapping paper for a bar of soap. Few of these items seem to have survived today.

Higgins pictures were marketed in several ways. Generally they were sold through several larger Maine department stores or through summer resorts throughout the Bath area. Other pictures were also sold to customers who stopped by the studio or who ordered

Charles Higgins also built and operated the Greenmoors Inn in Kittery, Maine. This establishment quickly became a popular shore dining resort. Its initial success as a restaurant led to Higgins broadening its services to include lodging as well.

Higgins was extremely active in local community affairs, both in Bath and his winter home in later years, Frostproof, Florida. He was a member of the Poplar Star Lodge, the Masons, Montgomery and St. Bernard, R.A.C., Dunlap Commandry, K.T. and the Council in Brunswick, Kora Temple, Mystic Shrine of Lewiston, and the Bath Elks Lodge.

Charles Higgins died of a heart attack in 1930 at the age of 67.

Higgins Collecting Tips:

* Because of their relatively limited marketing area, Higgins's pictures are rarely found outside of New England.

* In addition to colonial interior and exterior pastoral pictures, Higgins also sold scenes with children, Indians, boats, seascapes, and even a stagecoach scene.

* Although the quality of Higgins's pictures were better than many other early photographers, we have seen few that approached some of Nutting's better pieces.

* In many Higgins's pictures, the *Chas R Higgins* signature appears within the mat indentation while the title appears below the indentation line.

A Charles Higgins paper label

Hodges's Racquet Lake
Birches, $65.

An authentic Higgins label may add 10 – 15% to the value of a picture.

* Recent Sale Prices:

Birches on the Bank	9x12"	Ext.	$10	3.5	3/97
By the Fireside	18x24"	Int.	$165	3.5	9/96
Close-framed horse					
& carriage	4x6"	Horse	$66	4	11/95
Close-framed interior	10x13"	Int.	$45	4	3/97
Colonial Stairway, A	6x10"	Int.	$65	4	3/97
Fireside Reflections	9x15"	Int.	$75	4	11/95
Going Shopping	11x12"	Misc. Un.	$70	4	3/97
Grandfather's Clock	7x10"	Int.	$28	3	11/95
Highway and Byway	10x16"	Cow	$121	4	10/94
In Colonial Days	13x16"	Misc. Un.	$95	3	3/97
Near Sugar Mill	8x12"	Ext.	$39	4	9/96
November Sunset, A	10x16"	Ext.	$65	4	9/96
Road by the River	11x14"	Ext.	$23	3	3/97
Rocky Shore, A	10x13"	Sea	$30	3	11/95
Slow Fire, A	12x15"	Int.	$90	4	4/95
Spring on the Old Farm	10x12"	Misc. Un.	$53	4	4/95
Lane, The	9x12"	Ext.	$85	4	3/96
Old Chaise, The	15x19"	Horse	$230	4	3/97
Tower Surf	10x13"	Sea	$33	3	3/97
Twin Birch	7x12"	Ext.	$25	3.5	4/95
Untitled exterior	5x7"	Ext.	$20	3	4/95
Untitled fisherman's cove	8x13"	Misc. Un.	$50	4	4/95
Untitled girl by house	8x12"	Misc. Un.	$60	4	3/97
Untitled girls by house	18x22"	Misc. Un.	$30	3	11/95
Untitled girls on street	9x12"	Misc. Un.	$50	5	10/94
Untitled interior	4x9"	Int.	$22	4	10/94
Untitled seascape	7x11"	Higgins	$44	4	9/96
Winding Stair, A	7x14"	Int.	$28	4	6/96
Winter Sunset, A	7x11"	Snow	$30	3.5	3/97

HODGES (first name not known)
* New York State and New England pictures
* Shot pictures at Racquette Lake
* Recent Sale Prices:

Raquette Lake	10x13"	Ext.	$45	4	3/97
Raquette Lake	10x13"	Ext.	$55	3.5	3/97
Raquette Lake Birches	11x14"	Ext.	$65	4.5	6/96
Untitled lake	9x12"	Ext.	$15	3	3/97
Wannamaker Falls	10x12"	Ext.	$23	4	3/97

HOMER (first name not known)
* No other information available

HUDSON (first name not known)
* No other information available
* Recent Sale Prices:

Autumn Arrayed	11x14"	Ext.	$75	4	4/95
Wissahickon Waters	11x14"	Ext.	$45	4	4/95

KATTLEMAN (first name not known)
* No other information available

KNAFFLE & CO.
* No other information available
* Recent Sale Prices:

The Ferry	9x12"	Misc. Un.	$22	4	11/95

KNOFFE (first name not known)
* No other information available
* Recent Sale Prices:

Twilight	11x14"	Ext.	$5	3.5	3/96

KRABEL (first name not known)
* No other information available

HAND-COLORED

LAKE (first name not known)
* No other information available

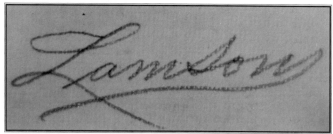

Lamson pencil signature

Lamson's Grazing Sheep, $55.

LAMSON (first name not known)
* Portland, Maine
* Lamson's business was purchased by Fred Thompson Art Co. prior to 1910.
* Recent Sale Prices:

Cliff, The	9x15"	Sea	$17	2	9/96
Full Sail	8x10"	Ship	$110	4	3/96
Grasp of Winter	8x12"	Snow	$160	4	3/96
Grazing Sheep	7x14"	Sheep	$55	4	3/97
Lakeside Mansions	8x14"	Misc. Un.	$22	4	9/96
Noon Time Rest	8x10"	Cows	$30	3	9/96
Placid Waters	6x10"	Ext.	$25	3	3/96
Sailing ship by rock	8x14"	Misc. Un.	$55	4	3/97
Tea Time	10x14"	Int.	$44	3	9/96
Untitled snow scene	8x14"	Snow	$28	4	3/97
Woodland Road	11x14"	Ext.	$13	3	3/97

Leand's Baby's Welcome, $55.

LEAND, DAVID
* No other information available
* Recent Sale Prices:

Baby's Welcome	14x17"	Child	$55	3.5	11/95

LIGHTSTRUM, M.
* No other information available
* Recent Sale Prices:

Nassau	6x8"	Misc. Un.	$19	4	9/96

MACKINAE, ROSSILER
* No other information available
* Recent Sale Prices:

Untitled exterior	7x12"	Misc. Un.	$22	4	9/96

MERRILL (first name not known)
* No other information available
* Recent Sale Prices:

Two Canoes	7x9"	Misc. Un.	$3	3.5	9/96

MURRAY (first name not known)
* No other information available

MEYERS (first name not known)
* No other information available
* Recent Sale Prices:

Untitled Exterior	8x14"	Ext.	$3	3.75	9/96

MOEHRING, WILLIAM
* His signature looks almost exactly like the typical Wallace Nutting signature.
* Recent Sale Prices:

Decked for Spring	10x12"	Ext.	$25	3.5	3/96

MOELINING (first name not known)
* No other information available
* Recent Sale Prices:

Untitled country road	8x10"	Ext.	$20	4	12/96

MORAN (first name not known)
* No other information available
* Recent Sale Prices:

Cooling Drink, A	9x12"	Misc. Un.	$33	3.5	4/95
Midst the Flowers	9x12"	Misc. Un.	$40	4	3/96

MURREY (first name not known)
* No other information available

NELSON, LYMAN
* Portland, Maine
* Purchased by Fred Thompson prior to 1910

Neviller's Lilacs and Bride Wreath, $75.

NEVILLE, J. ROBINSON
* New England, primarily New Hampshire
* Recent Sale Prices:

Autumn in New England	13x16"	Ext.	$25	4	3/96
Lilacs and Bride Wreath	13x17"	Ext.	$75	4.5	5/97
Spanning the River	9x11"	Ext.	$50	4	3/96

NEWCOMBE (first name not known)
* No other information available
* Recent Sale Prices:

Untitled birches	8x14"	Ext.	$15	3	4/95

PARKER, N.A.
* No other information available
* Recent Sale Prices:

Untitled street	9x12"	Ext.	$4	3	10/94

PATCH (first name not known)
* Patch's studio, Randolph, VT
* Recent Sale Prices:

The Flame, White Mts.	9x12"	Ext.	$15	4	9/96

PATTERSON (first name not known)
* No other information available

PERRY, OWEN
* Portland, Maine
* Purchased by Fred Thompson prior to 1910

PETTY, GEORGE B.
* Chicago, IL
* Recent Sale Prices:

Low Bridge	11x14"	Ext.	$6	3	10/94

PHELPS (first name not known)
* Gloucester, Massachusetts

PHINNEY (first name not known)
* No other information available
* Recent Sale Prices:

Autumn	11x14"	Ext.	$22	4	9/96
In Crawford Notch,					
White Mountains, NH	13x17"	Ext.	$17	4	11/95
Untitled exterior	6x9"	Ext.	$11	3	9/96

PRANG ART CO. (Also TABER-PRANG ART CO.)
* Louis Prang
* Hand-painted lithographs
* Recent Sale Prices:

Overhanging Pine	11x14"	Ext.	$30	3	10/94

REYNOLDS, P.
* No other information available

ROBBINS, F.
* No other information available
* Recent Sale Prices:

The Franconias, NH	10x14"	Ext.	$15	3.75	9/96

ROYCE (first name not known)
*St. Albans, Vermont

SANBORN (first name not known)
* No other information available
* Recent Sale Prices:

Blossoms & Country Road	5x7"	Ext.	$23	3	11/95

SCHEETZ, FRED'K
* Philadelphia, Pennsylvania area
* Primarily Fairmount Park area
* Recent Sale Prices:

Cresheim Creek	14x17"	Ext.	$25	4	3/96
Near Devil's Pool	11x14"	Ext.	$22	4	9/96
Valley Green, The	13x15"	Misc. Un.	$200	4	4/95

Sheldon's Wannamaker Falls, $25.

SHELDON, WALTER
* No other information available
* Recent Sale Prices:

Wannamaker Falls	10x12"	Ext.	$25	4	12/96

SHOREY STUDIOS
* No other information available
* Recent Sale Prices:

New Hampshire Birches	5x5"	Ext.	$3	3	9/96

SIMPSON, E.W.
* No other information available
* Recent Sale Prices:

Untitled girl in garden	10x12"	Misc. Un.	$30	3.5	11/95

Snow's Waiting (left) and Sunday Morning (right), $95 – 100.

SNOW, EDWARD G.
* No other information available
* Recent Sale Prices:

Sunday Morning	8x10"	Int.	$100	5	4/95
Waiting	8x10"	Int.	$95	5	4/95

Standley-assorted Colorado scenes, $35 – 45.

STANDLEY (first name not known)
* Primarily Colorado's Rocky Mountains
* Recent Sale Prices:

Untitled Colorado exterior	9x15"	Ext.	$45	4	11/95
Untitled Colorado exterior	9x15"	Ext.	$40	4	11/95
Long Peak, Estes Park, CO	6x11"	Ext.	$45	3	3/96
Royal Gorge, Canon City, CO	11x14"	Ext.	$48	4	3/96
Spanish mission	9x15"	Misc. Un.	$55	3.5	9/96

STOTT (first name not known)
* No other information available

Summers's Rock Bed of the Wissahickon, $20.

SUMMERS, W.R.
* Philadelphia, Pennsylvania Area
* Shot various scenes around the Wissahick-on Creek
* Recent Sale Prices:

Rock Bed of Wissahickon	11x14"	Ext.	$20	3	3/97
Wissahickon	12x14"	Misc. Un.	$25	3	11/95

SVENSON, ESTHER
* Framingham, Massachusetts
* Wallace Nutting's head colorist who sold a few items over her own name

TABER-PRANG ART CO. (Also PRANG ART CO.)
* Louis Prang
* Hand-painted lithographs

Florence Thompson's A Different Lesson, $75.

THOMPSON, FLORENCE
* Location Unknown
* Script Thompson signature
* If you see a script Thompson signature, it is most likely Florence Thompson, not Fred Thompson.
* Recent Sale Prices:

Different Lesson, A	8x10"	Child	$75	4	5/97
Incoming Tide, The	8x10"	Sea	$15	4	4/95

THOMPSON, THOMAS
* No other information available

TROTT, M.A.
* No other information available
* Recent Sale Prices:

Fairyland Gate, Bermuda	7x10"	Sea	$19	3	9/96

TULL, SANFORD
* Massachusetts
* Worked for Wallace Nutting
* Recent Sale Prices:

Manchester Byway	11x14"	Misc. Un.	$25	3	3/96

Turner's goin to within, $25.

TURNER (first name not known)
* No other information available
* Recent Sale Prices:

"goin to within"	9x11"	Misc. Un.	$25	4	3/97

Underhill's Dressing the Bride, $13.

UNDERHILL, NELSON
* Not a photographer, but an artist
* Sold hand-colored lithograph-type colonial interior scenes
* Recent Sale Prices:

Dressing the Bride	7x12"	Int.	$13	4	3/97
Old Melody	10x13"	Int.	$15	4	3/97

Villar's The Old Well, $40.

VILLAR (first name not known)
* No other information available
* Recent Sale Prices:

Day Dream	14x16"	Misc. Un.	$39	4	11/95
Shady Nook, A	14x17"	Misc. Un.	$28	3	9/96
Shallow Waters	11x14"	Ext.	$28	4	9/96
Spring Pastoral, A	11x14"	Horse	$50	4	4/95
Old Homestead, The	11x14"	Misc. Un.	$33	4	9/96
Old Well, The	12x14"	Misc. Un.	$40	4	3/97

Wapt's The Delaware, $45.

WAPT, J.R.
* Pennsylvania (Bucks & Montgomery Counties)
* Recent Sale Prices:

Delaware, The	8x14"	Ext.	$45	4	3/97
Perkiomen, The	12x14"	Ext.	$25	4	3/97

WARD, ARTHUR
* No other information available

HAND-COLORED

Watson's Long Bay, Bermuda, $30.

WATSON, EDITH
* Location not known
* Did various Bermuda scenes
* Recent Sale Prices:

Bermuda Seacoast	8x10"	Sea	$38	4	3/97
Long Bay, Bermuda	7x11"	Sea	$30	4	6/97
Triple Bermuda Scene	6x15"	Misc. Un.	$11	4	10/94

Wight's Roadside Birches, $8.

WIGHT (first name not known)
* No other information available
* Recent Sale Prices:

Roadside Birches	10x14"	Ext.	$8	3	3/97

WILLARD, STEPHEN H.
* Southwestern United States
* Recent Sale Prices:

Desert, The	15x20"	Ext.	$58	4.5	11/95
Sentinels of the Desert	15x20"	Ext.	$14	4.5	11/95

WILMOT (first name not known)
* No other information available
* Recent Sale Prices:

Everywhere Are Roses	9x12"	Misc. Un.	$3	3	9/96
Where Memories Tingle	9x12"	Misc. Un.	$11	3	9/96

WILSON, EDITH
* No other information available
* Recent Sale Prices:

Blossoms & Birches	6x6"	Misc. Un.	$30	4	3/96

WORSHAK, N.
* No other information available
* Recent Sale Prices:

Old North Shore, The	12x13"	Ext.	$25	3.5	11/95

WRIGHT (first name not known)
* No other information available
* Recent Sale Prices:

Silvery Seas	7x9"	Sea	$6	3	9/96

YATES (first name not known)
* No other information available
* Recent Sale Prices:

The Milford Lakes	6x8"	Ext.	$15	3	4/95

Assorted Pictures By Unknown Photographers

Close-framed seascape	1x2"	Sea	$50	5	3/96
1926 calendar	5x7"	Cal.	$15	3.75	4/95
1932 calendar		Misc	$6	4	9/96
Boothbay Harbor, ME	6x8"	Misc. Un.	$28	4	9/96
Bridal Path, The	10x12"	Misc. Un.	$83	4	11/95
California cypress trees	7x10"	Sea	$8	4	3/96
Calm lake	7x9"	Ext.	$8	4	11/95
Capistrano	5x6"	Misc. Un.	$5	3	3/96
Cast from Masonic Play	11x4"	Misc. Un.	$11	5	9/96
Children by blossoms	13x17"	Misc	$30	3	11/95
Close-framed house scene	7x9"	Misc. Un.	$11	4	11/95
Close-framed Mt.Ranier	7x10"	Snow	$10	4	3/97
Close-framed Seascape	8x14"	Sea	$28	4	4/95
Coast at East Point	7x9"	Sea	$10	4	3/97
Covered bridge	8x10"	Misc. Un.	$35	5	3/96
Desert (Southwest U.S.)	8x10"	Misc. Un.	$25	4	9/96
Dog (Boxer)	8x10"	Dog	$15	4	7/96
Douglas Camp Ground	7x9"	Ext.	$1	3	10/94
Early Spring	9x11"	Sheep	$18	4	3/96
Exterior	8x10"	Ext.	$18	4	11/95
Fading Light	11x15"	Int.	$10	3	3/96
Fisherman on Maine Dock	16x20"	Misc. Un.	$85	4.5	12/96
Fishing Village	13x16"	Misc. Un.	$25	4	11/95

Flag-Draped					
American Coffins	10x13"	Misc	$17	4	9/96
Girl in Flower Garden	7x9"	Child	$77		10/94
Girl with Flowers	6x10"	Int.	$25	3	4/95
Grand Canyon	15x29"	Misc. Un.	$50	4	9/96
Granny at Rest	6x10"	Misc. Un.	$11	4	10/94
Green Mts. of Vermont	5x8"	Misc	$39	4	9/96
Harbor, Provincetown, The	8x10"	Ships	$23	3.75	4/95
Horizontal mirror with					
exterior scene	10x27"	Mirror	$41	4	11/95
Lady by Mirror	4x5"	Print	$8	3	10/94
Land of Midnight Sun					
and Mission			$3	3	9/96
Lighthouse	5x14"	Sea	$85	4	4/95
Man by Car	8x10"	Man	$20	4	7/96
Man Watering in Garden	8x11"	Man	$25	4	3/96
Man with Golf Club	6x9"	Misc. Un.	$33	4	9/96
Men Eating in Snow	8x10"	Men/Snow	$15	4	3/96
Miniature exterior	3x4"	Misc	$14	4	9/96
Mirror with exterior scene	5x14"	Mirror	$36	3.5	11/95
Mirror with exterior scene	5x20"	Mirror	$33	3.75	11/95
Mountain Trail, The	6x8"	Misc	$22	4	9/96
Natural Bridge			$8		4/95
Near Head of Bright					
Angel	14x16"	Ext.	$25	3	3/96
Pergola, Amalfi	11x15"	Italy	$25	3	3/96
Pocahontas House	8x10"	Misc. Un.	$28	4	9/96
Roadside Farm	6x8"	Misc. Un.	$19	4	10/94

Seaside Cliffs	8x10"	Sea	$17	4	9/96
Sheep in Field	7x9"	Sheep	$10	4	3/96
Skirting the Lake	11x14"	Ext.	$15	3	3/96
Streamside Church	16x20"	Misc. Un.	$13	3	3/96
Take Tahoe	5x6"	Ext.	$14	3	10/94
Tall Waterfalls	16x20"	Ext.	$39	4	11/95
Triple Colorado grouping	13x17"	Misc. Un.	$14	4	10/94
Triple exterior grouping	8x13"	Misc	$18	4	4/95
Triple exterior grouping	6x16"	Misc	$40	4	3/97
Triple exterior grouping	12x39"	Misc. Un.	$18	4	3/97
Triple exterior grouping	4x16"	Misc. Un.	$55	4	11/95
Twin Palms, Florida	10x12"	Ext.	$22	3	10/94
Two Men on Horseback	10x12"	Men	$45	4	3/96
Untitled country road	7x11"	Ext.	$18	3	4/95
Untitled cows	11x14"	Cows	$25	4	3/97
Untitled cross	12x14"	Misc. Un.	$8	3	9/96
Untitled exterior	10x11"	Ext.	$11	3	9/96
Untitled exterior	10x13"	Ext.	$15	4	9/96
Untitled house	11x14"	Misc. Un.	$10	4	4/95
Untitled interior	11x13"	Int.	$6	4	9/96
Untitled seascape	8x8"	Sea	$5	3	4/95
Untitled seascape	6x8"	Misc. Un.	$19	4	9/96
Untitled seascape	11x14"	Sea	$35	4	3/97
Untitled/unsigned					
seascape	14x20"	Sea	$30	3	3/96
Venice Canal scene	13x17"	Foreign	$19	3	11/95
Vermont card	5x8"	Card	$22	4	11/95
Village on Island	12x20"	Misc. Un.	$15	3.5	9/96

Desert (Southwest U.S.), $25.

Boxer Dog, $15.

Fishermen on Maine Dock, $85.

Fishing Village, $25.

Man by Car, $20.

About the Author

Michael Ivankovich has been collecting hand-colored photography for nearly 25 years. Buying his first picture in 1974, he started searching out Wallace Nutting pictures in garage sales, flea markets, antique shows, and local auctions. His interest in David Davidson, Fred Thompson, Sawyer, and other early 20th century photographers who sold hand-colored pictures soon followed. Shortly thereafter, he began purchasing entire collections. Today he is generally considered to be the country's leading authority on Wallace Nutting and Wallace-Nutting-like pictures, as well as Wallace Nutting books, furniture, and memorabilia.

This specialization in Wallace Nutting pictures led to his first book in 1984, *The Price Guide to Wallace Nutting Pictures* (1st Edition). Three additional editions of that book were released between 1986 – 91. His latest Nutting price guide, *The Collector's Guide to Wallace Nutting Pictures: Identification & Values*, was released by Collector Books in 1997. He has also authored three other books relating to Wallace Nutting including *The Alphabetical & Numerical Index to Wallace Nutting Pictures, The Guide to Wallace Nutting Furniture*, and *The Guide to Wallace Nutting-Like Photographers of the Early Twentieth Century*. Through his Diamond Press subsidiary company, he has also published three additional books on Wallace Nutting: *The Wallace Nutting Expansible Catalog, Wallace Nutting: A Great American Idea*, and *Wallace Nutting Windsors: Correct Windsor Furniture*.

His interest in popular early twentieth century American prints came more recently. Over the past five years while traveling and conducting expand-ed research into the area of hand-colored photography, he also began researching the works of many of the more popular twentieth century artists and illustrators whose works he often found hanging beside hand-colored photographs in antique shows and shops. He found these seemingly dissimilar subject areas surprisingly similar in many ways.

Mr. Ivankovich conducted the first all-Wallace Nutting consignment auction in 1988, in Framingham, Massachusetts. The enthusiasm generated by this auction has led to 31 more Wallace Nutting catalog auctions between 1988 and 1997, with four Michael Ivankovich Wallace Nutting and Nutting-like auctions taking place each year throughout the New England and Mid-Atlantic states. Starting in 1998, Mr. Ivankovich has added poplar early twentieth century American prints to his auctions.

These auctions have now become the national center of hand-colored photography activity. They provide Wallace Nutting and Nutting-like buyers with the opportunity to compete for a wide variety of Wallace Nutting items. These auctions also provide sellers of Wallace Nutting and Nutting-like pictures with the opportunity to place their consignments in front of the countrys leading and most knowledgeable collectors. And they provide all hand-colored photography enthusiasts with the opportunity to see the largest and most diverse assortment of Wallace Nutting pictures that they will probably ever see assembled all in one place.

A frequent lecturer on Wallace Nutting, Mr. Ivankovich has written articles for most major trade papers, has appeared on various radio and television programs, and is frequently consulted by antique columnists from throughout the country. He also provides Wallace Nutting appraisal services and exhibits at select antique shows.

Mr. Ivankovich is also a licensed auctioneer, conducting various antique and collectible, household and estate, general consignment, and fundraising auctions.

Together with his wife Susan (who has published four cookbooks, including *The Not-Strictly Vegetarian Cookbook* and *Cooking with Sundried Tomatoes*), they reside in Doylestown, Pennsylvania, with their four children Jenna, Lindsey, Megan, and Nash.

Other Wallace Nutting Reference Books

available from Michael Ivankovich

P.O. Box 2458 * Doylestown, PA 18901
(add $3.75 P&H for 1st book ordered, $1.25 for each additional book)

The Collector's Guide to Wallace Nutting Pictures: Identification & Values, 160 pgs ..$18.95

Wallace Nutting Expansible Catalog featuring nearly 1,000 Wallace Nutting Pictures, 160
pgs $14.95

The Guide to Wallace Nutting Furniture, by Michael Ivankovich, the #1 book on Nutting's
reproduction furniture, 160 pgs $14.95

The Wallace Nutting General Catalog, Supreme Edition, a great visual reference reprint of
Nutting's 1930 reproduction furniture catalog, 168 pgs $13.95

Wallace Nutting: A Great American Idea, a useful visual reference reprint of the 1923 reproduction furniture catalog covering Nutting's script branded furniture, 36 pgs...........$11.95

Wallace Nutting Windsor Furniture, a useful visual reference reprint of Nutting's 1918 Windsor
reproduction furniture catalog; Nutting's most complete Windsor catalog, 48 pgs ...$11.95